A TEXT BOOK OF

SURVEYING

FOR

SECOND YEAR DIPLOMA COURSE IN CIVIL ENGINEERING

SEMESTER – III

As per MSBTE's Revised Syllabus 'G' Scheme

With Effective From June 2013

Late V. S. GAJARE
M.I.E., C.E. (II)
Ex. Head of Civil Engineering Department,
Government Polytechnic,
Jalgaon.

S. V. GOSAVI
B.E. (Civil), M.I.E.
Lecturer, C.S. Department,
V.B.V. Polytechnic,
Vasai Road (W), Thane - 401 202

R. B. NARAHARI
B.E.(Civil)
Lecturer Selection Grade,
Bharati Vidyapeeth's J.N.I.O.T,
Pune-43

V. R. SAWANT
B.E. (Civil)
Ex. Lecturer, Civil Engg. Department,
Government Polytechnic,
Mumbai.

V. S. BHAGWAT
B.E. (Civil)
Lecturer, Civil Engg. Department,
K. K. Wagh Polytechnic,
Nashik - 03.

Price ₹ 195.00

N1931

S. Y. Dip. : Semester – III (Civil) : SURVEYING　　　　　ISBN 978-93-83073-19-1

Second Edition　　:　June 2014

Published By :
NIRALI PRAKASHAN
Abhyudaya Pragati, 1312, Shivaji Nagar,
Off J.M. Road, PUNE – 411005
Tel - (020) 25512336/37/39, Fax - (020) 25511379
Email : niralipune@pragationline.com

Printed By :
REPRO INDIA LTD.
50/2 TTC MIDC Industrial Area,
MAHAPE
Navi Mumbai

DISTRIBUTION CENTRES
PUNE

Nirali Prakashan
119, Budhwar Peth, Jogeshwari Mandir Lane
Pune 411002, Maharashtra
Tel : (020) 2445 2044, 66022708, Fax : (020) 2445 1538
Email : bookorder@pragationline.com

Nirali Prakashan
S. No. 28/25, Dhyari,
Near Pari Company, Pune 411041
Tel : (020) 24690204 Fax : (020) 24690316
Email : dhyari@pragationline.com
　　　　　bookorder@pragationline.com

MUMBAI
Nirali Prakashan
385, S.V.P. Road, Rasdhara Co-op. Hsg. Society Ltd.,
Girgaum, Mumbai 400004, Maharashtra
Tel : (022) 2385 6339 / 2386 9976, Fax : (022) 2386 9976
Email : niralimumbai@pragationline.com

DISTRIBUTION BRANCHES

NAGPUR
Pratibha Book Distributors
Above Maratha Mandir, Shop No. 3, First Floor,
Rani Jhanshi Square, Sitabuldi, Nagpur 440012,
Maharashtra, Tel : (0712) 254 7129

BENGALURU
Pragati Book House
House No. 1, Sanjeevappa Lane, Avenue Road Cross,
Opp. Rice Church, Bengaluru – 560002.
Tel : (080) 64513344, 64513355,
Mob : 9880582331, 9845021552
Email:bharatsavla@yahoo.com

JALGAON
Nirali Prakashan
34, V. V. Golani Market, Navi Peth, Jalgaon 425001,
Maharashtra, Tel : (0257) 222 0395
Mob : 94234 91860

KOLHAPUR
Nirali Prakashan
New Mahadvar Road,
Kedar Plaza, 1st Floor Opp. IDBI Bank
Kolhapur 416 012, Maharashtra. Mob : 9855046155

CHENNAI
Pragati Books
9/1, Montieth Road, Behind Taas Mahal, Egmore,
Chennai 600008 Tamil Nadu, Tel : (044) 6518 3535,
Mob : 94440 01782 / 98450 21552 / 98805 82331, Email : bharatsavla@yahoo.com

RETAIL OUTLETS
PUNE

Pragati Book Centre
157, Budhwar Peth, Opp. Ratan Talkies,
Pune 411002, Maharashtra
Tel : (020) 2445 8887 / 6602 2707, Fax : (020) 2445 8887

Pragati Book Centre
Amber Chamber, 28/A, Budhwar Peth,
Appa Balwant Chowk, Pune : 411002, Maharashtra,
Tel : (020) 20240335 / 66281669
Email : pbcpune@pragationline.com

Pragati Book Centre
676/B, Budhwar Peth, Opp. Jogeshwari Mandir,
Pune 411002, Maharashtra
Tel : (020) 6601 7784 / 6602 0855

PBC Book Sellers & Stationers
152, Budhwar Peth, Pune 411002, Maharashtra
Tel : (020) 2445 2254 / 6609 2463

MUMBAI
Pragati Book Corner
Indira Niwas, 111 - A, Bhavani Shankar Road, Dadar (W), Mumbai 400028, Maharashtra
Tel : (022) 2422 3526 / 6662 5254, Email : pbcmumbai@pragationline.com

www.pragationline.com　　　　　　　　　　　　　　　　　　info@pragationline.com

Dedicated to,

My father and my teacher

Late Vijay Shankar Gosavi

&

My mother

Shrimati Suman Vijay Gosavi

Sureshchandra Vijay Gosavi

Dedicated to,

My mothor and first Guru

Smt. R. B. Bharathi

Narahari R. B.

PREFACE

It gives us immense pleasure to present a text book on **"Surveying"** as per MSBTE G-Scheme Syllabus effective from June 2013 for the students of Diploma Second Year (Civil).

All basic concepts of the subjects are explained clearly in lucid manner with neat sketches, varieties of problems from MSBTE examination have been solved with illustrative theory portion. A large number of theory questions and numerical problems from MSBTE examination are also been included at the end of each chapter.

During preparation of this book a number of text book written by Indian and Foreign authors have been referred, authors are sincerely thankful to them.

Necessary care has been taken to avoid errors and misprints in this edition. However if they brought to notice will be rectify the same in coming edition.

Authors are thankful to the publisher Mr. Dineshbhai Furia, and Pradeep Furia and Mr. Sashikant Patel and also thanks to staff Mrs. Anagha Kaware, Mr. Santosh Bare and Mrs. Deepa Sawant and other staff of Nirali Prakashan for bringing out this book in good manner.

Authors

SYLLABUS

1. INTRODUCTION (06 Hours, 08 Marks)

- Definition of survey, Objects of different surveys, Uses of surveys.

- **Classification of surveys :** Primary and Secondary, Primary division-plane and geodetic surveys, Secondary - Based on instruments used, Nature of field and objective. Principles of survey.

- Conventional symbols in survey plans/maps.

2. LINEAR MEASUREMENT (09 Hours, 12 Marks)

- Study and use of instruments for linear measurements - Metric chain, Measuring tapes and its types, Ranging rod, Arrow, Peg, Digital tape, Methods of linear measurements - By pacing, By speedometer, By changing, By digital tape.

- **Ranging :** direct and indirect ranging and procedure, Code of signals used in ranging.

- **Chaining :** Procedure on plane and sloping ground. Correction of linear measurements for incorrect length of chain/tape. (Simple problems)

3. CHAIN TRIANGULATION AND CROSS-STAFF SURVEY (10 Hours, 16 Marks)

- **Principles of chain survey :** Triangulation, Survey station types and their selection, Survey line, Base line, Check line, Tie line.

  Offset, Types of offset : Long, Short, Perpendicular and oblique, Instrument for setting offsets - Open cross-staff, Optical square, Principle of optical square, Setting offset with open cross-staff and optical square. Survey field book and recording entries.

- Chain and cross-staff survey for finding area of the field. Simple numerical problems.

  Types of obstacles in changing and methods of overcoming them. Simple numerical problems.

4. COMPASS TRAVERSE SURVEY (15 Hours, 24 Marks)

4.1 Principle of compass survey - Traversing, Prismatic compass - Component parts and their functions, Setting of compass, Meridian - True meridian, Magnetic meridian and Arbitrary meridian. Magnetic declination, Dip of needle. Bearing of a line - True bearing, Magnetic bearing and Arbitrary bearing, Systems of bearing - Whole circle bearing and Quadrantal bearing, Force and back bearing of line and their relationship. (12)

4.2 Compass traversing - Open and close traverse, Local attraction and its detection. Correction for local attraction and finding corrected bearings and included angles. Numerical problems. Plotting the compass traverse and its graphical adjustment by Bowditch rule, Sources of error in compass survey.

- Principle of plane table survey. Different accessories of plane table and their use. Setting of plane table, Telescopic alidade and its advantages.

- Orientation of plane table - Back sighting and magnetic meridian. Methods of plane table surveys - Radiation, Intersection and Traversing, Merits and demerits of plane table survey.

| 6. | **LEVELLING** | **(16 Hours, 28 Marks)** |

6.1 **(8)**

- Concept of levelling. Meaning of terms used in leveling - Level surface, Level line, Horizontal surface and line, Vertical line, Datum line, Reduced Level, Bench Mark and its types.

- Levelling instruments - Dumpy level and Auto level. Dumpy level - Component parts, Line of collimation, Axis of telescope, Axis of bubble-tube and their relationships, temporary adjustment, permanent adjustment of dumpy level (only relationship of different axes of dumpy level). Auto Level - Component parts and temporary adjustments. Advantages of Auto Level. Leveling Staff-Telescopic.

6.2 **(8)**

- Fore Sight, Back Sight, Intermediate Sight, Negative staff reading, Change point, Height of plane of collimation, Station point, Rise and Fall, Level book and its recording,

- Methods of leveling - Simple levelling, Differential levelling, Profile and Cross-sectioning, Fly levelling, Check levelling and reciprocal levelling

6.3 **(12)**

- Method of reduction of level - Height of instrument, Rise and Fall method. Arithmetic check. Numerical problems.

- Sources of errors in levelling, precautionary measures.

❑❑❑

CONTENTS

❑❑❑

1...

Introduction

Contents

1.1 Introduction
1.2 Definition of Surveying and Levelling
1.3 Objects of Surveying
1.4 Uses of Survey
1.5 Principles of Surveying
1.6 Primary Classification of Surveying
1.7 Secondary Classification of Surveying
1.8 Conventional Symbol of Survey
    Solved Examples
    Important Points
    Practice Questions

1.1 INTRODUCTION

- *Surveying* is a branch of civil engineering and it is used to represent the general features of land in their proper relative positions.
- From these measurements, the drawings are prepared which may be in the form of a plan or a map.

1.2 DEFINITION OF SURVEYING AND LEVELLING

(S-05, 09, 10, 12 W-10, 11)

Surveying :

- "The process of making measurements on the earth surface to determine the relative positions of the points upon it, so that the points may be represented on a plan or a map" is known as surveying.
- It deals with the measurements in horizontal plane.

Levelling

- The branch of surveying for determining the relative heights or elevations of different points on the surface of the earth with reference to some datum is known as levelling.
- It deals with the measurements in vertical plane.
- Surveying and levelling are two distinct operations, but in a broad sense, surveying includes levelling.

1.3 OBJECTS OF SURVEYING   (S-08, 11; W-07, 08, 09)

- The main object of surveying is to prepare a map or a plan of the area surveyed.

- The map or plan is the horizontal projection of area on a horizontal plane.

- On plan, horizontal distances only are shown.

- Vertical distances between the points can be shown by contour lines. These distances can be clearly shown by drawing sections.

- When the scale used is small, drawing is called a map, such as map of India and when the scale used is large, drawing is called a *plan*, - such as a plan of a building. Surveying is important for determining the boundaries of land.

- It is very useful for the purpose of designing engineering projects, such as dams, head works, canals, roads, railways, water-supply schemes drainage schemes etc.

- The successful completion of any engineering project mainly depends upon accurate surveying.

1.4 USES OF SURVEY   (S-12)

The surveys may be plane or geodetic, but they have wide scope and utility. The following are the various uses of' the different surveys :

Uses of Plane Surveying :   (W-07, 08)

(i) It is basically useful for measurement of areas.

(ii) It is useful for other purposes, such as engineering, architectural, commercial, scientific, geographical, exploratory, military, navigational etc.

(iii) It can be used for making of plans in connection with legal documents.

(iv) It is used for both the location as well as construction of different classes of work, which may include making of plans and the reverse process of working from the plan for setting out works.

(v) It is also useful for other routine works of surveying and levelling.

Uses of Geodetic Surveying :

(i) Accurate maps of wide areas and controls for all other surveys are obtained by this survey.

(ii) Information regarding the positions of points, heights above sea-level, true bearings etc. is provided by this survey.

(iii) It is useful for obtaining the most useful checks at various stages for survey work carried out by an engineer or a surveyor.

(iv) It enables local surveys to be laid down and plotted on the official printed maps and plans.

(v) In case of dispute of property, certain plans may be used as legal documents.

1.5 PRINCIPLES OF SURVEYING (S-08, 10; W-07, 08, 09, 10; S-11, W-11, S-12)

The two main principles of surveying are :

(1) To work from the whole to the part.

(2) To locate a point by at least two independent processes-

    (a) Linear measurement,

    (b) Angular measurement, or

    (c) Both linear and angular measurement.

(1) To Work from the Whole to the Part

[According to work form whole to part] :

- It is essential to fix first, system of control points with high precision of the whole area to be surveyed.

- This area is divided into large traverse or triangles or both, and further subdivided into smaller ones by locating other control points in-between the main control points with less precision.

- The details are then located.

- By this method, minor errors are controlled and localized. Accumulation of errors is thus, avoided.

- On the other hand, if we work from part to the whole, small errors will increase in process of expansion and thus, become uncontrollable at the end. The whole survey then will go wrong.

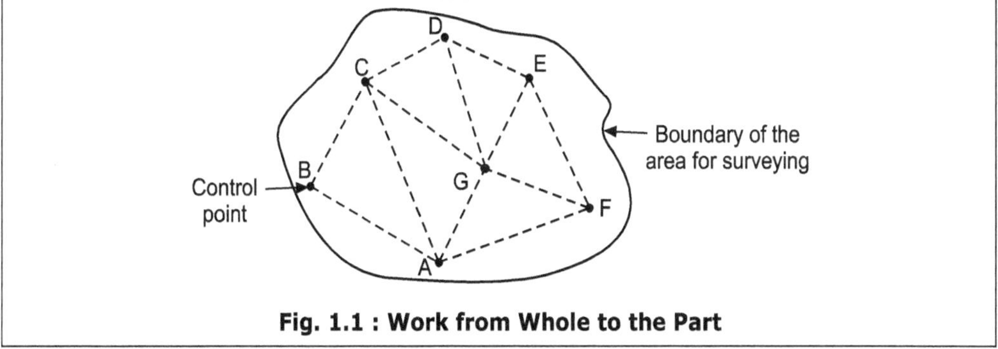

Fig. 1.1 : Work from Whole to the Part

- Suppose a very large area like town is to be surveyed. Firstly fixed the control points A, B, C, D, E, F with grate core.

- This area is divided into number of triangles. The details within these triangles are surveyed with less accurate method.

(2) To Locate a Point by At Least Two Points of References :

- In this method, two points are selected in the field and distance between them is measured. The relative positions of the points can be located from these reference points.

- To locate a point M with respect to two more given points of references say A and B, the following methods are used.

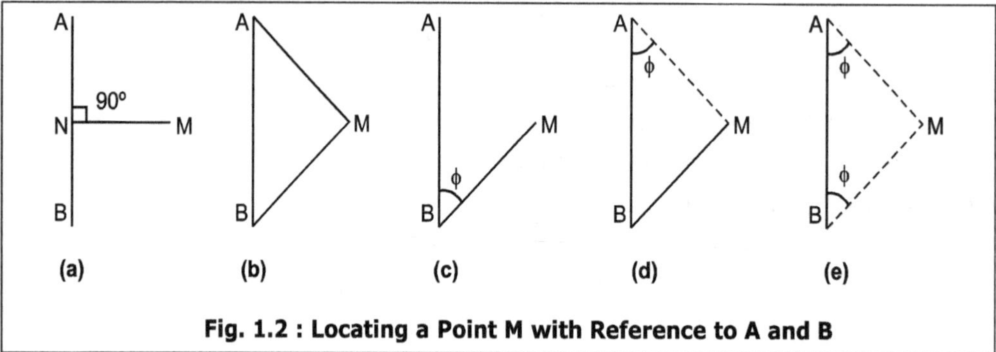

Fig. 1.2 : Locating a Point M with Reference to A and B

The position of point M can be located by any one of the methods described below :

(a) A perpendicular MN can be dropped on the reference line AB and lengths AN and NM are measured. The point M can then be plotted and measured. This principle is used in chain surveying for defining details.

(b) Distance AM and BM can be measured and point M can be plotted by swinging the two arcs to the same scale to which AB has been plotted. The principle is very much used in chain surveying.

(c) The distance BM and angle ABM can be measured and point M is plotted either by means of a protractor or trigonometrically. This principle is used in traversing.

(d) An angle MAB and distance BM is measured and point M is plotted either by protracting an angle and swinging an arc from B or plotted trigonometrically. This is used in traversing.

(e) In this method, the distances AM and BM are not measured, but angle MAB and angle MBA are measured with angle measuring instrument. Knowing the distance AB, the point M is plotted either by means of a protractor or by solution of triangle AMB. The principle is very much used in triangulation and for extensive work.

1.6 PRIMARY CLASSIFICATION OF SURVEYING

(S-05, 08, 10; W-07, 10; S-11)

(1) Plane Survey :

- *In plane surveying,* the effect of curvature of earth is not considered.

- The surface of the earth is taken as plane.

- The lines connecting any two points are considered as straight lines and the angles of polygon are plane angles. Plane surveys are carried out for small areas.

- The degree of accuracy is comparatively low. It involves plain trigonometry.

- The extent of surveys up to 260 km^2 are considered as plane surveys.

- Plane survey can be carried by any agency concerned.

(2) Geodetic Survey :

- In *geodetic surveying,* the curvature of earth is taken into consideration as the surveys extent for large distances and areas.

- It involves spherical trigonometry and hence, it is also called *trigonometrical survey.*

- It is carried out for locating distant control points and for surveying large areas i.e. beyond 260 sq.km. It is generally, performed by Government agencies.

- In India, it is done by Great Trigonometrical Survey (G.T.S.) department.

- It is carried out with a high degree of precision or accuracy to obtain data concerning the size and shape of earth.

1.7 SECONDARY CLASSIFICATION OF SURVEYING **(W-10, W-11)**

Classification based on the Nature of Field :

(1) Land Surveying :

(i) *Topographical surveys :* It deals with to determine the natural features of country, such as rivers, lakes, hills etc. and artificial features such as roads, railway, canals, towns and villages.

(ii) *Cadastral surveys* are plotted on larger scale than topographical surveys. It deals with to determine additional details, such as boundaries of fields, houses and other properties.

(iii) *Engineering surveys* are carried out for the determination of quantities or to collect data for designing of engineering works, such as roads, reservoirs, water-supply and sewage disposal. This can be also called as city surveying.

(2) Astronomical Surveying :

It deals with determine the absolute location of any point or the absolute location and direction of any line on the surface of the earth astronomical survey is used.

(3) Marine Survey :

It deals with bodies of water for purpose of navigation, water supply etc. It is also called as hydrographic survey.

Classification based upon the Instruments or Methods Employed –

(a) Chain survey.

(b) Theodolite survey.

(c) Traverse surveys - closed or unclosed.

(d) Triangulation survey.

(e) Plane table surveys.

(f) Tachometric surveys.

(g) Photographic surveys.

(h) Aerial surveys.

Classification based on Object of Survey :

(a) Engineering survey.

(b) Geological survey.

(c) Military survey.

(d) Archaeological survey.

(e) Mine survey.

1.8 REPRESENTATIVE FRACTION (R.F.)　　(W-11, S-11)

Definition :

- The scale is defined as the ratio of plan distance to corresponding ground distance.

- Thus, if 10 m on the ground represents 1 cm on the drawing paper, the scale is 1 cm = 10 m.

- The plan of a building, bridge, dam or a map of town etc. cannot be prepared in full size on a drawing sheet.

- For convenience, it is generally necessary to draw them to a reduced size, this operation is known as *"Drawing to scale"*. Thus, 1 cm on the plan represents 20 m on the ground, the scale of plan is 20 m to 1 cm. It is written as 1 cm to 20 m. This is called as Engineer's scale (1 cm=20 m)

- The scale is expressed as a fraction whose numerator is always unity. This fraction is known as Representative Fraction. (R.F.)

$$\text{Representative Fraction} = \frac{\text{Plan or map distance}}{\text{Corresponding ground distance}}$$

In R.F., both the numerator and denominator should be in the same units.

$$\text{i.e.1 cm = 20 m; R.F.} = \frac{1 \text{ cm}}{20 \times 100 \text{ cm}} = \frac{1}{2000}$$

Similarly, for 1 cm $=$ 1 kilometre

$$\text{R.F.} = \frac{1 \text{ cm}}{1 \times 1000 \times 100 \text{ cm}} = \frac{1}{100000}$$

Also, from a given R.F. the scale can be found out.

Hence RF is the ratio of plan distance to corresponding ground distance which is independent of units.

1.8.1 Scales Recommended for Survey Maps

(1) Geographical maps, from 1 cm = 160 km to 1 cm = 5 km.

(2) Topographical maps, from 1 cm = 2.5 km to 1 cm = 0.25 km.

(3) The large scale maps, R.F. $= \dfrac{1}{10000}$ to $\dfrac{1}{20000}$.

(4) Location maps, R.F. $= \dfrac{1}{2500}$ to $\dfrac{1}{500}$.

(5) Cadastral map, R.F. $= \dfrac{1}{1000}$ to $\dfrac{1}{25000}$.

(6) Forest map, R.F. $= \dfrac{1}{25000}$.

(7) Earth work, R.F. $= \dfrac{1}{2500}$ to $\dfrac{1}{100}$.

(8) Longitudinal section

$$\text{Horizontal scale R.F.} = \frac{1}{25000} \text{ to } \frac{1}{1000}$$

$$\text{Vertical scale R.F.} = \frac{1}{200} \text{ to } \frac{1}{100}$$

For cross-section of earth work, horizontal and vertical scale should be the same.

1.9 CONVENTIONAL SYMBOL　　(S-06, 08; W-06, 07, 09, S-12)

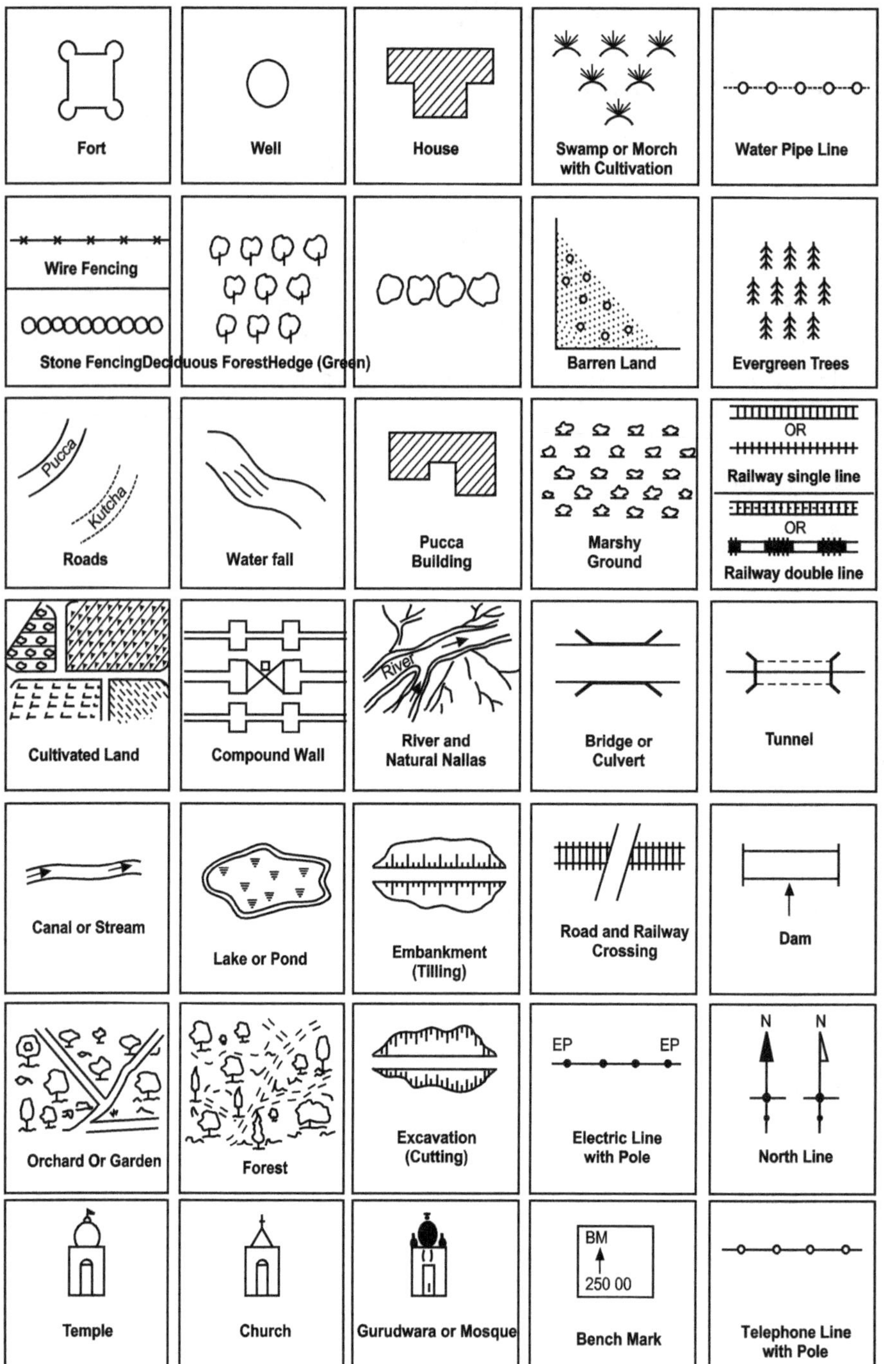

Fig. 1.3 : Conventional Symbol

SOLVED EXAMPLES

Example 1.1 : A rectangular plot measures 30 cm × 20 cm on the village map drawn to a scale of 1 cm = 80 m.

(a) What is the area in hectares ? What is the R.F. of Village map ?

(b) What will be its area on a toposheet drawn to a scale of 1 cm = 0.5 km ? What is the R.F. of toposheet ?

Solution : (a) Village map is drawn to a scale of 1 cm = 80 m.

∴　1 cm² on the map = 80 × 80 m² = 6400 m² on the ground

The area of plot on map is 30 cm × 20 cm = 600 m²

∴　The area plot on ground = 600 × 6400 = 3840000 m² =   384 hectares

$$\text{R.F. of the scale of village } = \frac{1}{80 \times 100} = \frac{1}{8000}$$

(b) Toposheet is drawn for a scale of 1 cm = 0.5 km.

∴　　　　1 cm² on toposheet = 0.5 × 0.5 km²

　　　　　　　　　　　　　　　= 0.25 km²

　　　　　　　　　　　　　　　= 0.25 × 1000 × 1000 m²

$$\text{i.e. } \frac{3840000}{0.25 \times 1000 \times 1000} = 15.36 \text{ cm}^2$$

$$\text{R.F. of the scale of toposheet } = \frac{1}{0.5 \times 1000 \times 100} = \frac{1}{50000}$$

Example 1.2 : Scale on map is 1 cm = 0.5 km. What is R.F. ?

$$\textbf{Solution :} \qquad \text{R.F.} = \frac{\text{Distance on map}}{\text{Distance on ground}} = \frac{1 \text{ cm}}{(0.5 \times 1000 \times 100) \text{ cm}}$$

$$= \frac{1}{50000}$$

Example 1.3 : 1.5 sq. km. area on the ground is represented by 15 sq. cm. in the map. What is its R.F. ?

Solution :　150 sq. cm. = 1.5 sq. km

　　　　　　　150 sq. cm. = 1.5 × 1000 × 1000 sq. m

$$1 \text{ sq. cm.} = \frac{1.5 \times 1000 \times 1000}{150}$$

　　　　　　　1 sq. cm. = 10000 sq. m

Hence, 1 cm = $\sqrt{10000}$ m

Scale : 1 cm = 100 m

$$\therefore \qquad \text{R.F.} = \frac{1 \text{ cm}}{(100 \times 100) \text{ cm}}$$

$$\text{R.F.} = \frac{1}{10000}$$

Important Points

- "The process of making measurements on the earth surface to determine the relative positions of the points upon it, so that the points may be represented on a plan or a map" is known as surveying.
- It deals with the measurements in horizontal plane.
- The branch of surveying for determining the relative heights or elevations of different points on the surface of the earth with reference to some datum is known as levelling.
- It deals with the measurements in vertical plane.
- The two main principles of surveying are :
  (1) To work from the whole to the part.
  (2) To locate a point by at least two independent point of reference.
- *In plane surveying,* the effect of curvature of earth is not considered.
- In *geodetic surveying,* the curvature of earth is taken into consideration as the surveys extent for large distances and areas.
- **The scale** is defined as the ratio of plan distance to corresponding ground distance.
- RF is the ratio of plan distance to corresponding ground distance which is independent of units.

Practice Questions

1. State the primary divisions of surveying. Describe it in brief.
2. State the meaning of the following terms :
   (i) a scale of plan, (ii) drawing to scale, (iii) representative fraction.
3. What is the difference between "drawing to scale" and "not to scale" ?
4. What is a Vernier ? Explain the principle of direct vernier. How is it constructed ?
5. Explain the method of constructing a vernier scale of the theodolite from the given data.
   (i) Smallest division on main scale is 20 minutes, and
   (ii) Least count of vernier is 20 seconds.
6. State the vernier used in the following instruments :
   (i) Abney Level
   (ii) Transit Theodolite
   (iii) Astronomical sextant
   [**Ans.** (i) Extended vernier
   (ii) Direct vernier
   (iii) Extended vernier]
7. What is remote sensing in surveying ?
8. Give the designations of the following scales :
   (i) $\dfrac{1}{10000}$, (ii) $\dfrac{1}{3000}$, (iii) $\dfrac{1}{100000}$.
   [**Ans.** (i) 1 cm = 100 m. (ii) 1 cm = 30 m. (iii) 1 cm = 1000 m.]
9. An area of 60 cm^2 of a map represents an area of 7260 m^2. What is the R.F. ?
   [**Ans.** R.F. = 1 : 1100].

MSBTE Questions & Answers

Summer 2008

1. Define Surveying and levelling. State the object of Surveying.
Ans. Refer Section 1.2 and Section 1.3.
2. State the basic difference based on earth surface between plane survey and geodetic survey. **(S-05, 10; W-07)**
Ans. Refer Section 1.6.
3. State two uses of surveying based on plan surveying.
Ans. Refer Section 1.4.
4. Give the classification of surveys (name only) based upon
   (i)   Nature of field survey, (ii) The object of survey, (iii) The instrument used.   **(W-06)**
Ans. Refer Section 1.7.
5. State the principles of surveying. Explain it in detail. **(W-07, 09)**
Ans. Refer Section 1.5.
6. Classify surveying (i) based on instruments and (ii) objects. **(S-09; W-09)**
Ans. Refer Section 1.7.

Winter 2008

1. Define surveying and levelling. State the object of surveying.
Ans. Refer Section 1.2 and Sectoin 1.3.
2. State two uses of surveying based on plan surveying.
Ans. Refer Section 1.4.

Summer 2009

1. Define surveying and levelling.
Ans. Refer Section 1.2.
2. State the principles of surveying. Explain it in detail.
Ans. Refer Section 1.5.
3. Classify surveying : (1) based on instrument and (2) objects.
Ans. Refer Section 1.7.

Winter 2009

1. Define surveying and levelling. State the object of surveying.
Ans. Refer Section 1.2 and 1.3.
2. State the principles of surveying. Explain it in detail.
Ans. Refer Section 1.5.

Summer 2010

1. State the objectives of surveying.
Ans. Refer Section 1.3.
2. State the principles of surveying.
Ans. Refer Section 1.5.

Summer 2011

1. Write the objects of surveying.
Ans. Refer Section 1.3.
2. What is representative fraction of scale ?
Ans. Refer Section 1.8.
3. Explain the primary classification of surveying.
Ans. Refer Section 1.6.
4. Write the main principles of surveying ?
Ans. Refer Section 1.5.

Winter 2011

1. Define surveying.
Ans. Refer Section 1.2.
2. Write the importance of scale in surveying.
Ans. Refer Section 1.8.
3. Write secondary classification of surveying.
Ans. Refer Section 1.7.
4. Write principle of surveying.
Ans. Refer Section 1.5.
5. Differentiate between 'Plain survey' and 'Geodetic survey'.
Ans. Refer Section 1.6.
6. Show conventional signs for cutting, embankment, road over railway line, cultivated land.
Ans. Refer Fig. 1.3.
7. Define : (i) Surveying.
Ans. Refer Section 1.2.

   (ii)   Levelling.
Ans. Refer Section 1.2.

Summer 2012

1. Write two uses of surveying.
Ans. Refer Section 1.1.
2. Define "surveying".
Ans. Refer Section 1.2.
3. State the basic principles of surveying. Explain any one in brief.
Ans. Refer Section 1.5.
4. Draw conventional sign for : (i) Road bridge, (ii) Embankment, (iii) Cutting, (iv) Lake.
Ans. Refer Fig. 1.3.

Winter 2012

1. Define surveying.
Ans. Refer Section 1.2.
2. State the principle of surveying.
Ans. Refer Section 1.5.
3. What are the primary divisions of surveying ?
Ans. Refer Section 1.6.
4. Draw conventional symbol for : (i) Embankment, (ii) Cutting.
Ans. Refer Fig. 1.3.
5. What is representative fraction of scale ? An area of 58 square centimeter of map represents an area of 4698 square meter ? What is its RF?
Ans. Refer Section 1.8.

Summer 2013

1. Write two uses of surveying.
Ans. Refer Section 1.4.
2. Define surveying.
Ans. Refer Section 1.2
3. State the basic principles of surveying. Explain any one in brief.
Ans. Refer Section 1.5.
4. Draw conventional sign for : (i) Road bridge, (ii) Embankment, (iii) Cutting, (iv) Lake.
Ans. Refer Section 1.9.

2...

Linear Measurements

Contents

2.1 INTRODUCTION

There are two types of measurements :

(a) Linear measurement and (b) Angular measurements.

(a) Linear Measurements : Linear measurement are dividing in two parts :

(i) *Horizontal distances* – distances measured in horizontal plane.

(ii) *Vertical distances* – distances measured in vertical plane.

The different methods of linear measurements are :

(1) Direct measurement.

(2) Measurement by optical means.

(3) Electronic methods.

(b) Angular Measurements : It is divided into two parts.

(i) *Horizontal angles* – angular measurements made in horizontal plane.

(ii) *Vertical angles* – angular measurements made in vertical plane.

2.2 INSTRUMENTS USED FOR MEASURING DISTANCES   (W-10)

(1) Chain,   (5) Arrows,

(2) Tape,   (6) Pegs,

(3) Ranging rods, (7) Plumb bob.

(4) Offset rods,

2.2.1 Chain

- Now-a-days, metric chains are used for measuring distances.

- These chains are made of 20 m and 30 m. The 20 m chain is composed of 100 links of 20 cm each and 30 m chain is composed of 150 links of 20 cm each.

"

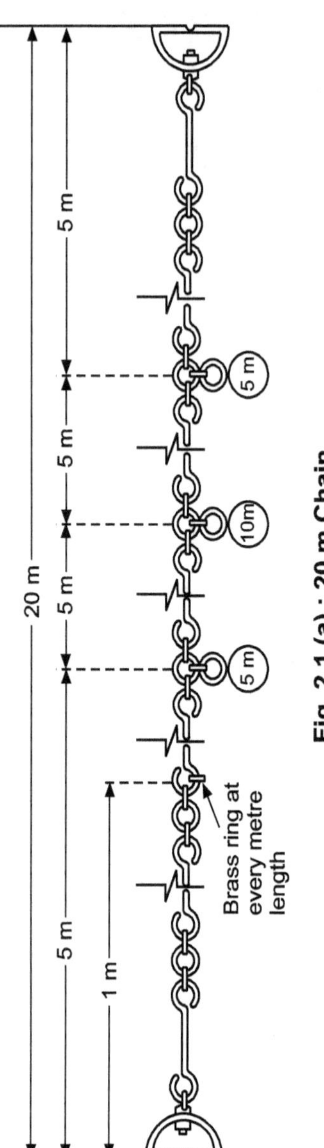

Fig. 2.1 (a) : 20 m Chain

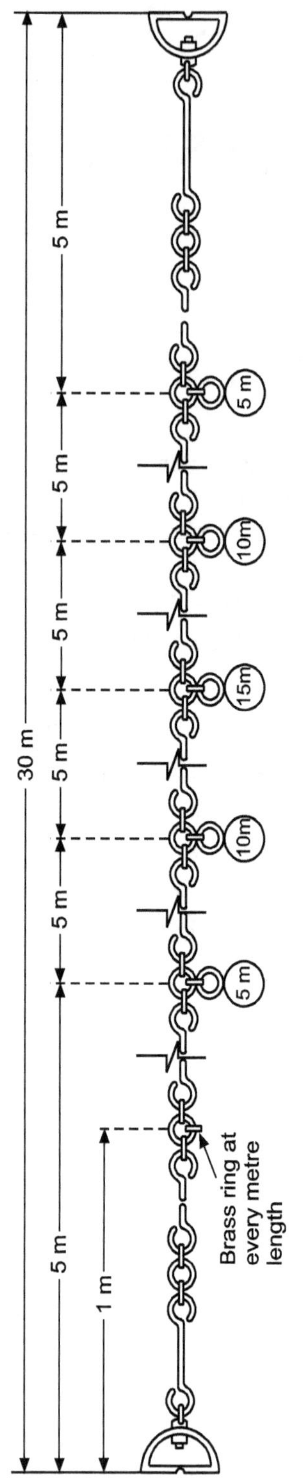

Fig. 2.1 (b) : 30 m Chain

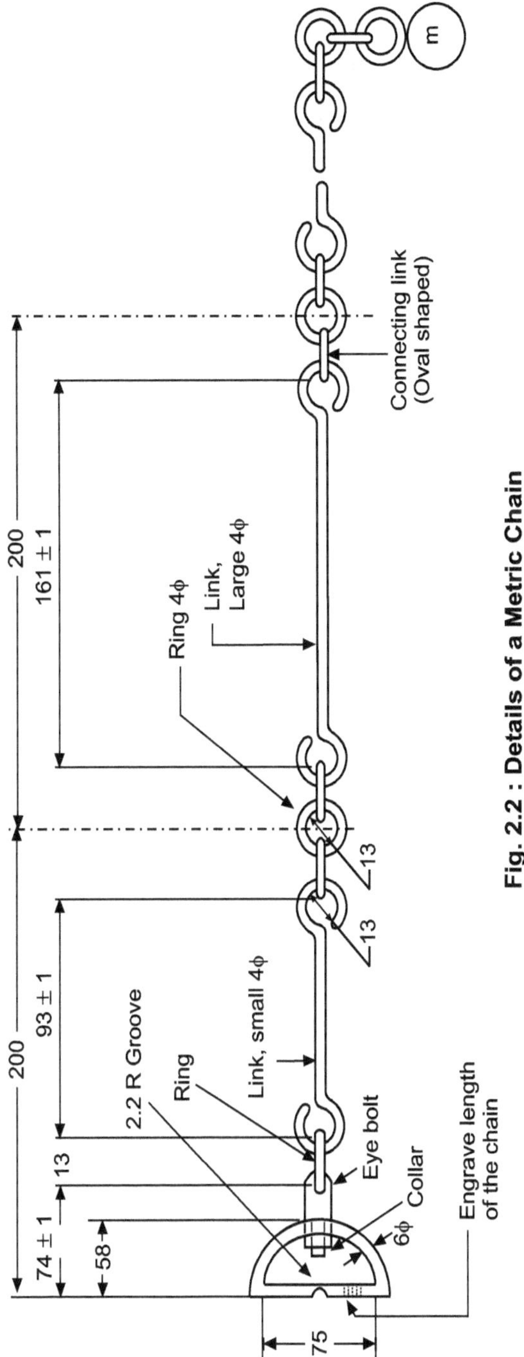

Fig. 2.2 : Details of a Metric Chain

- The length of a link is the center to center distance between two consecutive middle rings. The length of one link is 20 cm.

- The ends of each link are bent into loop and connected together by means of three oval rings which afford flexibility to the chain.

- The ends of chain are provided with brass handles for pulling the chain on ground over which the length of the chain is marked.

- The joint between the first link and the handle has a swivel joint which affords turning round the chain without twisting.

- To facilitate holding the arrows in position with the handle of the chain, a groove is cut on the outside surface of handle whose diameter is normally half the diameter of the Arrow. The tallies are used for measuring the distances in chain with ease.

- The letters 5 m, 10 m in case of 20 m chain and 5 m, 10 m, 15 m, in case of 30 m chain are marked.

- The 20 m chain and 30 m chain are shown in the figures 2.1 (a) and (b).

Testing the Chain :

- The correct length of metric chain should be 20 m or 30 m.

- Due to continuous use, the length of chain is either shortened or elongated. Its length is shortened due to bending of links and elongated due to joints, opening out of small rings or due to wear of wearing surfaces.

- Therefore, it is necessary to check the length before commencing each day's work.

- The chain is tested by comparing it with standard test gauge or with the steel tape. A permanent test gauge is established in some public buildings and the chain is tested comparing with it.

- In the field, test gauge is formed by driving two pegs at the required distance say 20 m or 30 m and nails are inserted into the top of these pegs to mark the exact point as shown in the Fig. 2.3 :

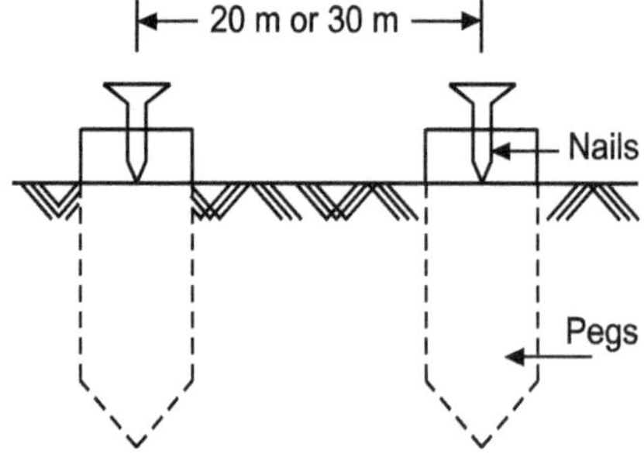

Fig. 2.3 : Field Test Gauge for 20 m OR 30 m Chain

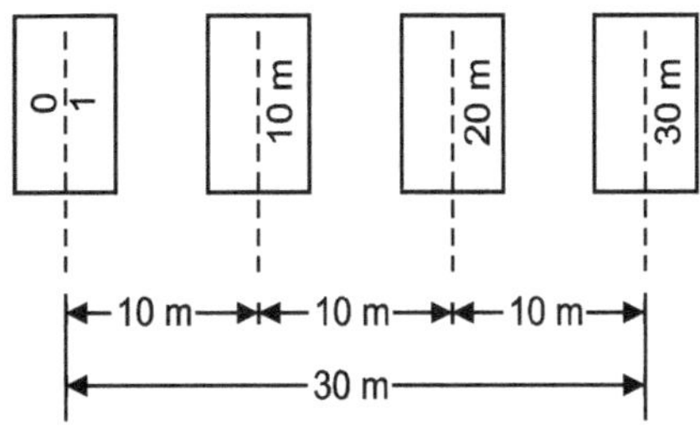

Fig. 2.4 : Permanent Test Gauge

Adjusting the Chain :   (W-11)

The incorrect length of chain may be adjusted as below :

(a) When the chain is found too long then the chain is adjusted -

(i)   By closing up the joints of the opened ring.

(ii)   By hammering back to the original shape of the flattened oval rings.

(iii) By replacing some of the worn rings.

(iv) By adjustable links at the handles.

(b) When the chain is found too short then the chain is adjusted -

(i)   By straightening the bent-up ring.

(ii)   By flattening some of the rings.

(iii) By replacing some of the rings by larger ones.

(iv) By the adjustable rings at the handles.

(v)   By adding new rings as required.

The adjustment in both the cases should be carried out without changing the position of central tag.

The overall length of chain shall conform to the following limits :

20 m chain, error shall not be more than ± 5 mm.

30 m chain, error shall not be more than ± 8 mm.

Errors in Chaining :   (S-11)

There are three types of errors occurring in chaining :

(i)   Compensating Error.

(ii) Cumulative Error.

(iii) Personal mistakes.

(i) Compensating Errors :

- 'Errors which may occur in both directions (i.e. both positive and negative) and which finally tend to compensate are known as *compensating errors*'.

- These errors do not affect survey work seriously.

- They are proportional to $\sqrt{L}$, where L is the length of the line.

Compensating errors are caused by :

(a) Incorrect holding of the chain.

(b) The variation of pull applied for straightening the chain.

(c) Fractional parts of the chain or tape not being uniform throughout its length.

(d) In stepping method, incorrect marking of points on the sloping ground.

(ii) Cumulative Errors :

- Errors which may occur in the same direction and which finally tend to accumulate are said to be cumulative.

- They seriously affect the accuracy of the work and proportional to the length of the line (L). The errors may be positive or negative.

Positive Errors, Negative Errors and Their Causes :　　　　(W-09)

Positive Errors :

When the measured length is more than the actual length (i.e. when the chain is too short), the error is said to be *positive error*. Such errors occur due to :

(a) The length of chain or tape being shorter than the standard length.

(b) Slope corrects not being applied.

(c) Corrects for sag not being made.

(d) Measurement being taken with bad ranging.

(e) Measurement being taken in high winds with the tape in suspension.

Negative Errors :

- When the measured length of the line is less than the actual length (i.e. when the chain is too long), the error is said to be *negative error*.

- These errors occur when the length of chain or tape is greater than the standard length due to following reasons :

(a) The opening of the ring joints.

(b) The applied pull being much greater than the standard pull.

(c) The temperature during measurement being much higher than the standard temperature.

(d) Wearing of connecting rings.

(e) Elongation of the links due to heavy pull.

(iii) Personal Mistakes :

Errors occurring due to carelessness of the chairman are called 'mistakes'. The following are the few common mistakes.

(a) Displacement of arrows :

Once an arrow is withdrawn from the ground during chaining, it may not be replaced in proper position when required, due to some reason.

(b) Miscounting chain :

A full chain length may be omitted or added. This happens when arrows are lost or wrongly counted.

(c) Erroneous reading and booking :

A reading may be taken from the wrong end of the chain.

The number may be called wrongly. For example,"50.2" may be called as "fifty two" and recorded.

Precautions to be taken Against Errors and Mistakes :

The following precautions should be taken to guard against errors and mistakes :

1. The point where the arrow is fixed on the ground should be marked with a cross (X).
2. The zero end of the chain or tape should be properly held.
3. During chaining, the number of arrows carried by the follower and leader should always tally with the total number of arrows taken.
4. While noting measurement from the chain, tally should be verified with respect to the correct end.
5. The chainman should call the measurement loudly and distinctly and the surveyor should repeat them while booking.
6. Measurements should not be taken with the tape in suspension.
7. In stepping operations, horizontality and verticality should be properly maintained.
8. Ranging should be accurately done.
9. Care should be taken so that the chain is properly extended.

Degree of Accuracy in Chaining :   (W-09)

In practice, the following limits of errors are stated -

(1)	For ordinary measurements with steel band on flat ground.	1 in 2000
(2)	For ordinary measurements with a tested chain on fairly level ground.	1 on 1000
(3)	For all average conditions.	1 in 500
(4)	For measurements on uneven or hilly ground.	1 in 250

Errors due to Incorrect Chain :

The measurements taken with an incorrect chain will go wrong. If the chain is too long than the standard length, the measured distance will be less than actual distance and vice versa. However, the distances measured with incorrect length can be corrected by using the formula :

$$\text{The correct length of line} = \frac{L'}{L} \times \text{Measured length of line with incorrect chain or tape}$$

where, L' = The incorrect length of chain.

L = The standard length of chain.

For example : In case of 20 m chain $L = 20$ m;

On testing if it is found 5 cm too long then

$$L' = (20 + 0.05) = 20.05 \text{ m}$$

or say 10 cm too short, then

$$L' = (20 - 0.10) = 19.90 \text{ m}.$$

Errors in area due to incorrect chain –

$$\text{Correct area} = \left(\frac{L'}{L}\right)^2 \times \text{measured area}$$

Errors in volume due to incorrect chain –

$$\text{Correct volume} = \left(\frac{L'}{L}\right)^3 \times \text{measured volume}$$

Where, L and L' are having the same significance.

2.2.2 Tapes

Tapes are used for taking fractional distances which are less than a chain length. They are also used for taking offsets.

Tapes are made of various materials :

(a)   Cloth or linen tapes,

(b)   Metallic tapes,

(c)   Steel tapes, and

(d)   Invar tapes.

(a) Cloth or linen tape :

- It is made of cloth or linen of 12 to 15 mm in width. In this 'm' and 'cm' are calibrated on one side and feet and inches on the other side.

- It is very light and handy, but can be affected by damp.

- It shrinks when wet. It is likely to twist and break. It is used for short distances upto 10 metres. So, its use in engineering field is very much limited.

(b) Metallic tape :

- This tape is made from a varnished strip of cloth or lines 12 to 15 mm wide.

- The brass wires or copper wires are woven into it to prevent twisting and elongation.

- Due to reinforcement with brass wires or copper wires, it is called *metallic tape.*

- Metallic tapes are available in 10 m, 15 m, 20 m, and 30 m lengths. Each metre length is divided into decimeters and centimeters.

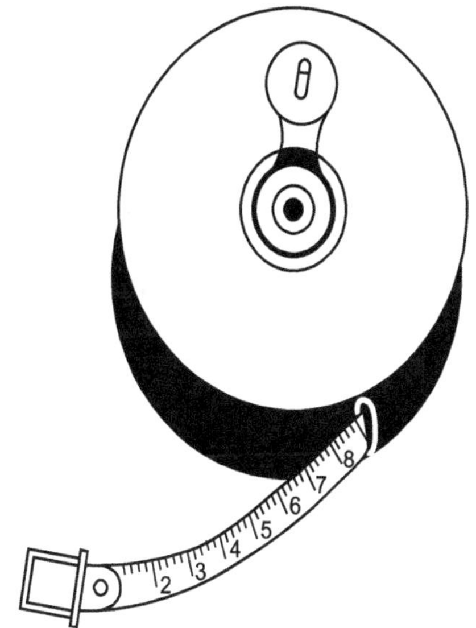

Fig. 2.5 : Metallic Tape

- It is available in leather case with winding device. The zero end of the tape is provided with metal ring. The details of metallic tape with method of graduation etc. are shown in Fig. 2.5.

- Metallic tapes are used in all engineering fields for taking offsets and subsidiary measurements excepts very precise measurements when accuracy is of prime importance.

(c) Steel tape :

- This tape is made of steel or stainless steel strip of width 6 mm to 16 mm. It is more accurately graduated.

- Each metre length is divided into two hundred equal parts, thus, each part of least count is equal to 5 mm.

- It is provided with brass ring at the zero end of the tape. The length of tape include this ring. Steel tapes are available in lengths of 10, 20, 30 and 50 m.

- It is wound either in a leather case or rust proof metal case of suitable winding device.

- For accurate measurements, steel tape is used. It is light and delicate and hence should be carefully handled.

- It should be wiped clean and dry after use and should be oiled with suitable mineral oil to prevent rusting. A graduated strip of steel tape is shown in the Fig. 2.6.

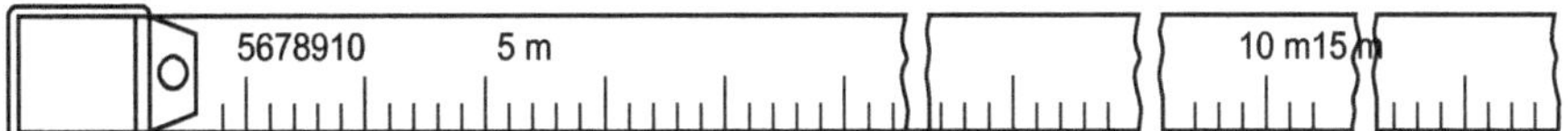

Fig. 2.6 : Steel Tape

(d) Invar tape :

- This tape is made-up of an alloy of steel (64 %) and nickel (36 %). It has a very low coefficient of thermal expansion (0.000000122 for 1°C) even less than 1/10 of that of steel.
- It is made in 6 mm strips and available in length of 20, 30, 50 and 100 m.
- It is very costly and very delicate.
- It must be handled with utmost care to avoid bending and kinking. It is only used for very accurate linear measurements.

2.2.3 Ranging Rods or Poles

- Ranging rods are used for ranging. Ranging is the process of locating the intermediate points between two survey stations when the length of survey line is more than the chain length.
- Ranging rods are made by seasoned teak or pine or deodar wood or steel pipes of 3 cm diameter.
- The length of ranging rod varies from 2 to 3 m and they are either circular or octagonal in section.
- An iron shoe is provided at the bottom of ranging rod to facilitate fixing into the ground. Ranging rods are painted in alternate red, black and white colours in length of 20 cm each as shown in Fig. 2.7 (a), so that they can be seen at distance.

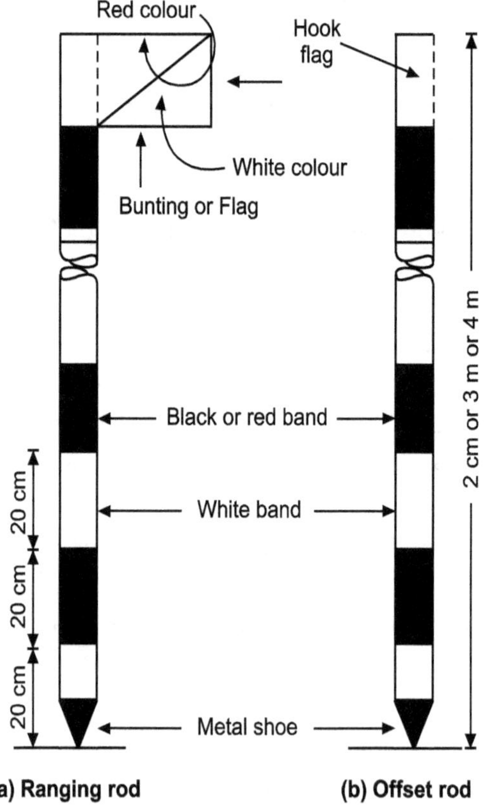

Fig. 2.7

- For better visibility, they are provided with coloured flags of 30 cm square at the top. Ranging rods are used for (i) ranging survey lines, and (ii) marking position of stations.

2.2.4 Offset Rods

- An offset rod is similar to ranging rod. It is usually 3 m long and is divided into parts, each of 0.2 m length.

- At the top, it is provided with a notch or hook for pulling or pushing the chain through a hedge or other obstruction. It is used for measuring the offsets roughly. [Fig. 2.7 (b)]

2.2.5 Arrows

- Arrows are also called 'marking pins'. They are used to mark the end of each chain during chaining.

- At the end of the changing, length of chain is multiplied by number of arrows to find total length. They are made of stout steel wire 4 mm (or 8 SWG) in diameter having length equal to 40 cm.

- They are pointed at one end for inserting into the ground and bent into a ring at the other end for carrying. Usually, ten arrows are supplied with one chain. Refer Fig. 2.8.

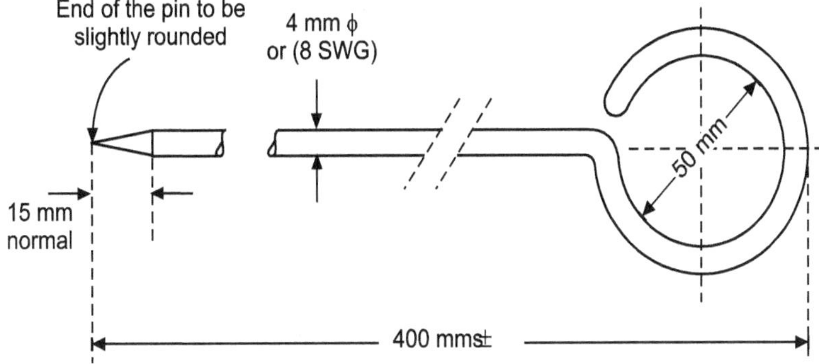

Fig. 2.8 : Steel Arrow

2.2.6 Pegs

- Pegs are made of hard timber usually 2.5 cm × 2.5 cm and 15 to 30 cm long. Iron pegs of 1 cm diameter are sometimes used instead of wooden pegs.

- In soft ground, large sized pegs of 30 to 50 cm are used. The pegs are tapered at one end and are driven into the ground with hammer.

- Pegs are used for making the positions of stations or terminal points of survey lines.

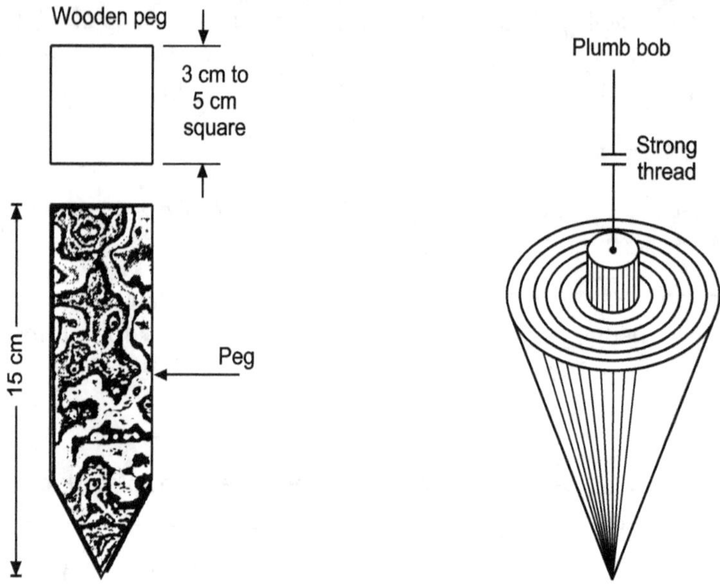

Fig. 2.9 : Wooden Peg   **Fig. 2.10 : Plumb Bob**

2.2.7 Plumb Bob

- Plumb bob is made of conical weight of metal (preferably brass) and is suspended from strong thread for testing the verticality of the objects.

- It is used to transfer the points to the ground while chaining on sloping ground as in method of stepping.

- It is also used for accurate centreing of the theodolite over the station point.

2.3 RANGING   (S-08; W-08, 09, S-12)

- The method of establishing intermediate points on a straight line between the two fixed points is known as *ranging*.

- It is done before chaining is started. It may be done by eye or by using some instruments such as line ranger or theodolite.

Methods of ranging : (1) Direct method or (2) Indirect method.

2.3.1 Direct Ranging   (W-11)

- Direct ranging is adopted when both ends of the survey line are intervisible. It is carried out by eye judgement or by using line ranger.

(1) Ranging by Eye Judgement :

- Let A and B be the two end points of survey line. The ranging of a line by eye is done by the surveyor and his assistant (Follower and Leader).

- The surveyor stands at point A with his ranging rod. Another ranging rod is fixed at point B.

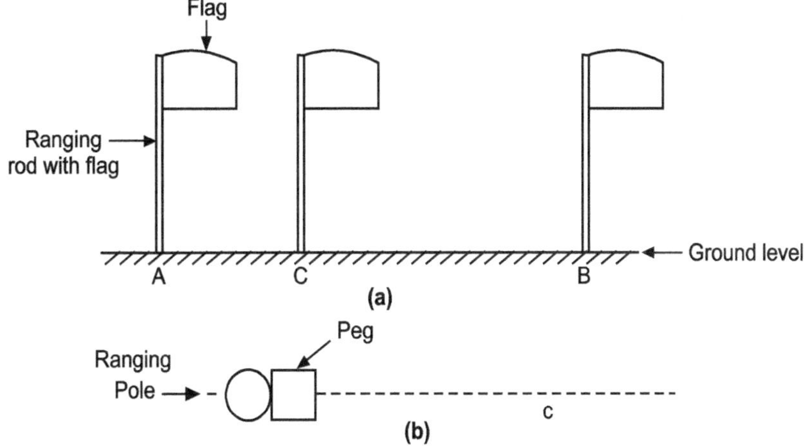

Fig. 2.11 : Ranging by Eye Judgement

- The assistant then goes with another ranging rod and holds at a point approximately in line with AB. This distance is less than the chain length from A.

- The surveyor at A then stands about half m behind A and directs the assistant to the right or left of the chain line till the pole appears in line with A and B.

- Now, points ACB will be in a straight line. The assistant examines the verticality of the pole and awaits for signal from the surveyor.

- Surveyor, on satisfaction, directs him to fix up the pole.

Code of Signals for Ranging (S-11) : In guiding the assistant into line, the surveyor should use the following code of signals :

Signal by the Surveyor (Follower)	Action by the Assistant (Feeder)
1. Rapid sweeps i.e. up and down movement with right hand on right side.	1. Move considerably to the right.
2. Rapid sweeps with left hand on left side.	2. Move considerably to the left.
3. Slow sweeps with right hand on right side.	3. Move slowly to the right.
4. Slow sweeps with left hand on left side.	4. Move slowly to the left.
5. Right arm extended.	5. Continue to move to the right.
6. Left arm extended.	6. Continue to move to the left.
7. Right arm up and moved towards right.	7. Make the rod vertical by moving towards right.
8. Left arm up and moved towards left.	8. Make the rod vertical by moving towards left.
9. Both hands above head and brought down.	9. Correct.
10. Both arms extended forward horizontally and then depressed briskly.	10. Fix the ranging rod.

(2) Ranging by Line Ranger :

- A line ranger is a small reflecting instrument used for fixing intermediate points on the survey line.
- It is used where survey line is too long and it is not convenient or possible to go either end for ranging by eye.

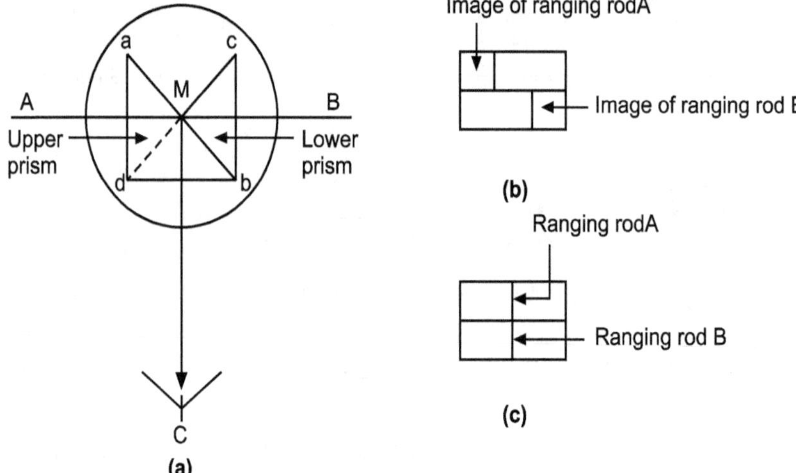

Fig. 2.12 : Line Ranger

Construction of Line Ranger :

- Line ranger consists of two right angled isosceles triangular prisms placed one above the other as shown in Fig. 2.12.
- To establish an intermediate point M in line with the terminal point A and B, the observer stands approximately in the line near M and holds the instrument at his eye level.
- The rays of light from signal A enter the upper prism are reflected from the hypotenuse, then enter the eye at right angles to the line AB.
- Similarly, the rays of light from signal B enter the lower prism and are reflected from the hypotenuse.
- It then enters the eye at right angle to the line AB. The images of A and B are then seen one above the other as shown in Fig. 2.12 (b).
- The observer then moves across the line until the two images appear exactly one above the other. The required point M is then marked on the ground as shown in Fig. 2.12 (c).

Adjustment of Line Ranger :

- One of the prisms is adjustable. For testing of line ranger, three points are fixed exactly in line.
- Hold the instrument over the middle point and observe the images of the two points; if they appear in exact coincidence.
- If not, move the adjustable prism until the images appear exactly in one vertical line.

2.3.2 Indirect Ranging or Reciprocal Ranging (W-05, W-10, W-11, S-12)

- Indirect or Reciprocal ranging is done when the ends of survey line are not intervisible due to high ground or a hill intervening.

- It is also done when ends of survey line are not clearly visible due to long distance between them.

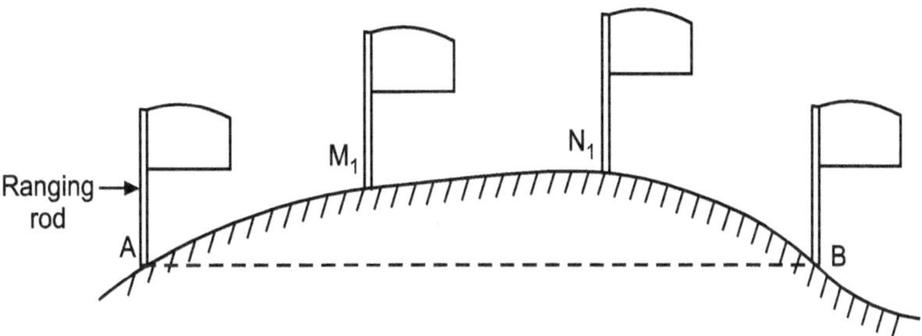

Fig. 2.13 (a) : High ground or hill

- Let A and B be two survey stations. They are not mutually visible due to high ground between them.

- It is required to measure the distance between A and B. Let two chain-man at M_1 and N_1 as shown in Fig. 2.13 (a).

- The chain-man at M_1 can see both the ranging rods at N_1 and B. The chain-man at N can see the ranging at M_1 and A.

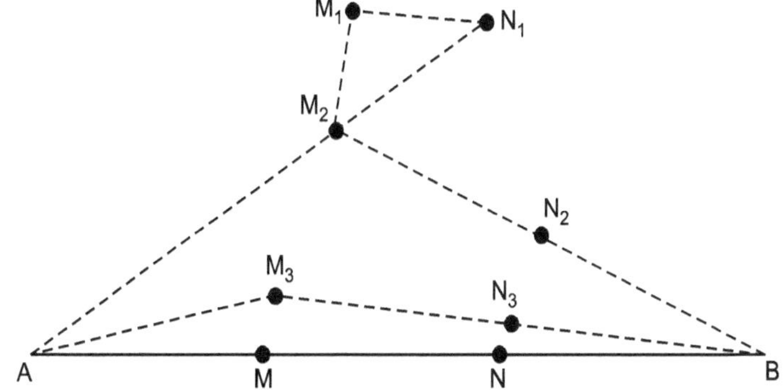

Fig. 2.13 (b) : Indirect ranging

- The two chain-men then direct each other alternately. The chain-man at N_1 directs the chain-man at M_1 to come in line with AN_1 to occupy position M_2.

- Then the chain-man at M_2 directs the chain-man at N_1 to come in line with M_2 B.

- By successively directing each other, they finally occupy position M and N on line AB. Now, AMNB are exactly in the same line.

- Other intermediate points can be fixed by direct ranging and the distance AB can be chained.

- This method can also be used in ranging a line across a valley.

Methods of Linear Measurements :

1. Pacing :

- Where approximate result is required, distance may be determined pacing. This method is used for reconnaissance survey, for preparation of military plans. Also used for approximate checking distance. The method consists of walking over a line and counting the number of paces the required distance may be obtained by multiplying the number of paces by the average length of pace.

The length of pace varies with the:

- Individual, age, height and physical condition.

- The nature of the ground (uphill and downhill).

- The slope of the country.

- The speed of pacing.

2. Speedometer :

- The Speedometer of an automobile may be used to measure distances approximately. It gives better results than pacing, provided the route is smooth.

- The distance covered will be equal to the product of the circumference of the wheel and the number of rotations of the wheel as in automobiles.

2.4 CHAINING　　　　　　　　(W-09, S-12)

- 'The method of measuring the distance with chain or tape' is called *chaining*.

- For measuring the length of line, two men are required. They are called chain-men.

- The chain-man at the forward end of the chain is called the 'leader' and the chain-man at the zero or rear end of the chain is a 'follower'.

- The follower is a more skilled man. To start with, the leader takes ten arrows in one hand and a ranging rod and handle of the chain in other hand.

- He marks the successive positions of his end of chain. The leader and the follower should each have ranging rod.

- Chaining involves the following steps :

    (i)　Fixing stations.

    (ii)　Unfolding the chain.

    (iii)　Ranging.

    (iv)　Measuring of distance.

    (v)　Folding the chain.

(i)   Fixing Stations : Stations are marked with ranging rods so that the stations are visible from long distances.

(ii) Unfolding the chain : The chain-man holds both handles in his left hand and throws out the chain with his right hand. With the help of his assistant, proceeds to free it from twists and knobs. Then the chain is roughly straightened. It is examined for bent links, badly opened joints before starting actual chaining.

(iii) Ranging : If a survey line i.e. chaining distance is large, then intermediate points are established for making the straight line is known as *ranging*.

(iv) Measuring of distance : The distance is measured by leader and follower by fixing arrows at the end point of chain by leader and again pulley the chain for measuring the further distance. At that time follower holds the rear end of chain where leader have fixed the arrow.

(v)   Folding the chain : After chaining is completed, the chain must be folded in particular manner to form a complete bundle which can be tightly held by a strap. By holding the middle end of the chain, it is roughly doubled. Each pair of link is folded oblique across to form a bundle. It is then tied with a strap.

Duties of Leader :

(1)   To hold ranging rod at the end of chain length.

(2)   To pull the chain forward.

(3)   To obey instructions of the follower.

(4)   To insert an arrow at the end of every chain.

Duties of Follower :

(1)   To direct the leader in line with ranging rod at forward end station.

(2)   To give instructions to the leader.

(3)   To carry the rear handle of chain.

(4)   To pick up the arrows inserted by the leader.

(5)   To transfer the arrows at the end of tenth chain length.

2.5 CHAINING ON SLOPING GROUND   (S-09, 10; W-10, S-12)

- For plotting, horizontal distances are required. On sloping ground, distances may be measured along the slope and then converted to horizontal equivalent distances.

- While chaining on sloping ground, horizontal distances can be computed by the following methods :

(1) Direct method - By stepping : （S-05）

- It consists of measuring the distance in small horizontal lengths.

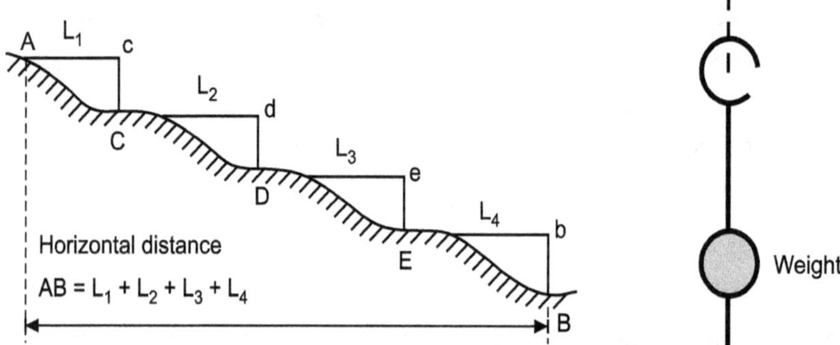

Fig. 2.14 : Step-by-Step Chaining

- Let the horizontal distance between A and B be measured by a chain or tape. A portion of chain say 2 m, 4 m, 5 m, 10 m is stretched horizontally with one end resting on the ground and the other end held in line at a convenient height say 1 m to 1.5 m, (say at point c).
- The point vertically below this end is then accurately marked with the help of plump bob (point C).
- The next step will then start from this point and the method is continued in the correct line with point B. It is used for small short slopes.

The following points should be kept in view while adopting this method :

(a)   The chain or tape should be stretched horizontally.

(b)   The length of step need not be the same throughout.

(c)   It is more convenient and gives better results, to chain down the hill than to chain up the hill.

(2) Indirect method :

- In case of regular or uniform slope the chaining is done along the slope.
- The angle of slope and difference in height between the two points is measured and horizontal distance is computed.
- Here horizontal distance is not determined on field directly so it is called indirect method.

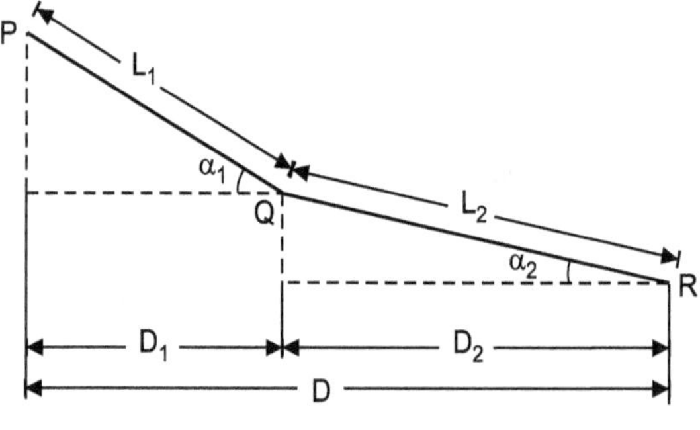

Fig. 2.15

In this method as shown in Fig. 2.15. L_1 is the inclined distance between P and Q. α_1 is the slope of line PQ

$$\therefore \qquad D_1 = L_1 \cos \alpha_1$$

L_2 is the inclined distance between Q and R. α_2 is the slope of line QR.

$$\therefore \qquad D_2 = L_2 \cos \alpha_2$$

$$\therefore \quad \text{Total distance } (D) = D_1 + D_2$$

2.6 DIGITAL TAPE

- A digital measuring tape is a device that measures length traditionally with tape but can be digitally. This type of device usually has a liquid crystal display (LCD) screen connected to a traditional measuring tape.

- When the type is extended and used to measure, the LCD screen will display the length. Owners also have the option of recording the lengths for future reference.

- A digital measuring tape allows its user to store and recall measurements that were taken using the tape.

- This can be useful during home repair or other projects that require frequent and numerous measurements.

- So the measurements can be recorded and referenced without having to be written down or manually recorded after each measurement.

- Common digital measuring tapes have an average length of 25 feet (7.5 m) but can come in virtually any length.

- The length of the digital measuring tape purchased likely will depend on the needs of its buyer. Those who have only small projects need not invest in a length digital measuring tape.

- The features of a digital measuring tape can vary from model to model. Devices can turn on automatically when the tape is extended or shut-off automatically when the tape is retracted, in order to conserve battery life.

- Many of the devices alert the user when batteries run low. Some models allow the user to have the measurement display for a longer period of time, and some advise the user of midway points with the touch of a button.

- Conversion between standard units and metric units can be a handy feature for someone using this type of device, as is the display of fractions.

- Some devices might also have the ability to record voice notes so that a builder can take notes while on the job or listen to previous notes.

- Some setting might even left users manipulate case lengths when taking interior measurements.

SOLVED EXAMPLES

TYPE-I : PROBLEMS ON CALCULATION OF TRUE LENGTH OR CORRECT DISTANCE

Example 2.1 :

Length of a survey line was measured with a 30 m chain and found to be 315.4 m. When the chain was compared with chain standard, it was found to be 0.2 m too short. Find correct length of the line.   **(S-08)**

Solution :

$$L = 30 \text{ m}$$

$$\text{Measured length} = 315.4 \text{ m}$$

$$L_1 = 30 - 0.2 = 29.8 \text{ m}$$

$$\text{True length} = \frac{L_1}{L} \times \text{Measured length}$$

$$= \frac{29.8}{30} \times 315.4 = 313.29 \text{ m} \qquad \textbf{... Ans.}$$

Example 2.2 :

A 30 m chain was tested before commencement of chaining work. Line PQ was chained by it and observed length of PQ was 1230 m. The chain was tested at the end of work and was found to be 12 cm too short. Find the correct distance PQ.

(W-10)

Solution :

$$\text{Correct distance} = \frac{L_1}{L} \times \text{measured distance}$$

$$\text{Error before commencement} = 0.0 \text{ m}$$

$$\text{Error at the end} = -0.12 \text{ m}$$

$$\text{Average error} = \frac{0 + (-0.12)}{2} = -0.06 \text{ m}$$

$$L_1 = 30 - 0.06 = 29.94 \text{ m}; \ L = 30 \text{ m}$$

$$\text{Measured distance} = 1230 \text{ m}$$

$$\therefore \quad \text{Correct length} = \frac{L_1}{L} \times \text{measured distance}$$

$$= \frac{29.94}{30} \times 1230$$

$$= 1227.54 \text{ m} \qquad \textbf{.... Ans.}$$

Example 2.3 :

A line was measured by a 20 m chain which was accurate before starting the day's work. After chaining 900 m, the chain was found to be 6 cm too long. After changing a total distance of 1575 m, the chain was found to be 14 cms too long. Find the true distance of the line.   **(W-06)**

Solution :

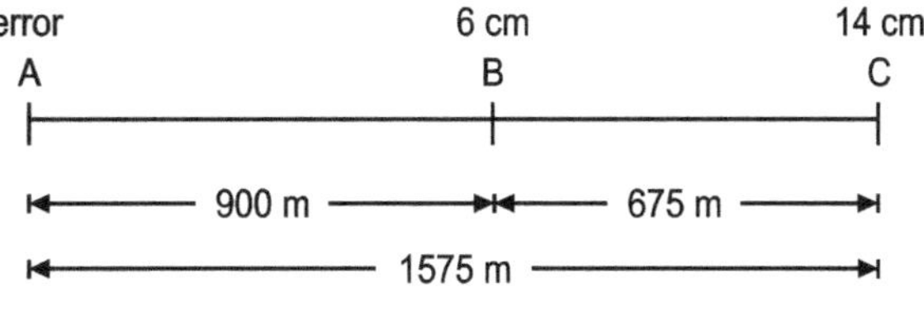

Fig. 2.16

For first 900 m :

$$\text{Average error} = \frac{0 + 6}{2} = 3 \text{ cm}$$

$$= 0.03 \text{ m}$$

$\therefore$ Length of the chain, L_1 = 20 + 0.03 = 20.03 m

$\therefore$ True distance $= \dfrac{20.03}{20} \times 900 = 901.35$ m

For next 675 m :

$$\text{Average error} = \frac{6 + 14}{2} = 10 \text{ cm} = 0.1 \text{ m}$$

$\therefore$ Incorrect length of chain, L_1 = 20 + 0.1 = 20.01 m

$\therefore$ True distance $= \dfrac{20.01}{20} \times 675 = 675.33$ m

$\therefore$ Total true distance of the line = 901.35 + 675.33 = 1576.68 m **... Ans.**

Example 2.4 :

A 20 m chain was found to be 0.05 m too long after chaining 1400 m. It was found to be 0.10 m too long after chaining next 2200 m. If the chain was correct before commencement of work, find the true distance chained. (W-07)

Solution :

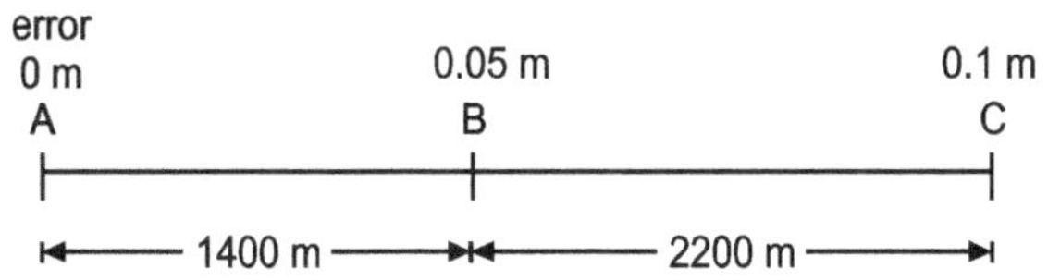

Fig. 2.17

(i) Chain was 0.05 m too long.

  Actual length (AB) = 1400 m

  Length of chain, L = 20 m

$$\text{Error} = \frac{0 + 0.05}{2} = 0.025 \text{ m}$$

  Mean length of chain, L_1 = 20 + 0.025

$$= 20.025 \text{ m}$$

$$\text{Correct length} = \frac{L_1}{L} \times 1400$$

$$= \frac{20.025}{20} \times 1400$$

$$= 1401.75 \text{ m} \qquad \text{... Ans.}$$

(ii) Chain was 0.10 m too long.

$$\text{Actual length (BC)} = 2200 \text{ m}$$

$$\text{Length of chain, } L = 20 \text{ m}$$

$$\text{Error} = \frac{0.05 + 0.1}{2} = 0.075$$

$$\text{Mean length of chain, } L_1 = 20.075$$

$$\text{Correct length} = \frac{L_1}{L} \times 2200$$

$$= \frac{20.075}{20} \times 2200$$

$$= 2208.25$$

$$\therefore \quad \text{Total distance} = 1401.75 + 2208.25 = 3610 \text{ m} \qquad \text{... Ans.}$$

Example 2.5 :

A 20 m chain was found to be 0.05 m too long after chaining 1500 m. It was found to be 0.1 m too long after chaining 3000 m. If the chain was correct before the commencement of the work, find the true distance.

Solution :

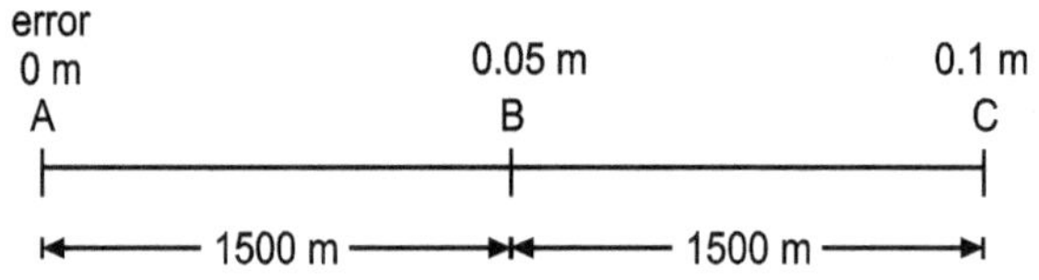

Fig. 2.18

$$\text{Error} = \frac{0 + 0.05}{2} = 0.025$$

$$\text{Correct distance} = \frac{L_1}{L} \times \text{measured distance}$$

For first 1500 m :

$$L_1 = 20 + \frac{0.025}{2} = 20.025$$

$$L = 20 \text{ m}$$

$$\therefore \quad \text{Correct distance} = \frac{20.025}{20} \times 1500 = 1501.875 \text{ m}$$

For next 1500 m (i.e. 1500 to 3000 m) :

Error in chain at 1500 m distance = + 0.05 m

Error in chain at distance 3000 m = + 0.1 m

$$\text{Average error} = \frac{0.05 + 0.1}{2} = 0.075 \text{ m}$$

$$L_1 = 20 + 0.075 = 20.075 \text{ m}$$

and

$$L = 20 \text{ m}$$

$\therefore$

$$\text{Correction distance} = \frac{L_1}{L} \times 1500 = \frac{20.075}{20} \times 1500$$

$$= 1505.625 \text{ m}$$

$\therefore$

$$\text{Total true distance} = 1501.875 + 1505.625$$

$$= 3007.5 \text{ m} \qquad \qquad \text{... Ans.}$$

Example 2.6 :

A 30 metre chain was tested before the commencement of the day's work and was found to be correct. After chaining a distance of 100 chains it was found to be 0.5 decimetre too short. At the end of the day's work after chaining a total distance of 180 chains, the chain was found to be 1 decimetre too long. What was the true distance chained ?

Solution :

1 chain = 30 m (for 30 m chain)

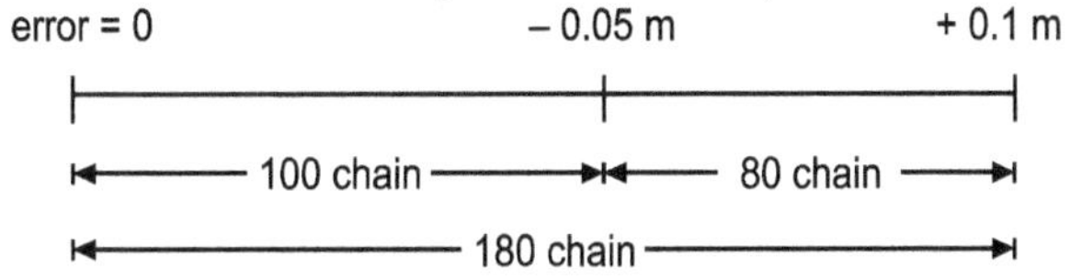

Fig. 2.19

For line AB :

$$\text{Error} = \frac{0 + (-0.05)}{2} = -0.025 \text{ m}$$

$$L_1 = 30 - 0.025 = 29.975 \text{ m}$$

$$\text{Measured length AB} = 100 \times 30 = 3000 \text{ m}$$

$$\text{True length of line AB} = \left(\frac{L_1}{L}\right) \times \text{Measured length}$$

$$= \left(\frac{29.975}{30}\right) \times 3000 = 2997.50 \text{ m}$$

For line BC :

$$\text{Error} = \frac{-0.05 + 0.1}{2} = 0.025$$

$\therefore$

$$L_1 = 30 + 0.025 = 30.025 \text{ m}$$

$$\text{Measured length of BC} = 80 \times 30 = 2400 \text{ m}$$

$\therefore$

$$\text{True length of line BC} = \left(\frac{L_1}{L}\right) \times \text{Measured length}$$

$\therefore$

$$\text{True length of line BC} = \left(\frac{30.025}{30}\right) \times 2400 = 2402 \text{ m}$$

$\therefore$

$$\text{Total true length} = l\,(AB) + l\,(BC)$$

$$= 2997.5 + 2402 = 5399.60 \text{ m}$$

TYPE II : PROBLEMS ON ERROR IN CHAIN

Example 2.7 :

A road is actually 4,250 m long but when measured by an incorrect chain which is 30 m long, was found to be 4,239 m long. What correction does the chain need ?

Solution :

$$L_1 = \frac{\text{Correct length of line}}{\text{Incorrect length of line}} \times L$$

$$= \frac{4250}{4239} \times 30$$

$$L_1 = 30.0778$$

$$L_c = 30.0778 - 30$$

$$= -0.0778 \text{ m}$$

i.e. the chain is too long by 7.78 cm.

∴   Correction needed for the chain is + 7.78 cm.   **... Ans.**

Example 2.8 :

A road actually 1410 m long was found 1406 m when measured by a defective 30 m chain. How much correction does the chain need ?   **(W-09)**

Solution :

$$\text{Actual length of road} = 1410 \text{ m}$$

$$\text{Incorrect length of road} = 1406 \text{ m}$$

$$\text{Length of chain, } L = 30 \text{ m}$$

$$\text{Incorrect length of chain, } L_1 = ?$$

$$\text{Correct length of road} = \frac{L_1}{L} \times \text{Incorrect length of road}$$

$$\therefore \quad 1410 = \frac{L_1}{30} \times 1406$$

$$\therefore \quad L_1 = 30.08$$

Now,   Correction in the chain = 30.08 – 30 m = 0.08 m

∴   Chain was 0.08 m too long.   **... Ans.**

Example 2.9 :

The length of a survey line was measured with a 20 m chain and was found to be equal to 1500 metres. As a check the length was again measured with a 30 m chain and found to be 1476 metres. If the 20 m chain was 5 cm too short, what was the error in 30 m chain ?   **(W-08)**

Solution :

$$\text{True distance} = \frac{L_1}{L} \times \text{Measured distance}$$

$$L = 20 \text{ m}$$
$$L_1 = 20 - 0.05$$
$$= 19.95 \text{ m}$$
$$\text{Measured distance} = 1500 \text{ m}$$

$\therefore$ $\text{True distance} = \dfrac{19.95}{20} \times 1500 = 1496.25 \text{ m}$ ... (i)

For 30 m chain, $L = 30 \text{ m}$

$$\text{Measured distance} = 1476 \text{ m}$$
$$L_1 = ?$$
$$\text{True distance} = 1496.25 \text{ m} \qquad \text{[From (i)]}$$

$\therefore$ $\text{True distance} = \dfrac{L_1}{L} \times \text{Measured distance}$

$$1496.25 = \frac{L_1}{30} \times 1476$$

$\therefore$ $L_1 = 30.411 \text{ m}$

$\therefore$ $30.411 - 30 = 0.411 \text{ m to long}$

The error in the 30 m chain was 0.411 m.   **... Ans.**

Example 2.10 :

The distance between two towns measured by 20 m chain was 1701 m and when measured by a 30 m chain, it was 8510 links. The tests show that both the chain were incorrect. What correction is required in the 20 m chain, if the 30 m chain is 0.4 link too long.

Solution :

[I] For 30 m chain.

30 m chain was 0.4 link too long and 1 link $= 0.20$ m.

$\therefore$ Error in 30 m chain $= 0.4 \times 0.20 \text{ m} = 0.08 \text{ m too long}$

$\therefore$ Length of chain with error,

$$L_1 = 30 + 0.08$$
$$= 30.08 \text{ m}$$

and $\text{True distance} = \dfrac{L_1}{L} \times \text{Measured distance}$

$$= \frac{30.08}{30} (8510 \times 0.20) = 1706.53 \text{ m}$$

[II] For 20 m chain.

Now, $\text{True distance} = 1706.53 \text{ m}$ (from case I)

and $\text{Measured distance} = 1701 \text{ m}$

$$\text{Length of chain, } L = 20 \text{ m}$$

We have,   True distance $= \dfrac{L_1}{L} \times$ Measured distance

$\therefore$ $1706.53 = \dfrac{L_1}{20} \times 1701$

$\therefore$ $L_1 = \dfrac{1706.53 \times 20}{1701}$

$\therefore$ $L_1 = 20.065$ m

$\therefore$ Error in 20 m chain $= 20.065 - 20$

$= 0.065$ m

The 20 m chain was 6.5 cm too long.   ... **Ans.**

TYPE III : PROBLEMS ON CALCULATION OF TRUE AREA

Example 2.11 :

A certain field was measured with a 20 m chain and found to be 45 sq. km. It was afterward found that the chain was 0.1 m too short, what is the true area of the field ?

Solution :

$$\text{True area} = \left(\dfrac{L'}{L}\right)^2 \times \text{ measured area}$$

$L' = 20 - 0.1 = 19.90$ m and $L = 20$ m

Measured area is 45 sq. km.

$\therefore$ True area of the field $= \left(\dfrac{19.90}{20}\right)^2 \times 45 = 44.5511$ km^2 ... **Ans.**

Example 2.12 :

A survey of field was plotted to a scale of 1 cm = 12 m. This plan was shrunk and area now obtained by planimeter is 294.4 cm^2.

It was found that a line measured 8 cm now, was originally 9 cm long. The 20 m chain used was 7 cm too short as per remarks mentioned on the plan. What is the true area of the plot.   **(S-09)**

Solution :

$$L = 9 \text{ cm}$$
$$L_1 = 8 \text{ cm}$$
$$\text{True area on paper} = \left(\dfrac{L_1}{L}\right)^2 \times \text{Measured area}$$
$$= \left(\dfrac{8}{9}\right)^2 \times 294.4 = 232.61 \text{ cm}^2$$
$$\text{Measured area} = 232.61 \times 12^2 = 576 \text{ m}^2$$
$$L = 20 \text{ m}$$
$$L_1 = 20 - 0.07 = 19.93 \text{ m}$$
$$\text{True area} = \left(\dfrac{L_1}{L}\right)^2 \times \text{Measured area} = \left(\dfrac{19.93}{20}\right)^2 \times 576$$
$$= 571.97 \text{ m}^2$$

... **Ans.**

Example 2.13 :

The plane of an old survey plotted to a scale of 1 cm = 10 m was found to have shrunk so that a line originally 10 cm long was found to measured 9.8 cm. There was a note on the plan that 30 m chain used was 0.03 m too short. If the area of the plan now measured with planimeter is 97.20 cm². Determine true area of survey. **(S-06)**

Solution :

Given : Scale in the map : 1 cm = 10 m

$$\therefore \quad 1 \text{ cm}^2 = 100 \text{ m}^2$$

Now, Original area of survey on paper $= \left(\dfrac{10}{9.8}\right)^2 \times 97.20 = 101.20 \text{ cm}^2$

$\therefore$ The area of plot measured on the ground $= 101.20 \times 100$

$$= 10120 \text{ m}^2$$

Note given on the map was '30 m chain used was 0.03 m too short'.

i.e. length of the chain, $L_1 = 30 - 0.03 = 29.97$ m

Hence,

Actual area on the ground $= \left(\dfrac{L_1}{L}\right)^2 \times$ Measured area $= \left(\dfrac{29.97}{30}\right)^2 \times 10120$

$$= 10099.77 \text{ m}^2 \quad\quad\quad\quad \textbf{... Ans.}$$

Example 2.14 :

The paper of an old map drawn to a scale of 100 m to 1 cm has shrunk, so that a line originally 10 cm has shrunk, has now become 9.6 cm. The survey was done with a 20 m chain 10 cm too short. If the area measured now is 71 cm². Find the correct area on the field. **(S-05)**

Solution :

10 cm line has shrunk to 9.6 cm.

Area measured $= 9.6$ cm

$\therefore$ Correct area of plane $= \left(\dfrac{10}{9.6}\right)^2 \times 71 = 77.04 \text{ cm}^2$

Scale used is, 1 cm $= 100$ m

$\therefore$ Measured area of survey $= (77.04)(100)^2 = 770400 \text{ m}^2$

Incorrect length of chain used $= 20 - 0.1$

$$= 19.9 \text{ m}$$

$\therefore$ Correct area $= \left(\dfrac{19.9}{20}\right)^2 \times 770400$

$$= 762715.26 \text{ m}^2 \qquad \text{... Ans.}$$

Example 2.15 :

The plan of an old survey, plotted to a scale of 1 cm = 40 m was found to be shrunk, so that a line originally 20 cm long measured 19.7 cm. There was also a note on the plan that the 20 m chain used was 0.1 m too short. If the area on the plan measured now by planimeter is 100 sq. cm. Find the true area of the survey plot in hectares.

Solution :

$$\text{Original Area (plotted)} = \left(\frac{20}{19.7}\right)^2 \times 100$$

$$= \frac{400}{388.09} \times 100 = 103 \text{ sq. cm on paper.}$$

The scale of the map was 1 cm = 40 m.

    i.e. 1 cm^2 represents 40 m^2 = 1600 sq. m.

    $\therefore$ The area of plot on the ground = $103 \times 1600 = 164800$ sq.m.

But there was a note on the map that 20 m chain was 0.1 m (10 cm) too short.

i.e. it was 20 − 0.10 = 19.90 only.

Hence,   actual area on the ground

$$= \left(\frac{L'}{L}\right)^2 \times \text{measured area}$$

$$= \left(\frac{19.90}{20}\right)^2 \times 164800 = 163156 \text{ m}^2$$

OR $\qquad \dfrac{163156}{10^4} = 16.3156$ Hectares $\qquad$ **... Ans.**

Example 2.16 :

A chain was tested before commencement of the work and was found to be exactly 20 m. At the end of the survey, it was found to measure 20.20 m. The area of the field drawn to a scale of 1 cm = 16 m was 60.25 sq.cm. Find the true area of the field in hectares.

Solution :   True length of chain = 20 m

    Length measured at the end of survey = 20.20 m

    Scale given is 1 cm = 16 m

$\therefore$ $\qquad\qquad$ 1 cm^2 = $(16)^2$ m^2

Now, measured area of the field = $60.25 \times 16 \times 16$

$$= 15424 \text{ m}^2$$

Area of the field measured with 20.2 m chain is 15424 m^2.

Now,   Length of the chain, L = 20 m

Length of the chain at the end of survey

$$= 20.20 \text{ m}$$

$\therefore$ $\qquad$ Mean length of chain $= \dfrac{20 + 20.20}{2}$

$$\therefore \qquad L_1 = 20.1 \text{ m}$$

True area measured by 20 m chain $= \left[\dfrac{L_1}{L}\right]^2 \times$ Measured area

$$\therefore \qquad \text{True area} = \left[\dfrac{20.1}{20}\right]^2 \times 15424$$

$$= 1.01 \times 15424 = 15578.24 \text{ m}^2$$

$$\therefore \qquad \text{True area} = \dfrac{15578.24}{10^4} \qquad [\because 1 \text{ hectare} = 10^4 \text{ sq.m}]$$

$$= 1.55 \text{ Hectares} \qquad\qquad \textbf{... Ans.}$$

Important Points

- There are two types of measurements :
  (a) Linear measurement and (b) Angular measurements.
- INSTRUMENTS USED FOR MEASURING DISTANCES
  (1) Chain,   (5) Arrows,
  (2) Tape,   (6) Pegs,
  (3) Ranging rods,   (7) Plumb bob.
  (4) Offset rods,
- **Chain :** The metric chains are used for measuring distances. These are made by 20 m and 30 m.

  (a) When the chain is found too long then the chain is adjusted -

  (i)   By closing up the joints of the opened ring.

  (ii) By hammering back to the original shape of the flattened oval rings.

  (iii) By replacing some of the worn rings.

  (iv) By adjustable links at the handles.

  (b) When the chain is found too short then the chain is adjusted -

  (i)   By straightening the bent-up ring.

  (ii) By flattening some of the rings.

  (iii) By replacing some of the rings by larger ones.

  (iv) By the adjustable rings at the handles.

  (v)   By adding new rings as required.

- **There are three types of errors occurring in chaining :**

  (i)   Compensating Error.

  (ii) Cumulative Error.

  (iii) Personal mistakes.

- Tapes are made of various materials :

  (a) Cloth or linen tapes,

  (b) Metallic tapes,

  (c) Steel tapes, and

  (d) Invar tapes.

- Arrows are used to mark the end of each chain during chaining.
- Pegs are used for making the positions of stations or terminal points of survey lines.
- Plumb bob is used to transfer the points to the ground while chaining on sloping ground as in method of stepping. It is also used for accurate centreing of the theodolite over the station point.
- The method of establishing intermediate points on a straight line between the two fixed points is known as *ranging*.
- Direct ranging is adopted when both ends of the survey line are intervisible.
- Indirect or Reciprocal ranging is done when the ends of survey line are not intervisible due to high ground or a hill intervening.

Practice Questions

1. Enlist the various instruments required for measuring distances. Describe each of them briefly.
2. Explain the construction and use of 20 m chain and 30 m chain. How is the chain tested and adjusted ?
3. State the various types of tapes used in engineering field. State the relative merits and demerits of each type.
4. Enlist the sources of errors in chaining ? What precautions would you take to guard against them ?
5. Explain any two Methods of setting out right angles from a point on the chain line with the help tape only.
6. Explain the following tape corrections along with formula :
   (i) Correction for slope, (ii) Correction for temperature.
7. State the four types of tapes along with specifications.
8. Find out the slope correction in links per 100 links of a 20 m chain for a line measured along a slope $10°30'$.
9. State the precautions to be kept in mind while chaining.
10. State the procedure for folding and unfolding of chain.
11. Describe the process of chaining.
12. What is normal pull ? State the formula for it with meaning and unit of terms used in it.
13. What is reciprocal raging ? Describe it along with a neat sketch.
14. Sketch and describe a line ranger. How is it used in the field ? How will you test it ?
15. The distance between two stations was measured with 20 m chain and found to be 1500 m. The same distance was measured with a 30 m chain and found to be 1497.19 m. If the 20 m chain was 0.05 too short, what was the error in 30 m chain ?
    [**Ans :** True distance = 1496.25, Error = 12 cm]
16. A 30 m chain found to be 6 cm too long after chaining a distance of 1800 m. It was 10 cm too long at the end of day's work, after chaining a total distance of 4800 m. If the chain was correct at the beginning of the work, compute the correct distance.
    [**Ans :** 4809.80 m.]

17. The area of the plan of an old map drawn to scale of 10 metres to 1 cm measures now as 100.2 sq. cm. as measured by planimeter. The plan is found to have shrunk so that a line originally 10 cm long now measures 9.70 cm only. There was also a note that the chain 20 m used was 8 cm too short. Find the correct area of the map in hectares.

[**Ans :** 105.642 cm^2]

MSBTE Questions & Answers

Summer 2010

1. The length of a line measurement with a 20 m chain was found to be 398 m. The true length of the line was known to be 400 m. Find out error in the chain.

Ans.

$$L = 20 \text{ m}$$

$$\text{Measured length} = 398 \text{ m}$$

$$\text{True length} = 400 \text{ m}$$

$$\text{True length} = \frac{L_1}{L} \times \text{mesured length}$$

$$400 = \frac{L_1}{20} \times 398$$

$$L_1 = 20.10 \text{ m}$$

$$\text{Error in chain} = 20.1 - 20 = 0.1 \text{ m}$$

The chain is 0.1 m too long.

Winter 2010

1. State four instruments used for linear measurements.

Ans. Refer Section 2.2.

2. Explain indirect ranging with neat sketch.

Ans. Refer Section 2.3.2.

3. Explain the process of changing on a sloping ground.

Ans. Refer Section 2.5.

4. A 30 m chain was tested before start of changing work. Line PQ was chained by it and observed to be 1230 m. The chain was tested at the end of the work and was found to be 12 cm too short. Find the correct distance PQ.

Ans. Refer Example 2.2.

Summer 2011

1. Give any four codes of signals used to direct assistant in ranging.

Ans. Refer Section 2.3.1.

2. Write any four mistakes in changing.

Ans. Refer Section 2.2.1.

3. A 30 m chain was tested before the commencement of the day's work and was found to be correct. After chaining a distance of 80 chains it was found to be 0.05 m too short. At the end of the day's work after changing a total distance of 162 chains the chain was found to be 0.1 m too long. What was true distance chained ?

Ans.

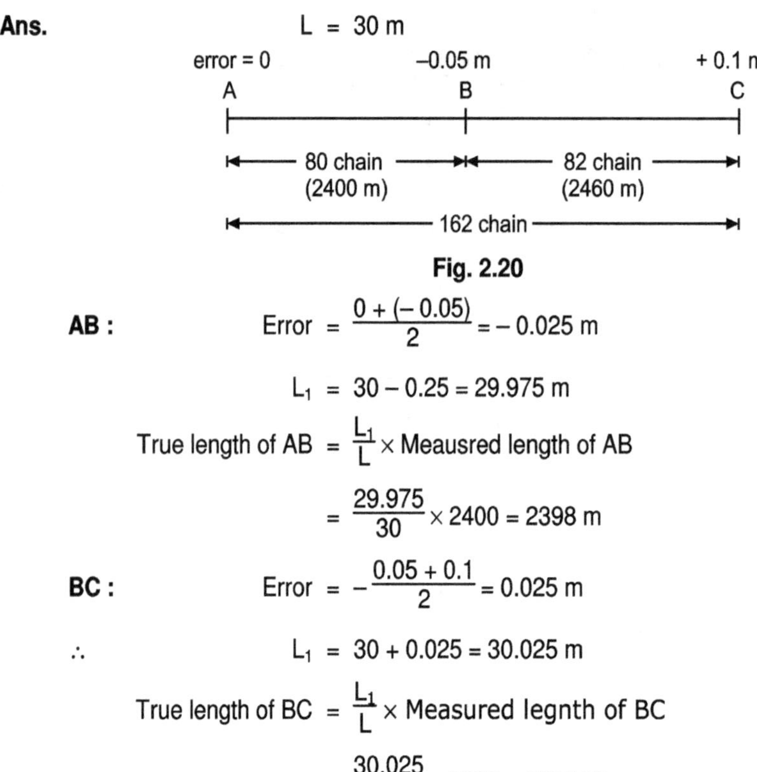

Fig. 2.20

AB :　　　Error $= \dfrac{0 + (-0.05)}{2} = -0.025$ m

$L_1 = 30 - 0.25 = 29.975$ m

True length of AB $= \dfrac{L_1}{L} \times$ Meausred length of AB

$= \dfrac{29.975}{30} \times 2400 = 2398$ m

BC :　　　Error $= -\dfrac{0.05 + 0.1}{2} = 0.025$ m

∴　　　$L_1 = 30 + 0.025 = 30.025$ m

True length of BC $= \dfrac{L_1}{L} \times$ Measured legnth of BC

$= \dfrac{30.025}{30} \times 2460 = 2462.05$ m

Total true length $= l(AB) + l(BC) = 3298 + 2462.05 = 4860.05$ m

---

Winter 2011

1. Write the use of following instruments in survey :

(i)　Ranging rod.

Ans.　Refer Section 2.2.3.

(ii)　Arrows.

Ans.　Refer Section 2.2.5.

(iii)　Pegs.

Ans.　Refer Section 2.2.6.

(iv)　Cross-staff.

Ans.　Refer Section

2. If measuring tape is not standardized then state what type of correction are necessary to apply to obtain true length.

Ans. Refer Page 2.8 (Formula for correction of tape and chain is same).

3. The down hill end of the 30 m tape is held 80 cm too low. What is horizontal length ?

Ans. Refer Section

Summer 2012

1. What is ranging ? State its types. Explain any one in brief.

Ans. Refer Section 2.3.

2. Define : (i) Chaining, (ii) Ranging.

Ans. (i)   Refer Section 2.4.

     (ii)   Refer Section 2.3.

3. Length of a survey line measured with a 20 meter chain was found to be 841.50 meter. When the chain was compared with a standard chain, it was found to be 0.10 meter too long. Find correct length of the line.

Ans.

$$L = 20 \text{ m}$$
$$\text{Measured length} = 841.50 \text{ m}$$
$$\text{Error} = 0.1 \text{ m}$$
$$L_1 = 20 + 0.1 = 20.1 \text{ m}$$
$$\text{True length} = \frac{L_1}{L} \times \text{Measured length}$$
$$= \frac{20.1}{20} \times 841.90$$
$$= 845.71 \text{ m}$$

Winter 2012

1. Explain method of chaining on sloping ground.

Ans. Refer Section 2.5.

2. A line was measured by 20 m chain which was accurate before starting the days work. After chaining 700 m the chain was round to be 6 cm too long. After chaining a total distance of 1500 m chain it was found to be 14 cm too long. Find true distance of the line.

Ans.

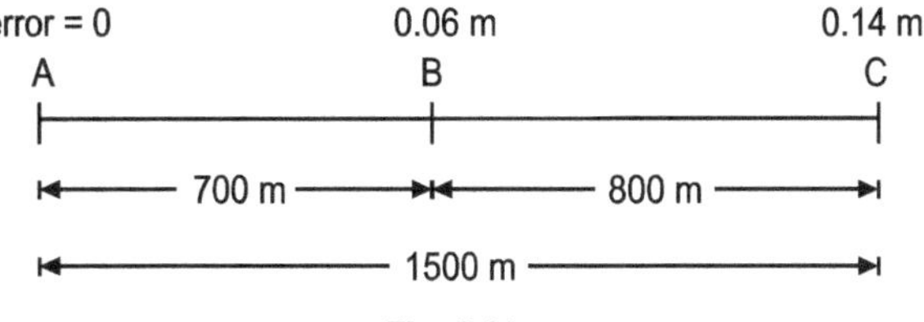

Fig. 2.21

AB :

$$L = 20 \text{ m}$$

$$\text{Error} = \frac{0 + 0.06}{2} = 0.03$$

$$L_1 = 20 + 0.03 = 20.03 \text{ m}$$

$$\text{True length of AB} = \frac{L_1}{L} \times \text{Measured length of AB}$$

$$= \frac{20.03}{20} \times 700 = 701.05 \text{ m}$$

BC :

$$\text{Error} = \frac{0.06 + 0.14}{2} = 0.1 \text{ m}$$

$$\therefore \quad L_1 = 20.1 \text{ m}$$

$$\text{True length of BC} = \frac{L_1}{L} \times l(BC) = \frac{20.1}{20} \times 800 = 804 \text{ m}$$

$$\text{Total true length} = 701.05 + 804 = 1505.05$$

Summer 2013

1. Define : (i) Changing, (ii) Ranging.

Ans. (i)   Changing : Refer Section 2.4. (ii) Ranging : Refer Section 2.3.

2. Describe procedure of indirect ranging with a neat sketch.

Ans. Refer Section 2.3.2.

3. Explain changing on sloping ground by method of stepping.

Ans. Refer Section 2.5.

4. Length of a survey line measured with a 20 meter chain was found to be 841.50 meter. When the chain was compared with a standard chain, it was found to be 0.10 meter too long. Find correct length of the line.

Ans. To solve this example please refer the solution of Example 2.1.

3...

Chain Triangulation and Cross-Staff Survey

Contents

3.1 INTRODUCTION (S-10)

- Chain surveying is a simple method of surveying in which the sides of triangles are measured directly in the field and no angular measurements are taken.

- This type of surveying is suitable for moderately small areas and also when the ground is fairly level and open with simple details i.e. there is no obstruction like building, tree etc.

- It is unsuitable for areas which are large, uneven and crowded with many details.

3.2 PURPOSE OF CHAIN SURVEYING

Chain surveying is adopted for the following purposes :

(a) To determine the area of the field.

(b) To locate the exact boundaries of land.

(c) To secure data for making a plan.

3.3 PRINCIPLE OF CHAIN SURVEYING　　　　(S-06, 08, 09, 11)

- The principle of chain surveying is *triangulation*.

- Triangulation consists of frame work of triangles. The whole area is divided into network of triangles.

- A triangle is the only simple plane figure which can be plotted by measuring its sides alone in the field.

- The frame work of triangles, to be adopted depends upon the shape and configuration of the ground and the natural obstacles.

- To obtain good results, the frame work should consist of triangles which are nearly equilateral as possible.

- Such triangles are known as well shaped or well conditioned triangles.

(1) In well-conditioned triangle : A triangle in which no angle is smaller than 30° and no angle is greater than 120° is known as well condition triangle.

(2) Ill condition triangle : A triangles having angles less than 30° or greater than 120° are known as *ill-conditioned triangles.*

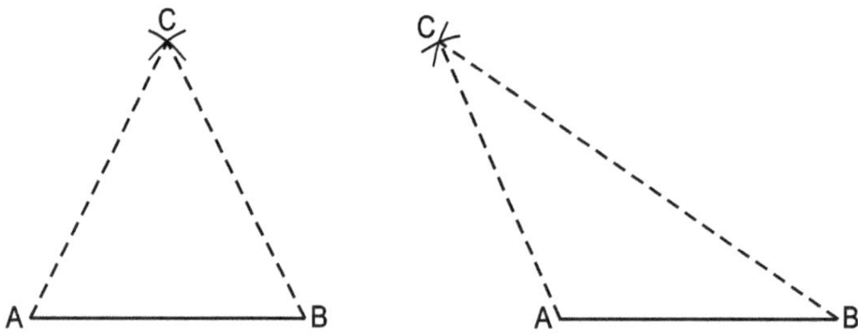

(a) Well-conditioned triangle　　　　**(b) Ill-conditioned triangle**

Fig. 3.1

- Well-conditioned triangles can be plotted more accurately than the Ill-conditioned triangles.

- Ill-conditioned triangles should always be avoided. If they are unavoidable great care should be taken in chaining and plotting.

3.4 SURVEY STATIONS

A survey station is an important point on the ground at the beginning and end of a chain line. There are two kinds of survey stations.

(1) Main stations, and

(2) Subsidiary stations or tie stations.

Main stations :

- A stations which are located at the ends of the chainline which command the boundaries of the survey is known as main station.
- The lines joining main stations are *called main survey lines or chainlines.*
- The biggest of the main survey lines, is called a *base line.*

Subsidiary or tie stations :

- A stations which are located at the points selected on main survey lines or subsidiary line subsidiary or tie lines to locate the interior detail such as buildings, fences, hedges etc. is known as subsidiary station.
- The lines joining these points are known as *tie lines.*
- The stations are usually denoted with a small circle round the station point. Thus, capital letters A, B, C etc. are used for main stations.
- Tie stations are represented by small letters such as a, b, c, or T_1, T_2 are subsidiary stations.
- Survey lines are indicated by AB, BC, ab, T_1T_2 etc. Sometimes the letters denoting the stations are written within the circle.
- The system of lines covering the area to be surveyed is termed as *skeleton or frame work* of survey.

3.5 SELECTION OF SURVEY STATIONS OR SURVEY LINES (S-08, 11)

The following points should be considered while selecting survey stations or survey lines :

(1) Main survey stations should be intervisible.

(2) If possible the survey lines should be run through a level ground and should be as close as possible to the boundaries to avoid long offsets.

(3) If possible a long line should be run roughly through the middle of area to form backbone of the skeleton.

(4) The survey lines should be as few as possible and should be so arranged as to avoid obstacles in ranging and chaining.

(5) The area should be divided into well-conditioned triangles, following the principle of surveying, i.e. working from whole to the part.

(6) Tie lines should be run to locate the details and to avoid long offsets.

(7) Each triangle in the skeleton should be provided with at least one check line.

3.6 SURVEY LINES (W-09)

The various types of survey lines are (i) Base line, (ii) Check line, (iii) Tie line.

(i) Base line : (S-08, W-11)

- The base line is generally the longest line running roughly through the middle of the area is known as base line.
- It is laid on a level ground as far as possible.
- The whole frame work is built upon this line.

- It fixes up the direction of all the survey lines. This being the most important line, it should be measured very accurately.

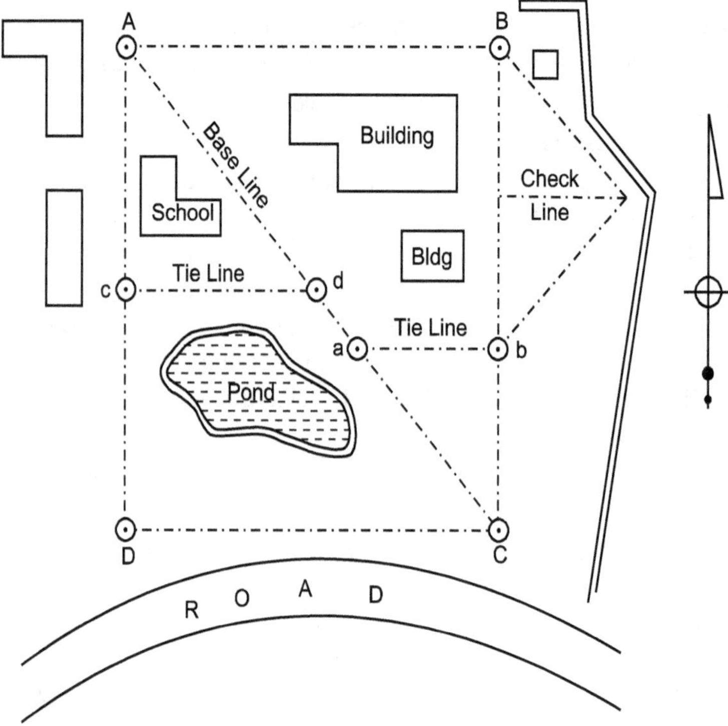

(1) A, B, C, D are main station.

(2) a, b, c, d are subsidiary station.

Fig. 3.2 : Different Survey Lines

(ii) Check line   (W-07)

- A is a line joining the apex of a triangle to some fixed point on the opposite side or a line joining some fixed point on any two sides of a triangle is known as check line.

- The length of check line measured in the field should agree with its length on the plan. Thus, it checks the accuracy of the frame work (Fig. 3.17).

(iii) Tie line :   (W-07)

- A is a line joining some fixed points as tie stations on the main chain lines is known as check line.

- It enables the surveyor to locate the interior details and also to check the accuracy of frame work (Fig. 3.2).

3.7 OFFSET   (W-08, S-12)

- The ground features such as buildings, boundaries, roads, nallas etc., are located with reference to the chain lines.

- Distances are measured from the chain lines to the objects right or left of the chain line. Such distances (lateral measurements) are called *offsets*.

- There are two types of offsets :   **(W-11, S-12)**

  (1) Perpendicular offsets.   (2) Oblique offsets.

- When the measurements are taken at right angles (90°) to the chain line, they are known as perpendicular *offsets* or simply offsets.

- The measurements taken at other angles than 90° angle, they are called *oblique offset*.

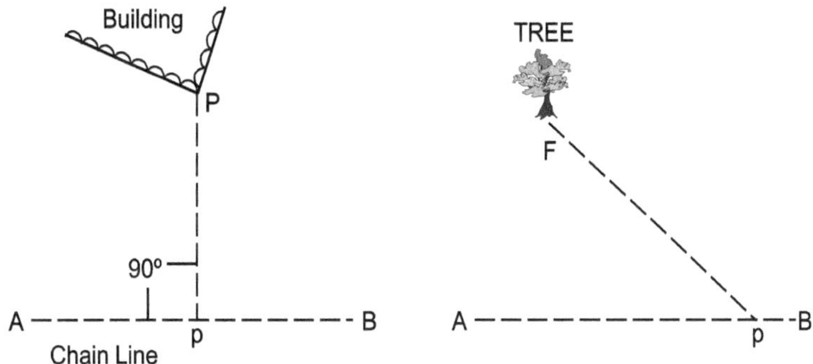

(a) Perpendicular offsets   **(b) Oblique offsets**

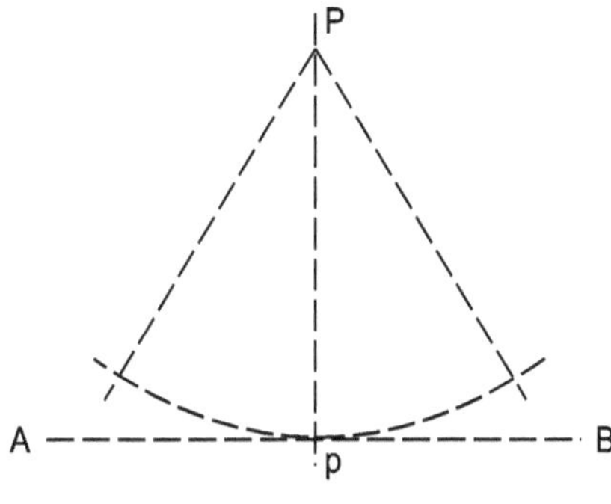

(c) Swing offset

Fig. 3.3

- The offsets are generally measured by metallic tape but when great accuracy is required a steel tape is used. Offset rod is sometimes used for short offsets.

- Every offset has two measurement boundaries :

  1. Distance along the chain line, called chainage (AP) and

  2. Length of offset (Pp). [Fig. 3.3 (c)]

- *Swing offsets* are taken by swinging the tape along the chain line. The position of the offset on chain line is located by the point where the arc is tangential to the chain.

- To take the offset from a point say P the leader holds the zero ends of the tape at P and the follower carrying the tape box swings it along the chain as shown in figure 3.3 (c). The minimum reading on the tape gives the foot of the perpendicular from P to p on a line AB. It is known as *swing offset*.

- Offsets up to a distance of 15 m are called *short offsets* and those which are more than 15 m are called *long offsets.*
- Short offsets may be taken by eye judgment or by swinging. Long offsets may be taken by means of cross-staff or optical square.   **(S-08)**

3.8 DEGREE OF ACCURACY IN TAKING OFFSETS

- The accuracy of taking offsets depends upon :

(1) Scale of plotting (2) Length of offset (3) Importance of object to which the offsets are taken.

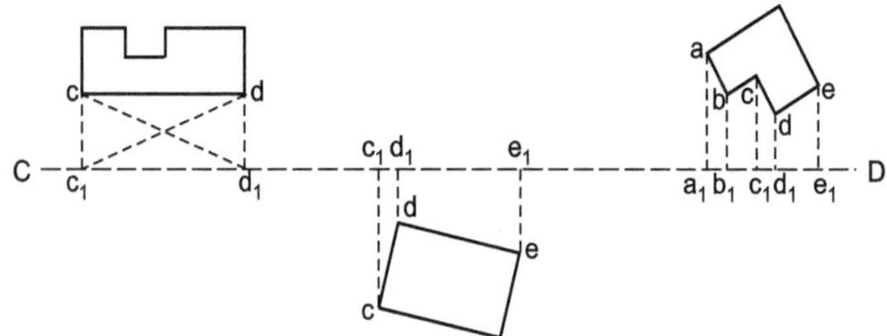

Fig. 3.4 : Locating Building

- It mainly depends on the scale of plotting. The smallest distance which can be plotted on drawing sheet is 0.25 mm.
- Knowing the scale of plotting the degree of accuracy required in measuring the offset distance can be decided easily.

3.9 INSTRUMENTS FOR SETTING OUT RIGHT ANGLES OFFSET

The following instruments may be used for setting out perpendicular to the chain line.

(1) Chain or tape.

(2) Cross-staff - (a) Open (b) French.

(3) Optical square.

(1) Right Angles with Chain and Tape :

- A chain or tape may be used for setting out right angle.
- The method is based on Pythagorus Theorem i.e. triangle whose sides are 'in proportion of 3, 4 and 5 is a right angled triangle; 6 m, 8 m, 10 m; or 30 links, 40 links and 50 links etc.

(i) To set out a perpendicular to a chain from a point on it.

- Let AB be the given chain line. It is required to set CD $\perp$ AB at C. Take 30 m chain (150 link).
- Measure CE = 40 links (8 m) on the chain line; pin one end of the chain at C and 70th link at E. Hold the chain, or tape at the end of 30th link (6 m) and put it on the ground until both sides CD and DE are tight. Mark the point D by fixing arrow, CD is required perpendicular to AB.

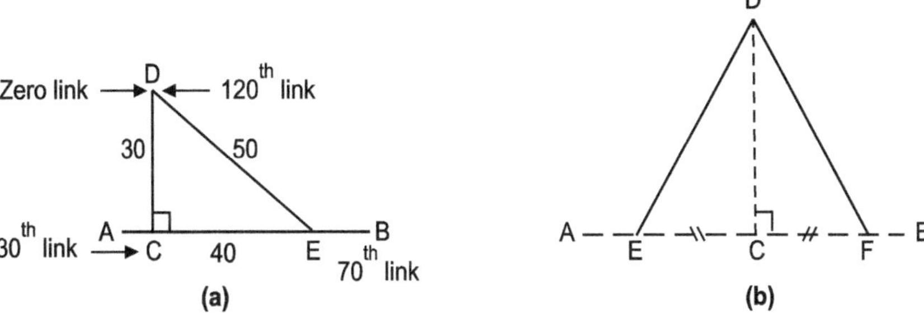

Fig. 3.5 : Right Angle with Tape or Chain

(ii) Select equidistant points on a chain line from a given point.

- Let AB be the chain line. It is required to select E and F points, equidistant from C. Pin the zero end of the tape at E and hold 20 m mark at F. Holding the middle mark of 10 m., stretch the tape tight to establish point D. CD is then the required perpendicular.

(2) Cross-Staff :

- It is the simplest instrument used for setting out perpendicular i.e. taking offsets from a chain line.
- It is easier and quicker method, but not very accurate.
- If great accuracy is desired, the work should be carried out by a theodolite.
- There are two types of cross-staff are in common use for chain survey (i) open cross-staff, (ii) French cross-staft.

(a) Open cross-staff :

- It is the simplest form of cross-staff. It consists of a head and leg. The head is made of wood or other material shaped as a cross (Fig. 3.6).
- The diameter or side of head is 15 cm and the thickness is 4 cm with two fine saw cuts at right angles to each other.
- The vertical slit is mounted at the end of each cut giving two lines of sight at right angles to each other.

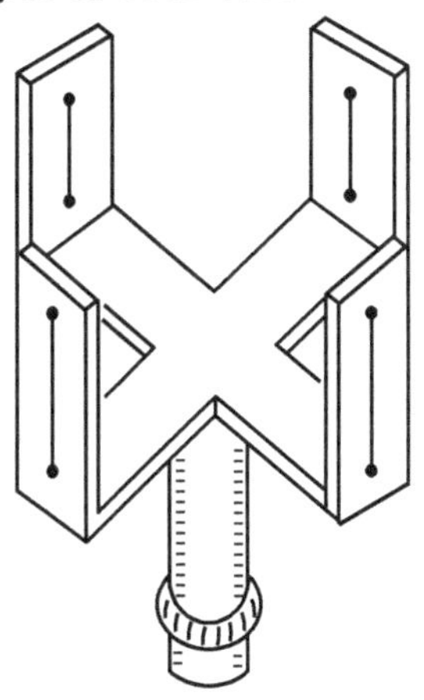

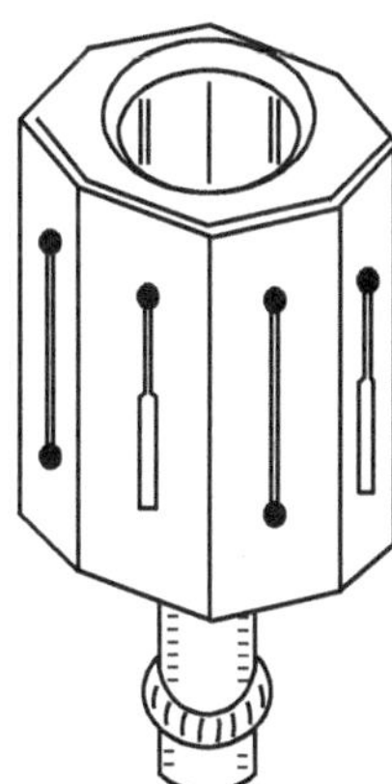

(a) Open Cross-Staff　　　　**(b) Trench Cross-Staff**

Fig. 3.6

- The head is mounted on the top of wooden pole about 2.5 cm diameter and 1.2 to 1.5 m long. It is provided with a conical metal shoe at the bottom for fixing it into the ground.
- Two persons are required to operate cross-staff.

Procedure : Ref. Fig. 3.28.

- The cross-staff is held vertically on the chain line where the offset is likely to occur. It is turned until one pair of opposite slits is directed to the ranging rod; say B.
- Through the other pair of slit, point P is seen.
- If it is not seen or bisected, cross-staff is moved forward or backward on the chain line AB until the object point P is seen.

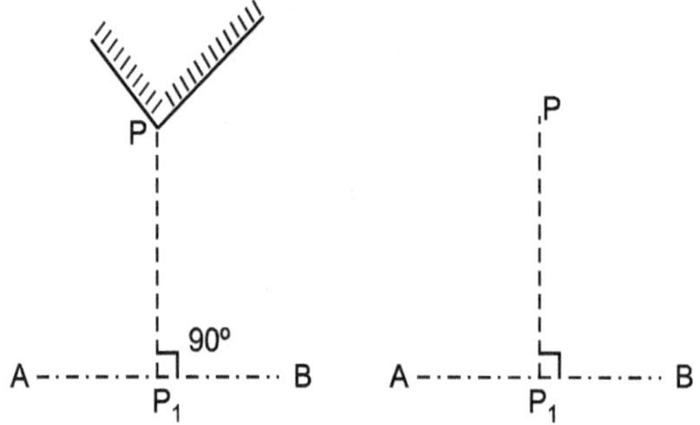

Fig. 3.7 : Measurement of Perpendicular Offset

- Then P_1 is the foot of perpendicular on the chain line.
- Care should be taken to hold the staff vertically and is not twisted round at the time of bisection.

(ii) To set out right angle at point on the chain line :

(b) French cross-staff or octagonal cross-staff :

- Another form of the instrument consists of a hollow octagonal box about 15 cm deep and 10 cm wide between opposite faces.
- Vertical sighting slits are cut in the middle of each face, such that the lines between the centres of opposite slits make angle of 45° with each other.
- It is, therefore, possible to set out angle of either 45° or 90° with this instrument Fig. 3.27. (b). This is also known as *French Cross-Staff.*
- A cross-staff is a non-adjustable instrument and is not capable of high accuracy.

(3) Optical Square   (S-10; W-07, 09)

- This is a more accurate instrument than a cross-staff. It is small compact and convenient instrument.
- It is used for setting out perpendicular to chain lines or finding the foot of perpendicular on a chain line.

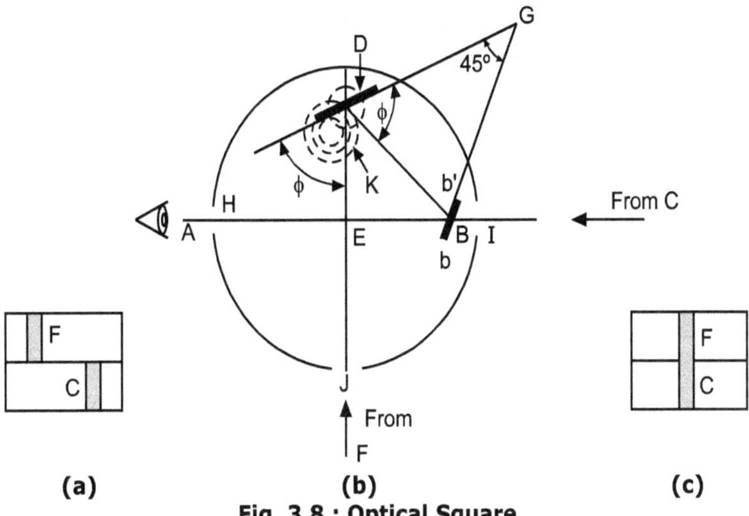

Fig. 3.8 : Optical Square

Principle

- In case of reflecting instrument, the angle between the first incident ray and the last reflected ray is twice the angle between the two mirrors.

- In case of optical square the angle between the two mirrors is 45° and hence the angle between the first incident ray and the last reflected ray is 90°.

Construction :

- It consists of a circular metal box about 5 cm diameter and 1.25 cm deep, in which three openings in the side at H, I and J are provided. bb' is horizon glass, half silvered. i.e. silvered at top and plane at bottom.

- Mirror D is set opposite to the opening J making an angle of 45° with the half silvered mirror bb'. Opposite of opening at J a silvered glass is fixed at D making an angle of 45° with the glass at B.

- Ray from ranging rod C passes through the plane glass directly to the eye of the observer at H and ray from ranging rod J falls on mirror at D i.e. index mirror and after reflecting falls on mirror at B and again reflects towards H.

- So the angle between the incident ray from F and the reflected ray towards A is 90°. The images of ranging rod at C and F are visible at A as shown in Fig. 3.8 (a).

- Now, the observer moves the optical square forward or backward on chain line so that the images of the ranging rods coinside.

- The point below this position of optical square is the point on the chain line where the offset can be dropped to meet point J as shown in Fig. 3.8 (c).

Use of Optical Square (S-09, 10) : The optical square is used –

(1) To find the foot of the perpendicular to the chain line and

(2) To set out a perpendicular to given chain line to find foot of perpendicular.

- If the object lies on the right hand side of the observer, the instrument is held in left hand and vice versa.

- Since a stand or tripod is normally not provided with this instrument care must be taken to hold the instrument exactly over the point on the chain line from which right angle is to be laid out.

- The best plan is to stand facing one end of the line with the heels touching and the feet making an angle of about 45° with one another and the middle point of the line joining toes coinciding with the point as shown in Fig. 3.30.

- By bending the head a little forward to the instrument when held to one eye will be approximately over the proper point. In using the instrument it should be held quite horizontal.

- The use of optical square is restricted to fairly level ground.

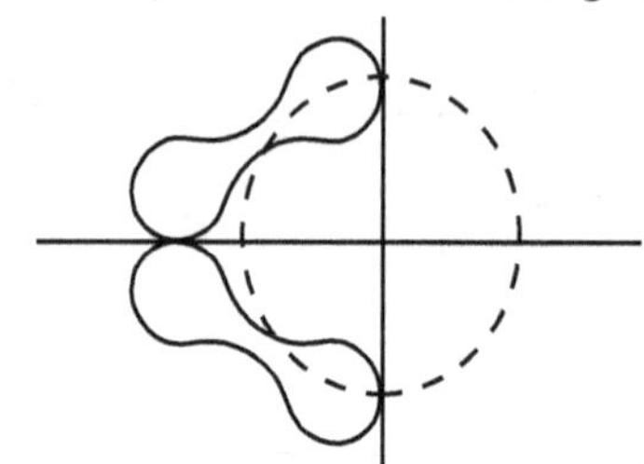

Fig. 3.9 : Setting Out Perpendicular

Testing and Adjusting the Optical Square :　　　(S-05, W-05)

- The optical square can be easily tested and adjusted if necessary, adjusted by the following method.

- Standing at an intermediate point O on the line AB, sight a pole held at the point 'A' and mark a point 'a'. It appears in the instruments to be at right angle to OA.

- Now turn round to face point 'B' and turn the instrument over in the hand. Sight the pole held at 'B'.

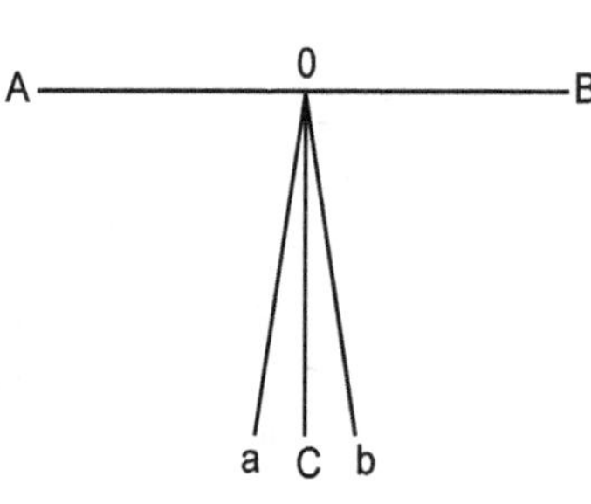

Fig. 3.10

- If the instrument is in adjustment the image of the pole at 'a' will coincide with the pole seen at B.

- If not; mark b as new position. Bisect the distance ab at C. Then OC is the true perpendicular at O to the line AB.

- The instrument can now be adjusted by means of a small milled head K in Fig. (3.10), and rotate the mirror D until B and the image of C appears coincident.

Indian Optical Square :

- Another form of optical square is shown in the Fig. 3.32. It is called the Indian optical square.

- It is used for the same purpose for which optical square, described above, is used.

- It is a brass wedge-shaped hollow box of 5 cm sides and about 3 cm deep with 7.5 cm long handle. Two mirrors are fixed at an angle of 45° to the inclined sides of the box.

- Two rectangular openings are provided above the mirrors for sighting. The open face is to be directed towards the objects to which offset is to be taken.

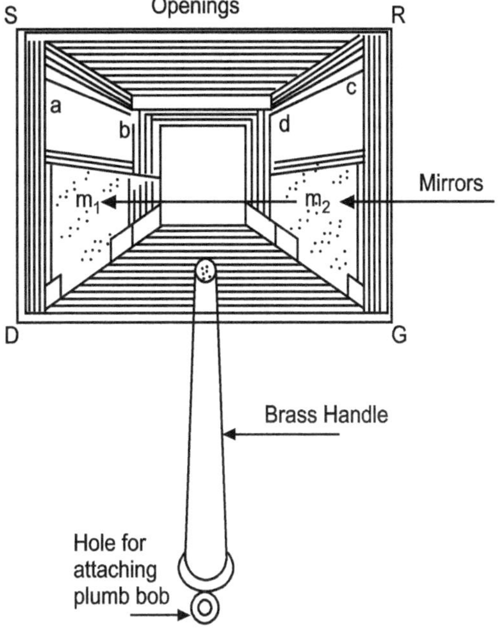

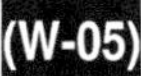

Fig. 3.11 : Indian Optical Square

Use of Indian Optical Square :

- To take an offset to the object O the observer holds the instrument in his hand and stands on the chain line AB.

- He turns the open face towards the object O. The forward station B is then sighted by looking through the opening, which according to the object O is to his right and walks along AB forward or backward until the image of the object appears exactly in line with the ranging rod at B.

- The point vertically under the instrument is the required point.

3.10 THE FIELD BOOK (W-05)

- This is a stiff covered note book of about 20 cm × 12 cm to 20 cm × 15 cm size in which survey work is recorded by measurements and sketches.

- The chain line is represented either by a ruled single line or by two lines, spaced at about 1.25 to 1.5 cm at the centre of each page.

- Single line field book is used for large scale and detailed dimensioned work.

- The double line field book is commonly used for normal work.

- A chain line is started from the bottom of the page and required upwards.

- The chainages are entered in the column and the sketches of the objects are drawn on either side of the chain line. The pages of field book are machine numbered.

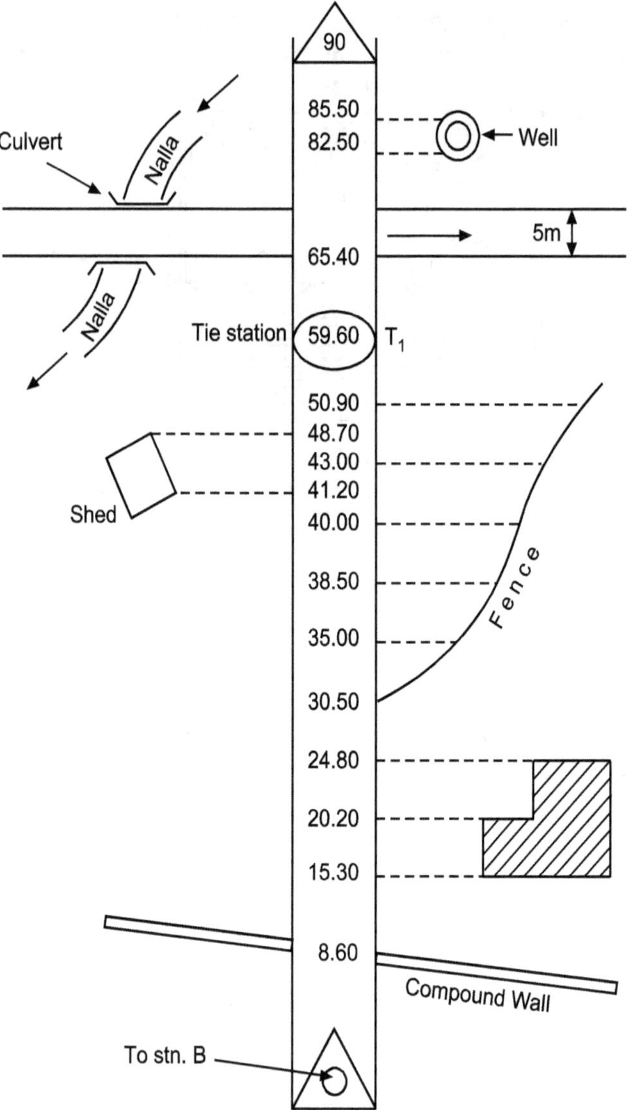

Fig. 3.12 : Showing Page of Field Book

How to record the field book ?

The following entries are taken in the field book at the starting of a chain line.

(1) Name of chain i.e., 20 m or 30 m,

(2) Name or number of station,

(3) The symbol 'Δ' denoting the station.

Recording of Field Book :

The rules relating to recording of chain survey field book are as follows :

1. The key plan of lines should be sketched in at the beginning to show the exact arrangement of survey lines.

2. The distances along the chain line called chaining should be written in the central column.

3. The starting and closing chainages should be written in the symbol 'Δ' denoting the station.

4. Each chain line should be recorded on separate page.

5. The chainages of tie stations are enclosed in circle or ellipse.

6. Objects to the right of the chain line are entered to the right of the centre column in the field book and those to the left of the chain to the left of the centre column.

7. The sketch must not cross the centre columns. The features crossing the chain line are broken off at one side of the column and continued horizontally opposite on its other side.

8. The sketching of the features is not to scale but only proportional.

9. Offset measurements are written against the features to which they refer.

10. Full description of all features must be written in the field book.

11. Entries should be recorded with good quality pencil.

12. The field book should be kept neat and clean.

Complete record of survey should include :

(a) Title of survey.

(b) General sketch of area surveyed.

(c) Location sketches of the main and the tie stations.

(d) Record of chain lines.

(e) Date of survey.

(f) The names of party members.

(g) Page index of chain line and station.

3.11 CHAIN SURVEY FIELD WORK   (W-11)

Equipments : The following equipments are required for conducting a chain survey :

1. A chain 20 m or 30 m.

2. Ten arrows.

3. Metallic tape 15 m or 30 m.

4. 10 Ranging rods and an offset rod.

5. An instrument for setting out right angles; cross-staff or optical square.

6. Plumb bob.

7. Survey field book, pencil, eraser, set square etc.

8. Pegs, hammer, axe, chalk, nail, string etc.

9. Canvas bag for carrying small articles such as pegs, hammer, optical square etc.

Chain Survey :

1. Reconnaissance :

- The preliminary inspection of area to be surveyed is called *reconnaissance*.

- Before starting the survey, the surveyor should walk over the whole area and observe main features and boundaries to fix best position of survey lines and survey stations.

- He should see the intervisibility of survey stations, and should prepare a neat sketch, called an *index sketch* in the field book showing the plan of ground, boundaries of land and important features such as buildings, roads, nallas etc.

- A careful reconnaissance provides fair knowledge of shape and extent of the area to be surveyed, difficulties arising in work and time required to complete the work.

2. Marking stations :

- During the reconnaissance survey, the positions of survey stations have been fixed. In next operation, these stations are marked on the ground in such a way that they can be discovered readily if required in future.

- The following methods are adopted to mark the survey stations :

(i) By fixing a ranging rod temporarily.

(ii) By driving wooden peg leaving a small projection 2.5 to 4 cm above the ground,

(iii) By using nails or spikes in case of roads or streets or by cutting a cross in case of hard surface.

(iv) By embedding a stone below the surface of the ground with a cross mark on its top in case of permanent marking of stations.

3. Reference sketch (Location sketch) (S-06) :

- Wherever possible a survey station should be fixed with reference to two or three permanent points such as building corner, tree, electric pole etc. and a reference sketch should be drawn in the field book as shown in Fig. 3.12.

- Reference sketches are necessary to retrace the positions of stations if required in future.

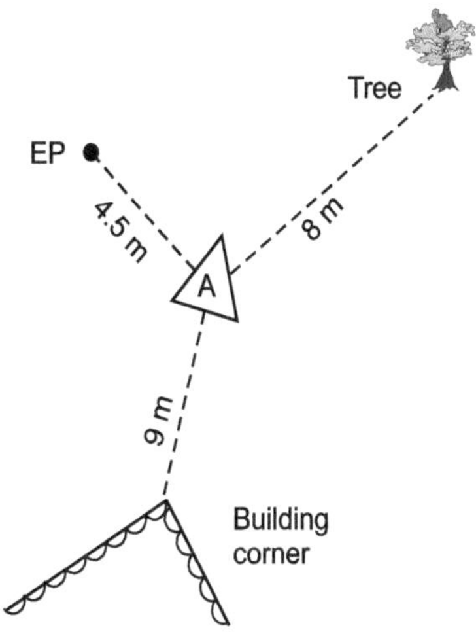

Fig. 3.13 : Location Sketch

4. Running Survey lines :

- Having completed the above three steps chaining may be started from the base line and carried through all the lines of the frame work. The work of running survey lines consists of -

  (i) to chain the line and

  (ii) to locate the adjacent details.

- The record of chaining and offseting is made in the field book.

3.12 CHAIN AND CROSS-STAFF SURVEY (S-11)

- The object of chain and cross-staff survey is to locate the boundaries of a field or plot and to find out its area.

- The instruments required for a cross-staff survey : (S-11)

  (i) Two chains 20 m or 30 m.

  (ii) Arrows

  (iii) Ranging rods

  (iv) A cross-staff or an optical square.

  (v) A plumb bob.

- To start the cross-staff survey, a chain line is run through the centre of the area to be surveyed.

- It is divided into right angled triangles and trapezoids. The perpendiculars to the boundaries are taken in order of their chainages.

- The area of the field is computed by the following formulae :

  (1) The area of a right angled triangle = $\frac{1}{2}$ base $\times$ height.

  (2) The area of a trapezoid = $\frac{1}{2}$ (Sum of parallel sides) $\times$ distance between them (base).

- A cross-staff or optical square is used to set out perpendicular offsets which are usually more than 15 m.

- Care should be taken that no offset is overlooked before the chain is removed.

- The chainages of the points of intersection of the chain line and the boundaries should be recorded.

- The lengths of boundary lines may be measured by direct measurement to check the accuracy of field work.

- After the field work is over, the survey is plotted to some convenient scale. The figure thus formed by the boundary lines is divided into triangles and trapezoids, the area of which can be computed in the tabular form as given below :

Sr. No.	Fig.	Chainage		Base	Mean	Area (m^2 base
		From	To	time	offset	× mean offset)

3.13 PLOTTING

- After carrying out the field work; office work for plotting the survey is done. It consists of preparation of plans and sections, computation of area etc.

- The field details should be complete in all respects so that there will not be any difficulty for plotting.

- For this, a suitable scale is selected, it is normally selected before starting the fixed work. The surveyor will then decide the size of paper required to contain the plan.

- While plotting conventional symbols are used. They play very important role for representing the different features of ground or land. They are very useful while reading different topographical maps.

- The survey should be plotted looking north to represent top, bottom, left and right as north, south; east and west respectively. The north line should generally be arranged upwards.

- To start with, a base line is first plotted accurately in proper solution. The intermediate stations on the base line are marked with a pencil point by accurately measuring their chainages.

- The triangles are then laid by intersection of arcs. Each triangle is then verified by measuring a check line on the plan and compared with its measured length in the field.

- Small errors may be suitably adjusted. If the errors are large, measurement may be repeated.

- Thus, the frame work is plotted. Offsets are then plotted by marking the chainages of offsets on the chain line and perpendiculars to the chain line are erected with the help of set square on either side.

- Great care should be taken to mark the accurate chainages and lengths of offsets.

3.14 OBSTACLES IN CHAINING   (S-09, S-12)

During chaining operations various obstacles such as rivers, hills, buildings, woods etc. are met with. But it is essential that chaining should be continued in a straight line.

Classification of Obstacles :

(1) Obstacles which can be chained across but cannot be ranged across.

(2) Obstacles which can be ranged across but cannot be chained across.

(3) Obstacles which can neither be ranged across nor be chained across.

(1) Obstacles to ranging :

Examples : Hill Intervening, rising ground. In this type, the ends of line are not intervisible.

There are two cases :

(a) Both ends may be visible from intermediate points on the line.

(b) Both ends may not be visible from any intermediate points.

- In case (a), the difficulty may be overcome by reciprocal ranging.

- We have discussed it in article 3.3.2.

- Case (b) occurs when it is required to chain forest, high crops or trees, preventing the fixing of intermediate points. Random line method is adopted here.

- We discuss here random line method.

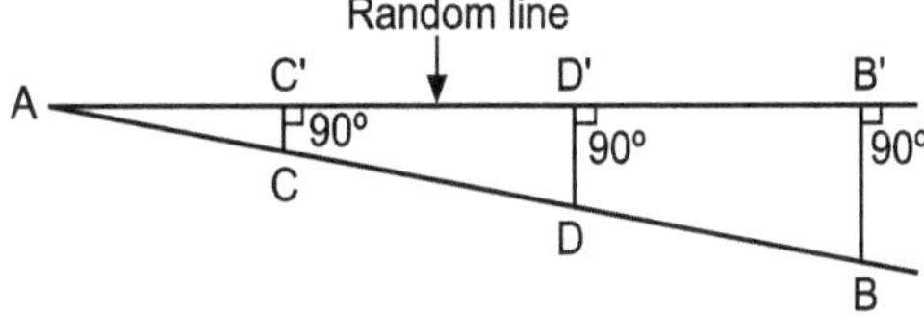

Fig. 3.14

- Let AB be the chain line whose length is required. From A to B' a line is run in any covenient direction, B is visible from B'. Such a line is called *random line*.

- BB' is perpendicular to AB'.

  Then, $AB = \sqrt{(AB')^2 + (BB')^2}$

- Similarly, $CC' = \dfrac{AC'}{AB'} \times BB'$ and $DD' = \dfrac{AD'}{AB'} \times BB'$ etc.

- Thus, the line is cleared and chained.

(2) Chaining obstructed vision free :　　　　　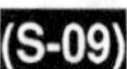

In this case the ends of the survey line are visible but chaining cannot be done across.

Example : River, Pond etc.

(i)　　When it is possible to chain round the obstacles; e.g. a pond, hedge etc.

(ii)　　When it is not possible to chain round the obstacles; e.g. river.

There may be several methods available. However, a few are described below :

Case (i) : (a) When the obstacle can be chained around.

Let PQ be the obstructed length. Erect perpendicular at P and Q so that PR = QS, measure the length RS which is equal to PQ.

(b) Erect perpendicular PR as shown in Fig. 3.15 (b) RQ line clears the obstacle. Then　　　　　$PQ = \sqrt{RQ^2 - PR^2}$

(c) By optical square or cross-staff set 90° angle at R as shown in Fig. 3.34 (c). Then　　　　　$PQ = \sqrt{PR^2 + RQ^2}$

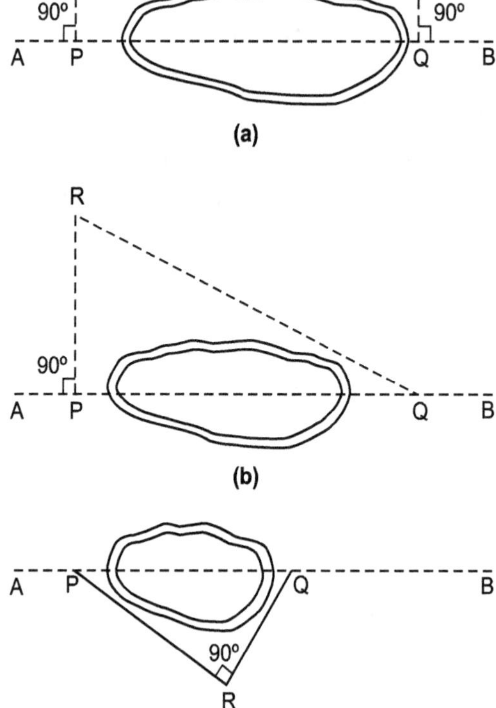

Fig. 3.15 : Chaining with Vision Tree Observation

Case (ii) : *When it is not possible to chain round the obstacle.*   **[S-06]**

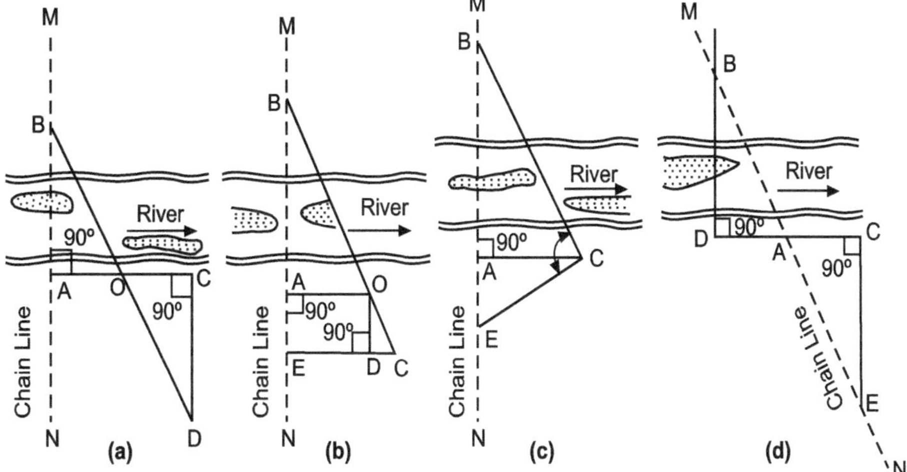

Fig. 3.16 : Vision Free Chaining Obstructed (Different Methods)

A and B are two points on opposite bank of river as shown in Fig. 3.16 (a).

Obstructed length is AB. On chain line MN, set AC perpendicular to AB and bisect at O. Erect perpendicular at C and mark a point D in line with BO. Measure the length CD. From the similar triangle ABO and CDO, AB = CD.

(b) Refer Fig. 3.16 (b). A and B are two points on the chain line. AB is the obstructed width. Select, another point E on the chainline, set out a perpendicular AO and EC in such a way that BO and C are in a straight line.

Measure length AO, EC and AE, Erect perpendicular OD.

Meeting D on EC.

Then,   DC = EC – ED

i.e.   DC = EC – AO

                 (AE = OD)

Triangles AOB and ODC are similar.

$$\frac{AB}{AO} = \frac{OD}{DC} \text{ or } AB = \frac{OD \times AO}{DC}$$

(c) Refer Fig. 3.16 (c). A and B are two points on either side of the river. Set out perpendicular AC at A of sufficient length. Erect perpendicular CE at C. Measure length of AC and AE.

Triangles ABC and ACE are similar.

$$\therefore \qquad \frac{AB}{AC} = \frac{AC}{AE} \text{ or } AB = \frac{(AC)^2}{AE}$$

(d) Refer Fig. 3.16 (d). The chain line crosses the river obliquely.

Let A and B be the two points on the chain line and on opposite bank of the river. Set out AD at right angle to BD by optical square or cross-staff. Produce DA to C such as AD = AC. Erect perpendicular CE at C so that E lies on line BA produced.

Triangle ABD and AEC are congruent. $\therefore$ AB = AE

(3) Both chaining and vision obstructed : Typical example of this case is a building obstructing the chain line. It is therefore required to prolong the line beyond the obstacle and then find out the distance across it. One common method is discussed below. Refer Fig. 3.17.

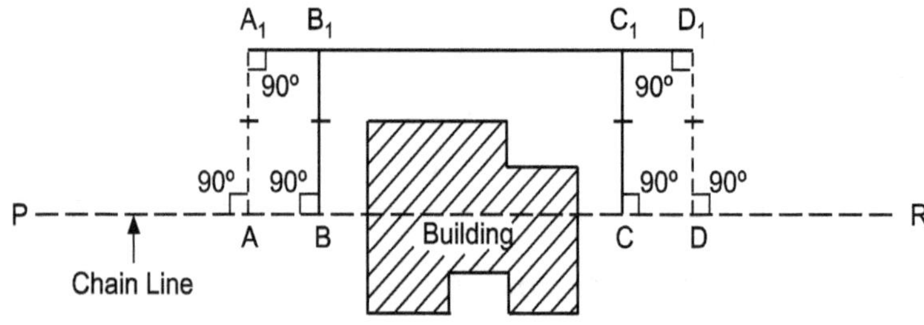

Fig. 3.17 : Chaining with Vision Obstructed

Let PR be the survey line. The obstruction of building prevents chaining from P to R. Select two points A and B at convenient distance apart. Measure the length of AB. Set out perpendicular AA_1 and BB_1, of equal length such that points A and B overcome the obstacle. Join $A_1 B_1$ and prolong the line $A_1 B_1$. Select two points C_1 and D_1 in line with $A_1 B_1$ produced. Set out perpendicular at C_1 and D_1 as CC_1 and DD_1 of equal length to AA_1.

Now, $AA_1 = BB_1 = CC_1 = DD_1$

Measure $B_1 C_1$ which is equal to obstructed length BC. The right angles should be set out accurately.

3.14.1 Chaining Across River　　　　(S-09, 10, 11)

(i)　Fix the end points of chain line M and N and intermediate points A and B by line ranger or eye judgement.

(ii)　Mark the perpendicular offset AC and ND.

(iii)　Mark mid-point of AC.

(iv)　Measure length CD, l (CD) = l (AB).

(v)　$\therefore$　l (MN) = l (NA) + l (AB) + l (BM).

SOLVED EXAMPLES

TYPE I : PROBLEMS ON IN MEASUREMENT CORRECTION

Example 3.1 :

Find out the slope correction in links per 100 links of a 20 m chain for a line measured along a slope of 10° 30'.

Solution :

We know that,

$$\text{Slope correction} = l\,(1 - \cos\theta)$$
$$= 100\,(1 - \cos 10° 30') = 100\,(1 - 0.9833)$$
$$= 1.67 \text{ links}$$

∴   Slope correction is 1.67 links.   ... **Ans.**

Example 3.2 :

An offset is laid out 5° from its true direction on the field. Find the resulting displacement of the plotted point on the paper.

(i) In a direction parallel to chain line.

(ii) In a direction perpendicular to the chain line given that the length of offset is 20 m and scale is 10 cm to 1 cm.

Solution :

Given : $l = 20$ m, $\alpha = 5°$. Scale : 10 cm = 1 m.

(i) Resulting displacement of the plotted point in a direction parallel to chain line

$$= l \sin\alpha$$
$$= 20 \sin 5°$$

∴   Displacement on paper $= \dfrac{20 \sin 5°}{10} = 0.17$ cm

[∵ Scale : 10 m = 1 cm] ... **Ans.**

(ii)   Resulting displacement in a direction perpendicular to the chain line

$$= l\,(1 - \cos\alpha)$$
$$= \dfrac{20\,(1 - \cos 5)}{10} = 0.0076 \text{ cm}$$

$$\left[\begin{array}{l}∵ \text{ Scale :}\\ 10 \text{ m} = 1 \text{ cm}\end{array}\right]... \textbf{Ans.}$$

Example 3.3 :

Find the maximum permissible error in a laying-off the direction of offset so that the maximum displacement may not exceed 0.25 mm on the paper, given that the length of the offset is 1 metres, the scale is 20 m to 1 cm and the maximum error in the length of the offset is 0.3 m.

Solution :

We know that,

$$\text{Displacement of the point} = l \sin\alpha$$
$$= 10 \sin\alpha$$

Given : Error in measurement $= 0.3$

Displacement may not exceed 0.25 mm i.e. 0.025 cm.

Now,   Total displacement $= \sqrt{(10 \sin \alpha)^2 + (0.3)^2}$ m

Displacement on paper $= \dfrac{\sqrt{(10 \sin \alpha) + (0.3)^2}}{20}$ cm

$\therefore \quad \sqrt{\dfrac{(10 \sin \alpha)^2 + (0.3)^2}{20}} = 0.025$

$\therefore \quad \sqrt{(10 \sin \alpha)^2 + (0.3)^2} = 0.025 \times 20$

$\therefore \quad \sqrt{(10 \sin \alpha)^2 + (0.3)^2} = 0.5$

Squaring both the sides, we get

$\therefore \quad (10 \sin \alpha)^2 + (0.3)^2 = 0.25$

$\therefore \quad (10 \sin \alpha)^2 = 0.25 - 0.09$

$\therefore \quad (10 \sin \alpha)^2 = 0.16$

$\therefore \quad 10 \sin \alpha = 0.4$

$\therefore \quad \sin \alpha = 0.04$

$\therefore \quad \alpha = 2° \, 17' \, 32''$ **... Ans.**

TYPE II : PROBLEMS ON OBSTACLES IN CHANING

Example 3.4:

B and C are two points on the opposite banks of a river along a chain line ABC which crosses the river at right angles to the bank. From a point P which is 42.270 m from B along the bank, the bearing of A is 215° 30' and the bearing of C is 305° 30'. If the length AB is 60.960 m, find the width of the river.

Solution :

Refer Fig. 3.18 :

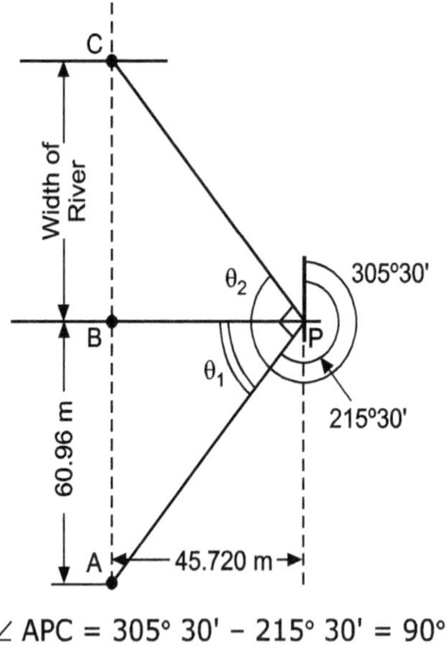

$\angle APC = 305° \, 30' - 215° \, 30' = 90°$

Fig. 3.18

Given : In $\triangle$ ABP l (AB) = 60.960 m

$\qquad\qquad\qquad\quad l$ (BP) = 45.720 m

$\therefore \qquad\qquad$ tan ($\angle$ APB) $= \dfrac{AB}{BP}$

$\therefore \qquad\qquad$ tan $\angle$ APB $= \dfrac{60.960}{45.720}$

$\therefore \qquad\qquad$ tan $\angle$ APB = 1.33

$\therefore \qquad\qquad \theta_1 = \angle$ APB = 53° 7' 48"

From Fig. 3.18

$\qquad\qquad\qquad \angle$ APC = 305° 30' − 215° 30'

$\qquad\qquad\qquad\qquad\quad$ = 90°

$\therefore \qquad\qquad \angle$ BPC = $\angle$ APC − $\angle$ APB

$\therefore \qquad\quad \theta_2 = \angle$ BPC = 90° − 53° 7' 48"

$\qquad\qquad\qquad\qquad\quad$ = 36° 53'

Now, from $\triangle$ BPC

$\qquad\qquad$ tan $\angle$ BPC $= \dfrac{BC}{BP}$

$\therefore \qquad\qquad\qquad$ BC = BP (tan $\angle$ BPC)

$\therefore \qquad\qquad\qquad$ BC = 45.720 (tan 36° 53')

$\therefore \qquad\qquad\qquad$ BC = 34.31 m

$\qquad$ Width of river, BC = 34.31 m. $\qquad$ **... Ans.**

Example 3.5 :

B and C are two points on the opposite banks of a river along a chain line ABC which crosses the river at right angles to the bank. From a point P which is 150 m from B along the bank, the bearing of C is 305° 30' and the bearing of A is 215° 30'. If the length AB is 200 m, find the width of river. **(S-05, W-05)**

Solution :

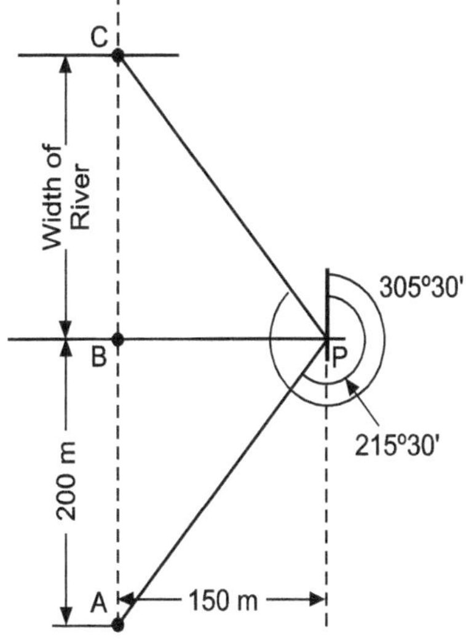

Fig. 3.19

From Fig. 3.19,

In $\triangle$ ABP, l (AB) = 200 m

                l (BP) = 150 m

$\therefore$ $\tan (\angle \text{APB}) = \dfrac{AB}{BP}$

$\therefore$ $\tan \angle \text{APB} = \dfrac{200}{150}$

$\therefore$ $\tan \angle \text{APB} = 1.33$

$\therefore$ $\angle \text{APB} = 53° \ 7' \ 48''$

From Fig.,

      $\angle \text{APC} = 305° \ 30' - 215° \ 30'$

$\therefore$ $\angle \text{APC} = 90°$

Now, $\angle \text{BPC} = \angle \text{APC} - \angle \text{APB}$

$\therefore$ $\angle \text{BPC} = 90° - 53° \ 7' \ 48''$

$\therefore$ $\angle \text{BPC} = 36° \ 53'$

Now, from $\triangle$ BPC,

      $\tan \angle \text{BPC} = \dfrac{BC}{BP}$

$\therefore$ $BC = BP \tan \angle \text{BPC}$

$\therefore$ $BC = 150 \tan 36° \ 53'$

$\therefore$ $BC = 112.555$ m

Width of river is 112.555 m.   **... Ans.**

Example 3.6 :

AD is chain line which crosses a lake, A and B are on the opposite sides of the lake. A line AB of length 175 m is ranged to the left of AD so that it is clear of the lake, similarly another line AC of length 230 m is ranged the right of AD. Further, the points B, D and C are collinear. The lengths of BD and DC are 110 m and 135 m respectively. The chainage of A is 1052.55 m. Calculate the chainage of D.

Solution :.

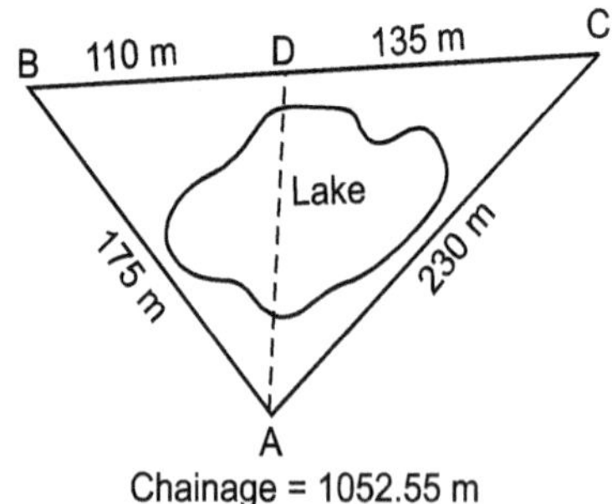

Fig. 3.20

From Fig. 3.20,

$$AD = \sqrt{\dfrac{AB^2 \times CD + AC^2 \times BD}{BC}} - BD \times CD$$

$\therefore\qquad AD = \sqrt{\dfrac{175^2 \times 135 + 230^2 \times 110}{(110 + 135)}} - (110 \times 135)$

$\therefore\qquad AD = 160.55$ m

Now, Chainage of D = Chainage of A + AD

       = 1052.55 + 160.55

       = 1213.10 m

Chainage of D is 1213.10 m. **... Ans.**

Example 3.7 :

To find out the width of a river, flowing west-east, two points P and Q are fixed along a bank 400 m apart. The bearing of a pole R on the other bank of the river as observed from P and Q are 30° and 315°. Determine the width of the river.

Solution :

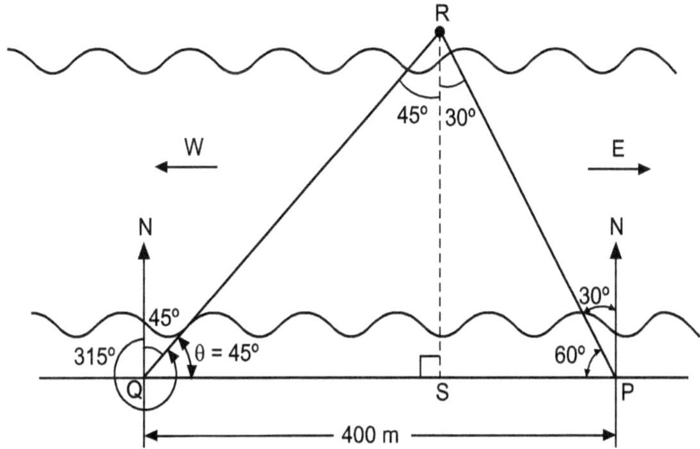

Fig. 3.21

From Fig. 3.21.

In $\triangle$ PSR $\tan 30° = \dfrac{PS}{SR}$

       $PS = SR \tan 30°$

and in $\triangle$ QSR $\tan 45° = \dfrac{QS}{SR}$

$\therefore$ $QS = SR \tan 45°$

or $PS + QS = SR \tan 30° + SR \tan 45°$

$\therefore$ $PQ = SR (\tan 30° + \tan 45°)$ $[\because PS + QS = PQ]$ from Fig. 2.38

$\therefore$ $400 = SR (0.577 + 1)$

$\therefore$ $400 = SR (1.577)$

$\therefore$ $SR = 253.65$ m

$\therefore$ Width of river, $SR = 253.65$ m **... Ans.**

TYPE III : PROBLEMS ON CROSS-STAFF SURVEY

Example 3.8 :

Calculate the area of a field from the following cross-staff survey.

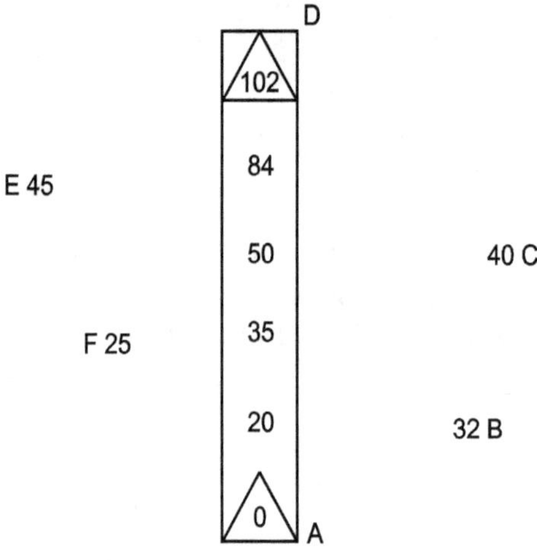

Fig. 3.22

Solution :

From the field data of Fig. 3.22 the area ABCDEF is sketched as shown in the Fig. 3.23. It is divided into right angled triangles and trapeziums. The chainages and offsets are entered in the following tubular form to compute the area.

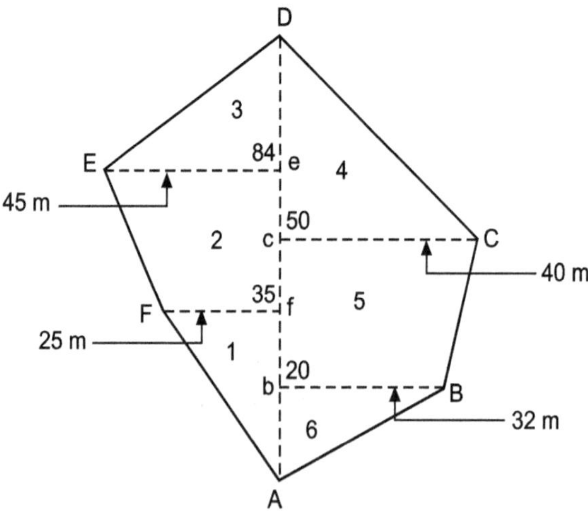

Fig. 3.23

Area Table

Sr. No.	Figure	Chainage in m.	Base in m.	Off-set in m.		Mean offset	Area in m^2 = (base × mean offset)
				O_1	O_2	$\dfrac{O_1 + O_2}{2}$	+ ve
1	2	3	4	5		6	7
1.	△ AfF	0 and 35	35	0 and 25		12.5	437.50
2.	▱ FfeE	35 and 84	49	25 and 45		35.00	1715.00
3.	△ EeD	84 and 102	18	45 and 0		22.50	405.00
4.	△ DCc	50 and 102	52	40 and 0		20.00	1040.00
5.	▱ cCBb	20 and 50	30	32 and 40		36	1080.00
6.	△ ABb	0 and 20	20	0 and 32		16	320.00
						Total	4997.5

Area of the field is 4997.5 m^2.   ... **Ans.**

Example 3.9 :

Plot the area of a field ABCDEF surveyed with reference to a chain line PQ. The station P and Q are beyond boundary of the field.

The area of the field ABCDEF is plotted as shown in Fig. 3.24.

In this type, the triangles i.e. AaM and EeN are beyond the boundary of field ABCDEF and hence their area is taken as negative area.

The chainages of point M and N may be measured, directly from the plotted figure or it can be calculated from similar triangles, so formed. The same can also be found in the field by ranging lines A to B and D to E. The chain line cuts at points M and N. The chainages of M and N are 15.55 and 80.55 respectively. The results are tabulated below to calculate the area of the field.

Solution :

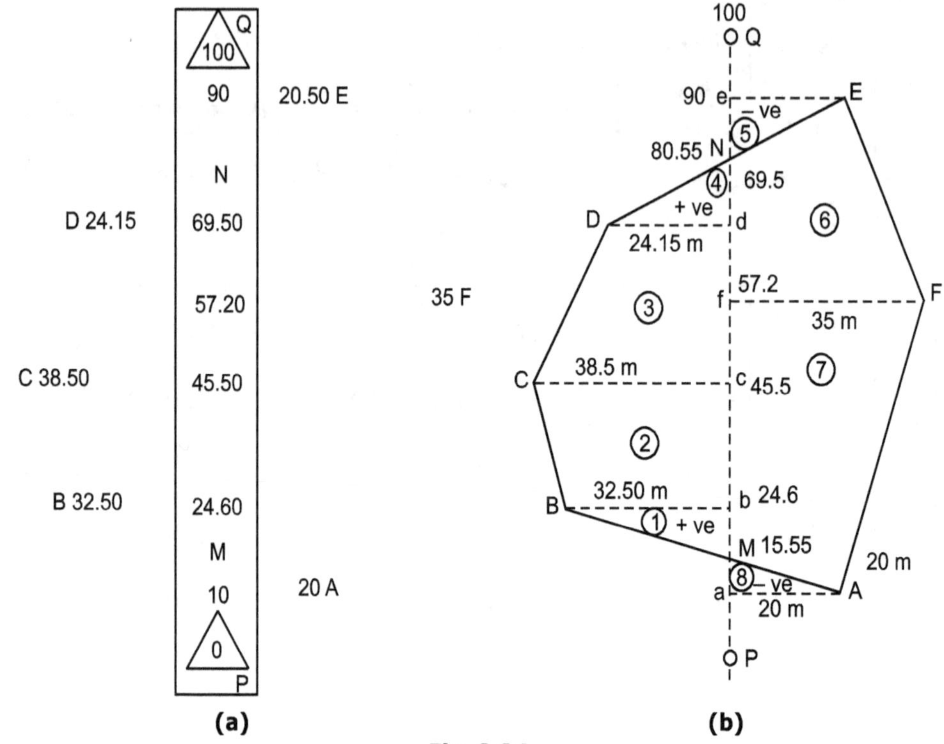

Fig. 3.24
Area Table

Sr. No.	Figure	Chainage in m	Base in m	Offfset in m	Mean offset	Area in m² Base × Mean offset
1.	△ Bbm	15.55 & 24.60	9.05	0 & 32.50	16.25	+ ve
2.	⬜ BbcC	24.60 & 45.50	20.90	32.50 & 38.50	35.5	147.06
3.	⬜ CcdD	45.50 & 69.50	24	38.50 & 24.15	31.325	741.95
4.	△ DdN	69.50 & 80.55	11.05	24.15 & 0	12.075	751.80
5.	△ eEN	90 & 80.55	9.45	20.50 & 0	10.25	133.43
6.	⬜ eEFf	90 & 57.20	32.80	20.50 & 35	27.75	−96.86
7.	⬜ fFAa	57.20 & 10.00	47.20	35 & 20	27.50	910.20
8.	△ aAM	15.55 & 10	5.55	20 & 0	10.00	− 55.50
					Total net area	= 3830.58

Area of the field ABCDEF = 3830.08 sq.m.   **... Ans.**

$$OR = \frac{3830.58}{10000} = 0.383 \text{ Hectare} \quad (\because 1 \text{ Hectare} = 10,000 \text{ sq.m})$$

Example 3.10 :

Plot the following cross-staff survey of field and calculate its area in m^2 as shown in Fig. 3.25.

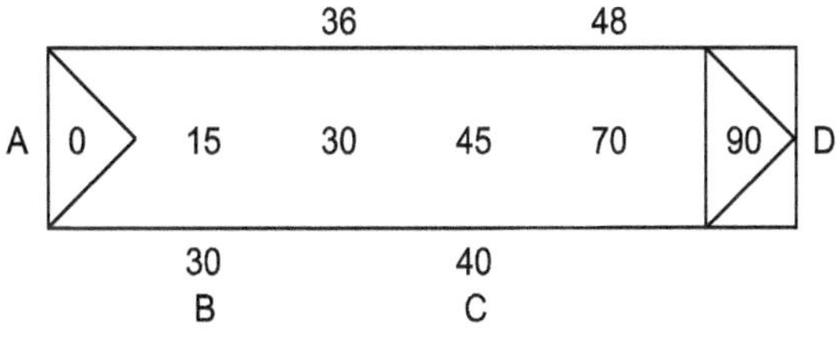

Line AD ⟶ All dimensions in metres

Fig. 3.25

Solution :

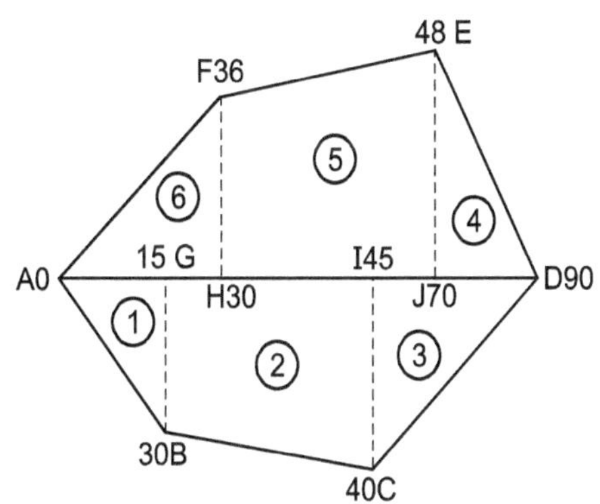

Fig. 3.26

Area Table

Sr. No.	Fig.	Chainages (m)		Base (m)	Offsets		Mean area (m)	Area sq.m.
		From	To		No. 1	No. 2		
1	△ ABG	0	15	15	0	30	15	225
2	☐ GBCI	15	45	30	30	40	35	1050
3	△ CID	45	90	45	40	0	20	900
4	△ DJE	70	90	20	0	48	24	480
5	☐ EJHF	70	30	40	48	36	42	1680
6	△ FHA	30	0	30	36	0	18	540
							Total Area =	4875 m²

Note : Area = base × mean offset

Example 3.11 :

Plot the following cross-staff survey of a field and calculate the area ABCDEF.

(W-08)

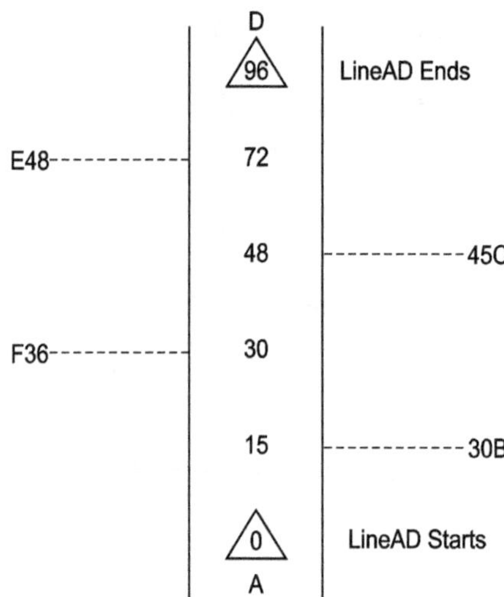

Fig. 3.27

Solution :

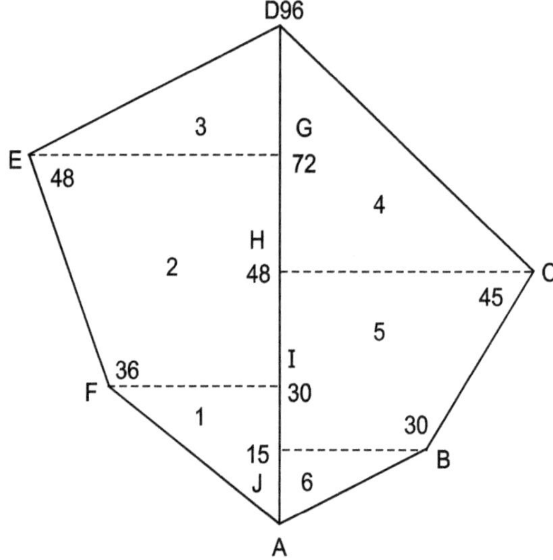

Fig. 3.28

Area Table

Sr. No.	Fig.	Chainages (m)		Base	Offsets		Mean offset	Area sq.m.
		From	To		O_1 No.1	O_2 No.2		
1.	△ AIF	0	30	30	0	36	18	540.0
2.	⬭ FEGI	30	72	42	36	48	42	1764.0
3.	◸ EGD	72	96	24	48	0	24	576.0
4.	◸ DHC	48	96	48	45	0	22.5	1080.0
5.	⬭ HJBC	15	48	33	30	45	37.5	1237.5
6.	◹ BJA	0	15	15	0	30	15	225.0
Total area = 5422.5 m^2								... **Ans.**

Example 3.12 :

Plot the cross-staff survey of the field and calculate the area of the Fig. ABCDEA in hectares. Find the area of Fig. ABCDEA. (All dimensions are in metres.)

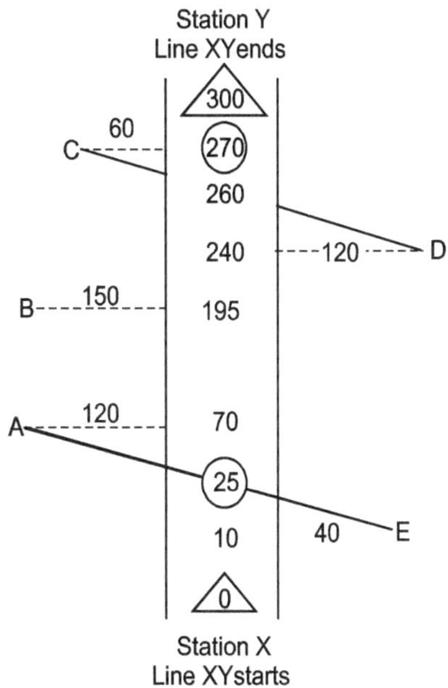

Fig. 3.29

Solution :

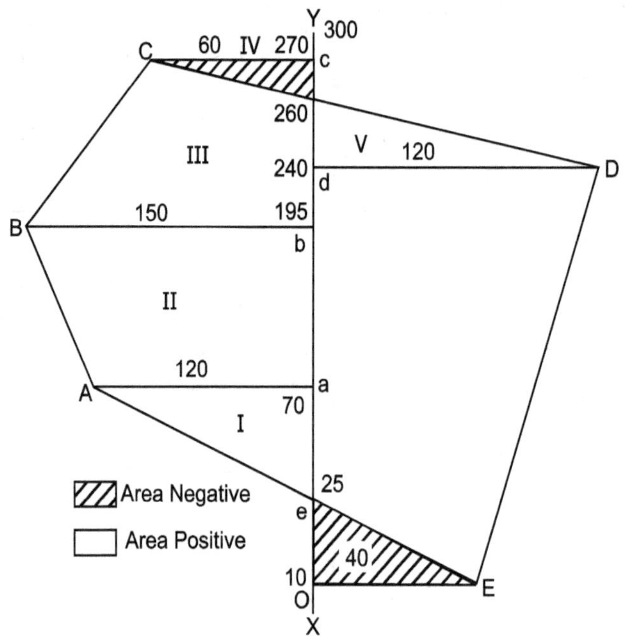

Fig. 3.30

Area Table

Sr. No.	Fig.	Chainages		Base	Offsets		Mean Area	Area (sq.m.)
		From	To		No.1	No.2		
1.	eaA	25	70	45	0	120	60	2700
2.	abBA	70	195	125	120	150	135	16875
3.	bcCB	195	270	75	150	60	105	7875
4.	VcC	260	270	10	00	60	30	−300
5.	dVD	240	260	20	0	120	60	1200
6.	OdDE	10	240	230	40	120	80	18400
7.	OeE	10	25	15	40	0	20	−300
Total area = 46450 m²								... **Ans.**

Important Points

- The principle of chain surveying is *triangulation*.
- Triangulation consists of frame work of triangles. The whole area is divided into network of triangles.
- **Well-conditioned triangle :** A triangle in which no angle is smaller than 30° and no angle is greater than 120° is known as well condition triangle.
- **Ill condition triangle :** A triangles having angles less than 30° or greater than 120° are known as *ill-conditioned triangles.*
- A survey station is an important point on the ground at the beginning and end of a chain line.
- Station which are located at the ends of the chain line much command the boundaries of survey is known as main station.
- A stations which are located at the points selected on main survey lines to run subsidiary or tie lines to locate the interior detail such as buildings, fences, hedges etc. is known as subsidiary station
- Distances are measured from the chain lines to the objects right or left of the chain line. Such distances (lateral measurements) are called offsets.
- When the measurements are taken at right angles (90°) to the chain line, they are known as perpendicular *offsets* or simply offsets.
- The measurements taken at other angles than 90° angle, they are called *oblique offset.*
- Principle of optical square states that in case of reflecting instrument, the angle between the first incident ray and the last reflected ray is twice the angle between the two mirrors
- The preliminary inspection of area to be surveyed is called *reconnaissance.*
- The instruments required for a cross-staff survey :　　　　**(S-11)**
  - (i)　Two chains 20 m or 30 m.
  - (ii)　Arrows
  - (iii)　Ranging rods
  - (iv)　A cross-staff or an optical square.
  - (v)　A plumb bob.
- **Classification of Obstacles :**
  - (1)　Obstacles which can be chained across but cannot be ranged across.
  - (2)　Obstacles which can be ranged across but cannot be chained across.
  - (3)　Obstacles which can neither be ranged across nor be chained across.

Practice Questions

1. Enlist the instruments required for conducting a chain survey. How is the chain survey executed in the field ?
2. Describe with neat sketches
   (a) Base line, (b) Location sketch, (c) Swing offset.
3. What do you understand by reconnaissance ? How does it helps in planning the chain survey ?
4. Distinguish between –
   Well-conditioned triangle and Ill-conditioned triangle.
   Why is it necessary to use well conditioned triangle ?
5. Name the instruments used for setting out right angles.

6. Explain with neat diagram the construction and working of prism square.
7. How the optical square is used in field ? How is it tested and adjusted ?
8. Describe the construction and use of open cross-staff and french cross-staff.
9. Explain with neat diagram the construction and working of cross-staff.
10. What do you understand by offset and oblique offset ? Why are they taken ? To what precision you will measure the offset if the plan of survey is to be plotted to a scale of
    (i) 1 cm = 5 m, (ii) 1 cm = 10 cm, (iii) 1 cm = 1 m ?
    [**Ans.** (i) 12.5 cm, (ii) 25 cm, (iii) 2.5 cm]
11. Set out clearly the precautions a surveyor should take in recording a field book of chain survey. Rule out a page of field book showing the chain line and record the following features on it :
    (a) A chain line crossing a road 20 m wide.
    (b) A building on right side of the chain line.
12. What should detailed instruction be given to a fresh trainee surveyor regarding the care and use of his field book for recording survey measurement ?
13. Explain any two methods of setting out right angles from a point on the chain line with the help of tape only.
14. An area is to be mapped by chain survey.
    (a) Explain clearly how the work is carried out in field and office.
    (b) Name the various equipments used in chain surveying and what is the function of each.
       Hints : (a) Explain briefly
       (i) Reconnaissance. (ii) Marking station.
       (iii) Running survey lines. (iv) Plotting or office work.
15. How can the chaining be continued past the following obstacles :
     (i) A hill, (ii) A tall building
16. State the various methods of overcoming obstacles in chaining for
    (a) Chaining free – vision obstructed.
    (b) Vision free – chaining obstructed.
    (c) Both chaining and vision obstructed.
17. Describe how will one continue chaining past the following obstacles :
    (i) Pond, (ii) River.
18. Describe how the chaining can be continued when the following obstacles meet :
    (a) A thick forest intervenes.
    (b) A river crosses a chain line.
19. What are the following :
    (i) Field work, (ii) Field book ?
20. Explain with neat sketches how you will locate the following with reference to the chain line :
    (a) A Nalla.
    (b) An irregular boundary.
    (c) A fair curve of railway line.
    (d) A road crossing the chain line obliquely.
    (e) A building situated at fairly long distance.

21. Write short notes on :
    (a) Location sketch.
    (b) Plotting of cross-staff survey.
    (c) Indian optical square-construction and use.
    (d) Booking field notes.
    (e) General principles of cross-staff survey.
22. State the method of plotting a chain survey. Mention the precautions you will take while plotting the chain survey.
23. An offset is laid out 5° from true direction on the field, find the resulting displacement of the plotted point on the paper (i) In a direction parallel to the chain line (ii) In a direction to the chain line given the length of offset is 20 m and scale is 10 m to 1 cm.
24. Find the maximum permissible error in a laying off the direction of offset so that the maximum displacement may not exceed 0.25 mm on the paper, given that the length of the offset is 10 metres, the scale is 20 m to 1 cm and the maximum error in the length of the offset is 0.3 m.
25. B and C are two points on the opposite banks of a river along a chain line ABC, which crosses the river at right angles to the bank. From a point P which is 45.720 m from B along the bank, the bearing of A is 215° 30' and the bearing of C is 305⁰ 30'. If the length AB is 60.960 m, find the width of the river.

MSBTE Questions & Answers

Summer 2010

1. List any eight instruments used in chain and compass surveying.
Ans. Refer Section 3.12.
2. Which important points should be considered in selecting survey stations for a closed traverse ?
Ans. Refer Section 3.5.
3. Calculate the area ABCDE in hectares. (Fig. 3.31)

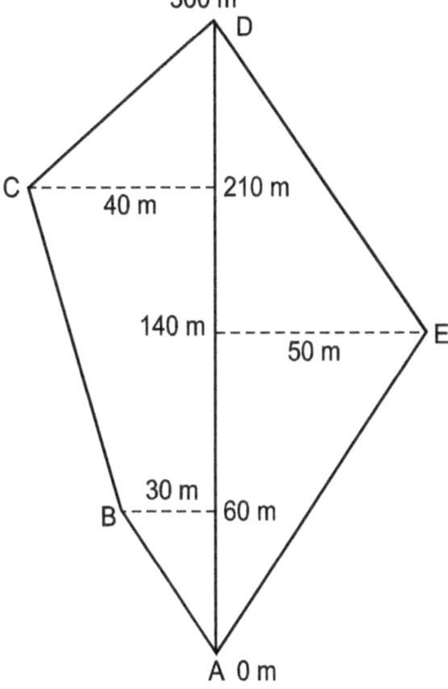

Fig. 3.31 (a)

Fig.	Chainage		Base	Offset		Average	Area
	From	To		No. 1	No. 2	offset	
1	0	60	60	0	30	15	900
2	60	210	150	30	40	35	5250
3	210	300	90	40	0	20	1800
4	140	300	160	50	0	25	4000
5	0	140	140	0	50	25	3500
							15450

$$\text{Area in ha} = \frac{15450}{10000} = 1.545 \text{ ha}$$

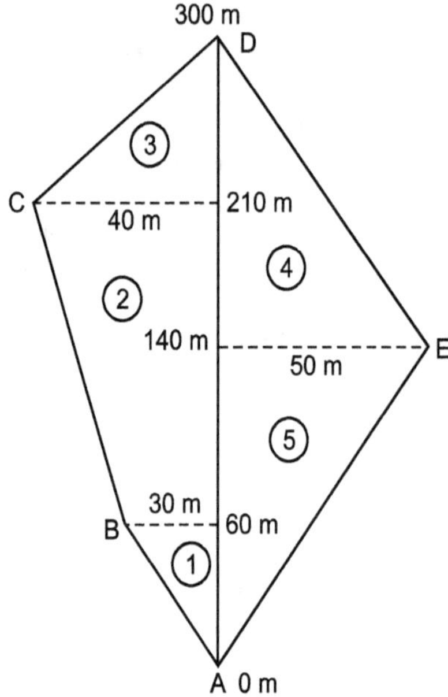

Fig. 3.31 (b)

Winter 2010

1. Calculate the area of a closed traverse ABCDEF from a page of a field book given in Fig. 3.32. All dimensions are in metres.

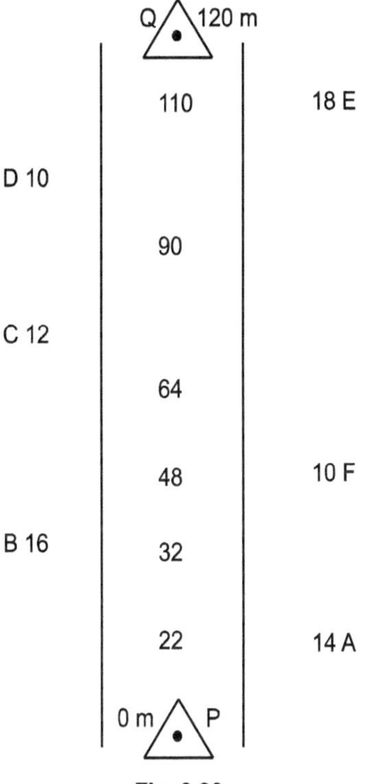

Fig. 3.32

Ans. 1.545 ha.

2. Define the following terms with the help of neat sketches :
   (i) Perpendicular offset.
   (ii) Oblique offset.

Ans. Refer Section 3.7.

Summer 2011

1. List the instruments required in doing chain and cross-staff survey.

Ans. Refer Section 3.12.

2. What is principle of chain surveying ?

Ans. Refer Section 3.3.

3. What are the different points considered while selecting survey stations ?

Ans. Refer Section 3.5.

4. How do you overcome the obstacle when chaining across a river ?

Ans. Refer Section 3.14 (2).

5. Prepare a page of field showing chain line with following details :
   (i) Length of chain line 96 m.
   (ii) A tree 30 m perpendicular from chainage 15 m at right.
   (iii) The corners of the building are 42 m and 48 m from chainage 60 m and 75 m respectively to the left of chain.

Ans. Refer Section 3.10.

Winter 2011

1. Define and write use of following :
   (i) Base line.
Ans. Refer Section 3.6 (i) on page no. 3.3.
   (ii) Offsets.
Ans. Refer Section 3.7.
2. Write different points to be considered while booking the field book in chain and cross-staff survey.
Ans. Refer Section 3.10.
3. How you overcome obstacles when both chaining and vision obstrcuted.
Ans. Refer Section 3.14.
4. Following figures shows page of field book of cross-staff survey. Plot the required figure and calculate area of figure ABCDE Refer Fig. 3.33.

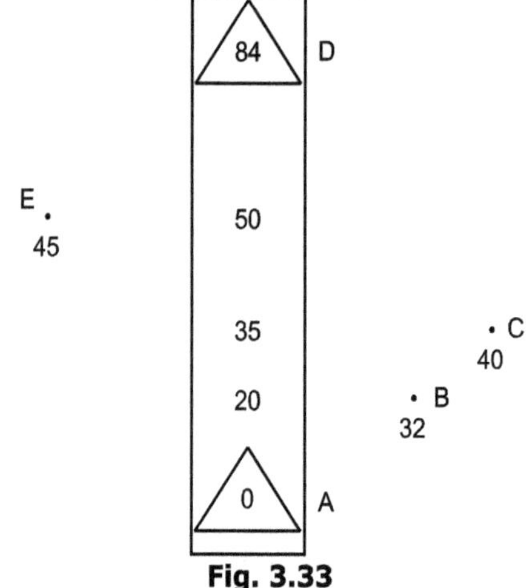

Fig. 3.33

Ans.

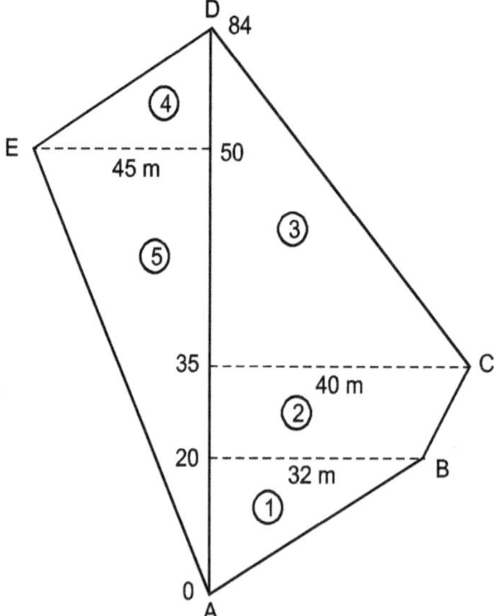

Fig. 3.34

Fig.	Chainage		Base	Offset		Average	Area
	From	To		No. 1	No. 2	offset	
1	0	20	20	0	32	16	320
2	20	35	15	32	40	36	540
3	35	84	49	40	0	20	980
4	50	84	34	45	0	22.5	765
5	0	50	50	0	45	22.5	1125
							3730

$$\therefore \ \text{Area} = 3730 \ m^2$$

Summer 2012

1. Differentiate between long-off set and short off-set.

Ans. Refer Section 3.7.

2. Explain principle and construction of a optical square with a neat sketch.

Ans. Refer Section 3.9.

3. State the types of obstacles in changing and explain one with neat sketch.

Ans. Refer Section 3.14.

Winter 2012

1. Difference between long off-set and short off-set.

Ans. Refer Section 3.7.

2. Plot the following cross-staff survey of field and calculate its area. (Fig. 3.35)

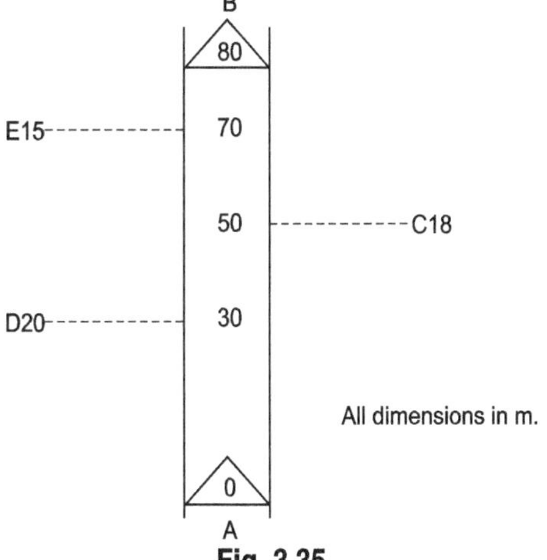

Fig. 3.35

Ans.

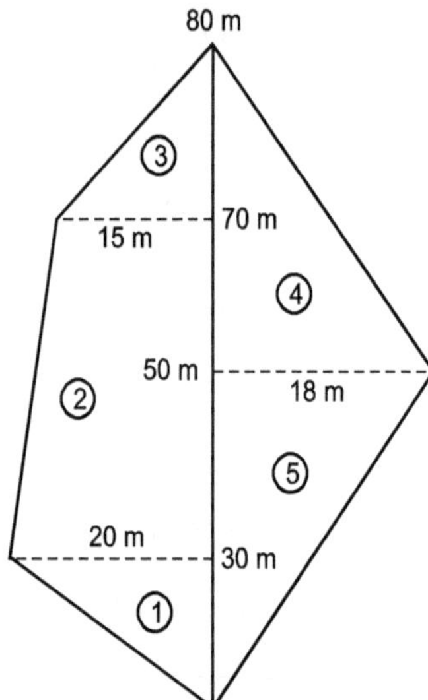

Fig. 3.36

Fig.	Chainage		Base	Offset		Average	Area
	From	To		No. 1	No. 2	offset	
1	0	30	30	0	20	10	300
2	30	70	40	20	15	17.5	700
3	70	80	10	15	0	7.5	75
4	50	80	30	18	0	9	270
5	0	50	50	0	18	9	450
							1795 m^2

$$\therefore \ AA = 1795 \ m^2$$

3. What is obstacles in chaining ? Explain briefly.

Ans. Refer Section 3.14.

Summer 2013

1. Differentiate between long off set and short offset.

Ans. Refer Section 3.7.

2. Explain principle and construction of a optical square with a neat sketch.

Ans. Refer Section 3.9 (3).

3. State the types of obstacles in chaining and explain any one with neat sketch.

Ans. Refer Section 3.14.

4...

Compass Traverse Survey

Contents

4.1 CHAIN AND COMPASS SURVEYING

- In chain surveying a network of triangles is found and no angular measurements are taken. It can be used when the area to be surveyed is comparatively small and is fairly flat.

- But in case of larger areas, methods of chain surveying alone are not sufficient and convenient and precise.

- Hence, it becomes essential to use fix the directions of survey lines by some instrument.

- In traverse surveying the area is divided into number of lines forming figures of more than four sides.

- The lengths are measured with chain or tape and the directions of survey lines are fixed by angular measurements such as prismatic compass, theodolite etc.

- The chaining and offsetting is done as in chain surveying. Running of check lines is not necessary.

4.2 COMPASS SURVEYING   (S-08, 09; W-07, S-12)

- It is a branch of surveying in which the bearing of sides of traverse are taken with prismatic compass or surveyor's compass and the lengths are measured with chain of tape.

- The principle of compass survey is Traversing, which involves a series of connected survey lines (may be open or closed) whose lengths and bearings are measured by linear and angular measuring instruments.

4.3 THE COMPASS

(i) A compass is a instrument is used for measuring horizontal angle.

The important parts of compass are :

(a) a box with graduated circle.

(b) a magnetic needle.

(c)   a line of sight.

- When the line of sight is pointed to a given point, the magnetic needle of compass points towards north (Magnetic meridian).

- The angle which this line of sight makes with the magnetic meridian is read on the graduated circle. It is known as magnetic bearing of the line.

There are two types of compasses :

(a) Prismatic compass (b) Surveyor's compass.

4.4 PRISMATIC COMPASS   (S-09; W-07, W-10; S-11, W-11)

- The prismatic compass is a very valuable instrument. It is usually used for rough surveys for measuring bearings of survey lines.
- It is used to measure angles between two or more relative points in horizontal plane.
- It is a portable form of magnetic compass is installed on a tripod stand.
- Principle of prismatic compass : To measure the angular measurement of closed or open traverse by tacking bearing of lines w.r.t. North.

Construction :   (S-08; W-09)

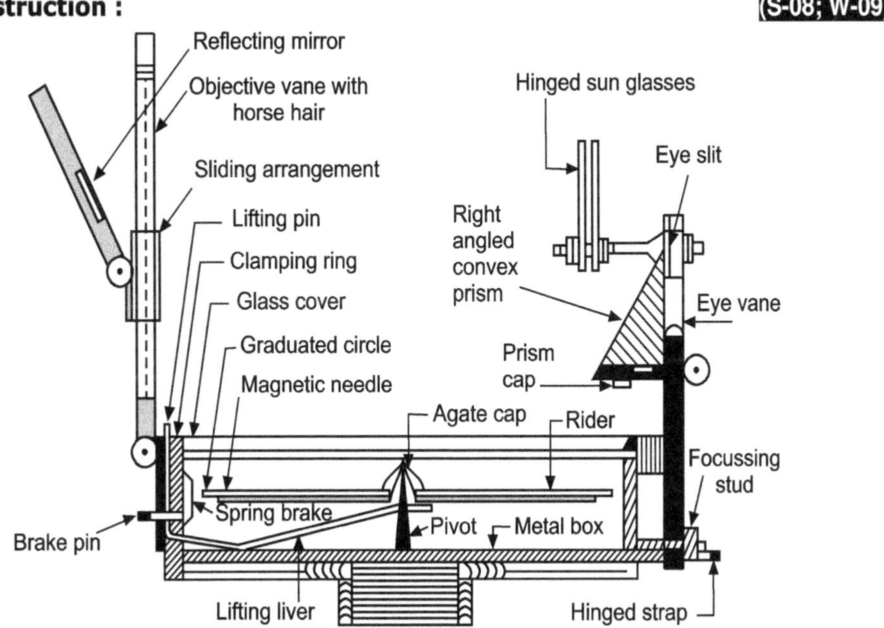

Fig. 4.1 (a) : The Prismatic Compass in Section

(i)   It consists of circular metal box about 85 mm to 110 mm diameter.

(ii) It has a hard steel pivot at the centre on which magnetic needle with graduated circle is balanced. The graduated circle is made of aluminium and it is numbered in degrees and half degrees. The figures are written inverted from 0° to 360°, but when we observe them through reflecting prism, they will be seen as direct on ring. The zero is marked at the south end of the needle and run clockwise 90° at west, 180° at north and 270° at east. The needle indicates the north direction. The least count is 30 minutes i.e. each part is equal to 30'. A freely suspended needle on the pivot always point towards the north pole or magnetic meridian.

(iii) Sighting vane and reflecting prism with a sighting slit at the top are fixed diametrically opposite to each other in the circular metal box.

    The sighting vane is linked to the box. A vertical horse hair of fine silk thread is stretched in the centre of it to bisect the objects. It can be folded to lie on the compass glass.

(iv) When the instrument is not in use the sight vane presses against the *lifting pin* which lifts the needle off the pivot and holds it against a glass lid; thus it prevents the undue wear of pivot point.

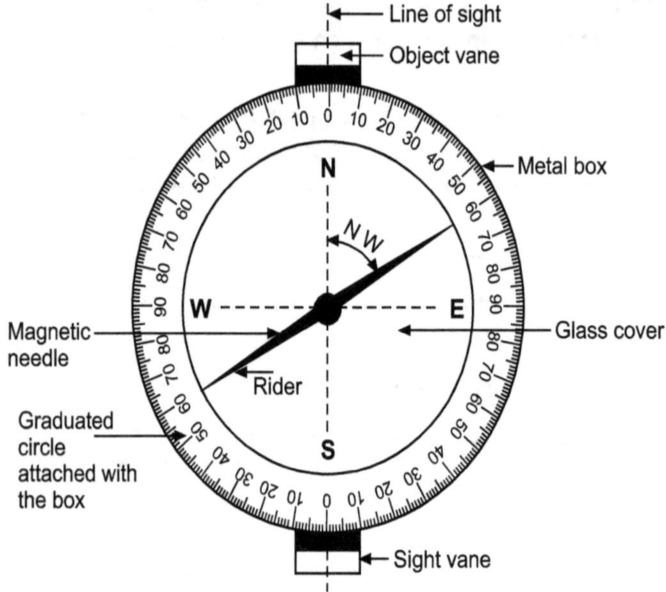

Fig. 4.1(b) : Surveyor's Compass and its Various Parts

(v) A light spring is fitted in the box to damp the oscillations of the needle and graduated circle when about to take the reading. It is called a *break pin* or *knob*. When pressed gently, it touches the edge of the graduated ring in order to bring it to rest and needle oscillations are stopped.

(vi) A reflecting prism is provided which can be adjusted to the eye sight of the observer by means of stud carrying it. The graduations on the ring below, are reflected from hypotenuse side to the eye. If the faces of the prism bring are convex, the graduations are seen magnified. Thus, looking through the prism, the observer can see the graduation erect and magnified.

(vii) The glass lid is provided on the top edge of box so that the graduations on the ring are visible. It also protects the instrument from dust. A *brass ring* is provided over the compass glass to keep it in position.

(viii) A sighting vane is provided with a hinged mirror (adjustable mirror) which can be adjusted upwards or downwards on the frame and can be slided along it as required. The adjustable mirror can be made to incline of any angle so that object too high or too low may be sighted by reflection. It can be lifted and refitted in the inverted position also, for example, to take bearing of a sun, the mirror is adjusted in such a way that its image is seen by reflection and the bearing can thus be taken.

(ix) Hinged sun glasses, generally, red and green or red and blue are attached to the frame of reflecting prism which can be interposed into the line of sight, when the sun or other luminous objects are to be sighted.

(x)　　A metal cover is provided over the glass lid and sighting vane when the compass is not in use.

(xi)　　A sliding rider is provided on the central plate of graduated circle above the needle, to balance the needle exactly in horizontal position.

(xii)　　The agate cap is mounted on the graduated ring at the center which rests against the pivot. The pivot point must be very sharp so that the needle swings freely in a horizontal plane and should come to rest in the magnetic meridian. To prevent undue wear, the needle when not in use should be lifted off the pivot by means of lever.

(xiii)　　The ball and socket arrangement is provided on the top of tripod stand by which the compass can be set in a horizontal position.

4.5 USES OF PRISMATIC COMPASS　　　(W-10)

(i)　　It is used for survey in wooded country, rough traverses, filling in details, preliminary surveys for roads, railways.

(ii)　　It is also used for sketching and right marching.

(iii)　　It is unreliable in places of magnetic rock or iron ore. It is less accurate than theodolite.

Graduations on compass　　　(S-08; W-09)

- In prismatic compass the graduations are numbered clockwise as shown in the Fig. 4.2. The zero at the south end of the needle, 90° at the west, 180° at the north and 270° at the east.

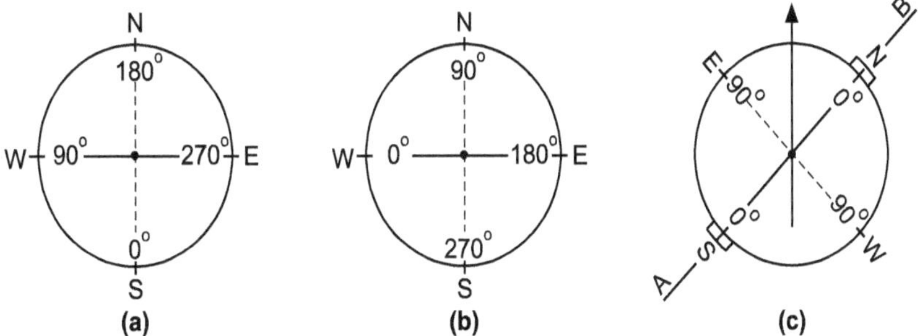

Fig. 4.2 : Graduations on Compass

The figures are engraved inverted.

The reason why zero is marked at south end of graduated circle :

- When the needle is freely swinging on the pivot it points towards North, the reading under the prism should be zero. But since the prism is placed exactly opposite the sight vane, the south end will be under the prism. Obviously, the zero of mark must be placed at the end of the needle. The bearings are thus obtained from north end in clockwise directions.

- In case of surveyor's compass Fig. 4.2 (b) the graduated circle is divided into four quadrants and the graduations are marked from 0° to 90° in each quadrant. The zero points are marked with letter N or S and 90° at E and W as in Fig. 4.2 (c). East-west are interchanged in the surveyor's compass.

4.6 THE LEVEL COMPASS

The compass attached to level is similar to the prismatic compass except the following.

(1) Sighting vane is not provided. The telescope is used to sight the objects.

(2) The prism is provided exactly at 90° to the line of sight. Hence, the zero is marked at West, 90° at the North, 180° at the East and 270° at the South as shown in Fig. 4.3 (b).

(3) Sharp point is provided to the side of the box below prism to point the reading.

(4) The objects are sighted through the telescope and bearings are taken through the prism.

4.7 TEMPORARY ADJUSTMENT OF COMPASS

- The prismatic compass may be held in hand and observations can be taken.

- But for accurate results, it is mounted on a light tripod which is provided with ball and socket arrangement.

- It enables to level the instrument quickly and to rotate it in horizontal plane.

- The following temporary adjustments are carried out at every set-up of the instrument before taking any observations.

(1) Centering (W-08) : Centering is the process of keeping the instrument exactly over the station. It is carried out by dropping a small piece of stone from the underneath of the compass, so that is falls on the top of the peg fixed at the station point.

(2) Levelling (W-08) : It is levelled by means of ball and socket arrangement provided to the tripod stand so that the graduated ring may swing freely. The instrument is then clamped.

(3) Focussing the prism : The reflecting prism is adjusted to the eye sight of the observer by raising of or lowering the stud, until the graduations are seen sharp and clear. The sighting of the object and reading of graduated circle are done simultaneously.

4.8 OBSERVING BEARINGS

Suppose bearing of a line AB is to be observed

(i) Set up the instrument at station A and carry out all the above temporary adjustments. Fix one ranging rod at B. [Fig. 4.3 (c)]

(ii) Turn the compass box until the ranging rod at station B is bisected by the horse hair when seen through the vertical slit above the prism.

(iii) When the needle comes to rest, bisect ranging rod at B exactly and note the reading. It gives the bearing of the line AB. Thus, in figure 4.4 the reading is 62° 30'.

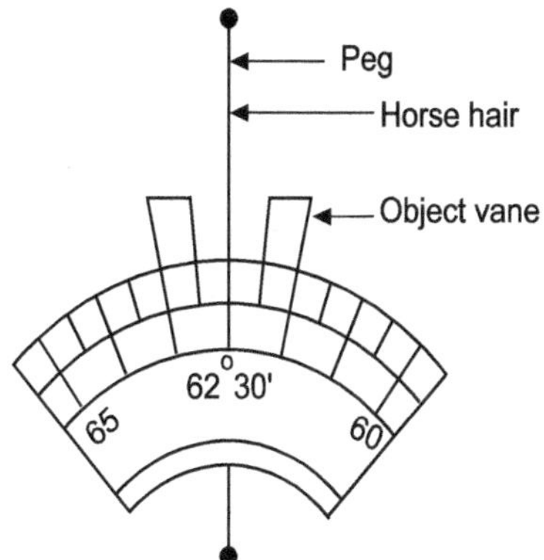

Fig. 4.3 : Reading on Compass

4.9 PERMISSIBLE ERROR IN COMPASS SURVEYING

- In case of prismatic compass, the smallest reading that can be observed by estimation is 15 minutes. Therefore, the permissible error should not exceed 15 minutes.

- The angular error of closure should not exceed $15 \sqrt{N}$, where N is the number of sides of a traverse. The relative error of closure should be between 1 in 300 to 1 in 600.

4.10 ERRORS IN COMPASS SURVEYING

The errors are classified as :

1. Instrumental errors.

2. Personal or Observational errors.

3. Errors due to External Influences (Natural errors etc.).

(1) Instrumental errors : These errors are due to faulty compass, not being in adjustment and perfect working order i.e.

(i) The needle not being perfectly magnetised, not pointing exact meridian.

(ii) The pivot being bent and not in the center.

(iii) The pivot being dull and not sharp.

(iv) The needle not being perfectly straight.

(v) The needle and graduated ring not being horizontal.

(vi) The object vane not being in plumb.

(vii) The horse hair being loose, not straight.

(2) Personal or Observational errors : The personal errors may be due to

(i) Inaccurate centering of compass over the station.

(ii) Inaccurate levelling of compass.

(iii) Inaccurate bisection of ranging rod or other objects.

(iv) Carelessness in taking readings.

(v) Carelessness in booking the readings in field book.

(3) **Errors due to External Influences (Natural errors) :** These errors may be due to :

(i)	Magnetic changes in the atmosphere on stormy days.

(ii)	Variations in magnetic declination.

(iii)	Local attraction due to proximity of magnetic substances like steel structures, electric lines etc.

4.11 PRECAUTIONS IN USING THE COMPASS

The following precautions should be taken in using the compass :

1.	Centering and levelling should be done carefully.

2.	Protect the pivot in every possible way. The needle should be kept off the pivot to prevent undue wear when compass is not in use.

3.	Stop vibrations of the needle by gently pressing the break knob to bring the needle to rest early.

4.	The North end of the needle should be red. Always look along the needle and not across it, thus avoiding parallax.

5.	Avoid taking reading in wrong direction, $35°$ to $25°$. Read always in rising direction of numbers on the graduated ring.

6.	The sources of local attraction should always be avoided.

7.	To detect local attraction fore and back bearing of every line should be taken.

8.	Tap the compass box after the needle has come to rest to overcome friction on the pivot.

9.	The bearing of important lines should be taken twice.

10.	Avoid touching the compass glass with moist fingers.

11.	If it is not possible to take the bearing of a line from its end the compass may be set-up over any intermediate point on the line.

12.	Due to obstructions in chain line, if it is not possible to observe the bearing of line, another line parallel to the chain line should be set and its bearing be observed.

4.12 TESTING AND ADJUSTING THE COMPASS

Before using the compass, it should be tested whether it is in good working order.

(1) **Needle :** Set-up the compass and level it carefully over the station, and see if graduated ring is perfectly horizontal. If not, slide the rider towards the high end to make it horizontal.

(2) **Pivot point :** To test whether the pivot is exactly in the centre of graduated ring, red both ends of the needle. The difference of reading shown by North and south ends should be exactly $180°$, provided the pivot is exactly in center and the needle is straight. If not make the needle straight and bend the pivot slightly so that the North and South end reading differ exactly by $180°$.

(3) Sight vane : The sight vane should be exactly vertical and diametrically opposite to the eye slit of prism. To test it, suspend a plumb line in front of the compass. Level the compass and bisect the hair. If the sights are vertical, eye vane, object vane and horse hair will be parallel and in the same line. If not adjust the affected vane by filing or inserting suitable packing under lower side. Repeat this adjustment until perfect.

(4) Sensitivity of needle : To see whether the needle is sensitive or the pivot is blunt, centre the compass and carefully level it over the station. Sight any object and note the reading. Now, disturb the compass and again sight the same object, the reading should be exactly the same. If not, the pivot point should be sharpended and the needle should be remagnetised. The sluggishness of the needle is more due to dullness of pivot, rather than to the loss of magnetism.

4.13 BEARING OF LINES

- The *bearing of a line* is 'the horizontal angle made by the survey line with some reference direction or meridian'.
- The reference direction or meridian may be
  - (i)   A true meridian.
  - (ii) A magnetic meridian.
  - (iii) An arbitrary or assumed meridian.
    - In geodetic surveys, true meridian or geographical meridian is adopted
    - In plane surveys Magnetic meridian is used.

(i) A true meridian :　　　　　　　(S-09; W-08, 09; S-11, S-12)

- The true to geographical meridian passing through a point on the earth's surface is the line in which the plane passing through the given point and the north and south poles intersects the surface of the earth.
- The true meridian or astronomic meridian is determined by astronomical observations. For any given point on the earth its direction is always the same.
- The horizontal angle between the line and true meridian is called a *true bearing of the line*. It is also known *azimuth.*

(ii) A magnetic meridian :　　　　　　(S-09; W-08, 09, 10, S-12)

- The direction indicated by a freely suspended and properly balanced magnetic needle unaffected by local attractive force is called the magnetic meridian.
- The angle made by the survey line with the *magnetic meridian* is called a magnetic bearing of the line or simply bearing of the line.

(iii) An arbitrary meridian :　　　　　　　　(S-09, W-10)

- Any convenient direction may be taken as a meridian for small survey.
- It may be a direction from a survey station to some well-defined permanent object or the first survey line.
- The angle made by a line with this meridian is called an *arbitrary bearing* of the line.

4.13.1 Differences

(1) Differentiate between True bearing and Magnetic bearing. (S-06; W-08)

Magnetic bearing	True bearing
1. The angle made by the survey line with the magnetic meridian i.e. north-south line is called magnetic bearing.	1. The horizontal angle between the line and true meridian is called true bearing of line.
2. There is variation in magnetic bearing.	2. True bearing at a point remains constant.

(2) Differentiate between Magnetic bearing and Arbitrary bearing. (W-08)

Magnetic bearing	Arbitrary bearing
1. The angle made by the survey line with the magnetic meridian is called magnetic bearing.	1. The angle made by the survey line with the arbitrary meridian is called arbitrary bearing.
2. Widely used for traversing and triangulation.	2. Rarely used for small survey.
3. Values of bearings are important.	3. Angles between lines are important than values of bearings.

4.14 DESIGNATION OF BEARINGS

(W-07, 09)

The bearings are commonly expressed as :

1. Whole circle bearing system.
2. Quadrantal bearing system (Reduced bearing).

4.14.1 Whole Circle Bearing System (W.C.B.)

In this system, the bearing of a line is measured in clockwise direction from the north. In this system the angle of bearing is from 0 to 360°.

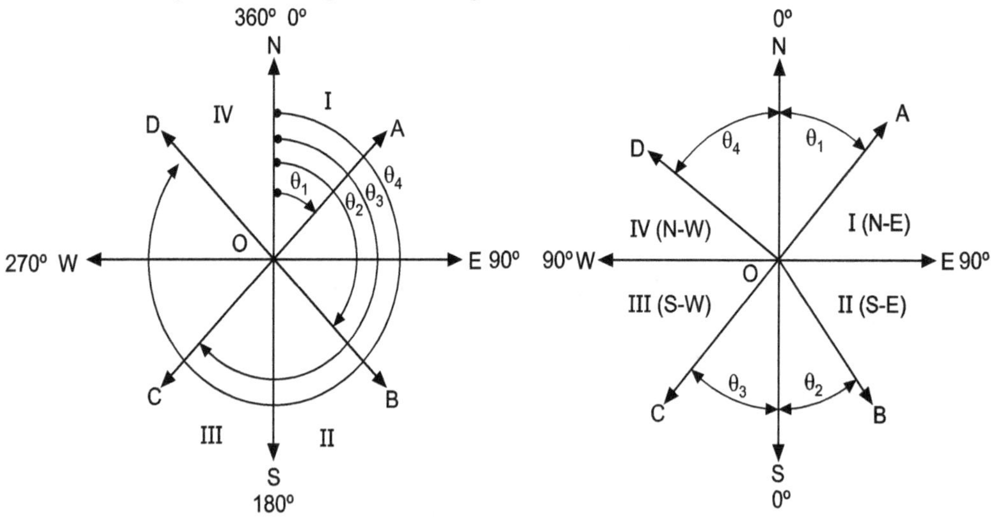

(a) Whole circuit bearing system   **(b) Quadrantal bearing system**

Fig. 4.4

It is called a whole circle bearing (W.C.B.). The value of the angle ranges from $0°$ to $360°$.

From the Fig. 4.4 (a)

W.C.B. of line OA is in I^{st} quadrant $= \theta_1 \ (0° < \theta_1 < 90°)$

W.C.B. of line OB is in IInd quadrant $= \theta_2 \ (90° < \theta_2 < 180°)$

W.C.B. of line OC is in IIIrd quadrant $= \theta_3 \ (180° < \theta_3 < 270°)$

W.C.B. of line OD is in IVth quadrant $= \theta_4 \ (270° < \theta_4 < 360°)$

Prismatic compass is graduated on this system.

4.14.2 Quadrantal Bearing or Reduced Bearing (RB) System

- In this system bearing of a line is measured clockwise or anticlockwise from the north or south pole whichever is nearer the line and towards east or west.

- It is, therefore, essential to state the quadrant in which the line lies. The letters N (north), S (South), E (east) and W (west) are used to represent the quadrant. [Fig. 4.4 (b)]

- These bearings are often called as *reduced bearings*. It never exceeds $90°$. Reduced bearings are observed by surveyor's compass.

- The quadrants are represented by letters as below :

  1st quadrant   N - E

  2nd quadrant   S - E

  3rd quadrant   S - W

  4rd quadrant   N - W

- The bearings of lines are written as below.

  'R.B.' or 'Q.B.' of line OA $= N \ \theta_1 \ E$

          Q.B. of line OB $= S \ \theta_2 \ E$

          Q.B. of line OC $= S \ \theta_3 \ W$

          Q.B. of line OD $= N \ \theta_4 \ W$

- The bearing must be written with letters denoting the quadrant, otherwise it is of no use.

4.15 CONVERSION OF BEARING FROM ONE SYSTEM TO THE OTHER

The bearing of a line can be easily converted from the one system to the other by using the given tables 4.1 and 4.2.

Table 4.1 : Conversion of W.C.B in R.B

Case	W.C.B. of line between	Rule for R.B.	Quadrant
I	$0°$ to $90°$	R.B. = W.C.B.	N - E
II	$90°$ to $180°$	R.B. = $180°$ – W.C.B.	S - E
III	$180°$ to $270°$	R.B. = W.C.B. – $180°$	S - W
IV	$270°$ to $360°$	R.B. = $360°$ – W.C.B.	N - W

Table 4.2 : Conversion of R.B. in W.C.B.

Case	R.B. in quadrant	Rule for W.C.B	W.C. B between
I	N - E	W.C.B. = R.B.	0° to 90°
II	S - E	W.C.B. = 180° – R.B.	90° to 180°
III	S - W	W.C.B. = R.B. + 180°	180° to 270°
IV	N - W	W.C.B. = 360° – R.B.	270° to 360°

- When the whole circle bearing of the line exceeds 90°, it may be reduced to the corresponding angle less than 90° which has the same numerical value to trigonometrical functions.

- This angle is known as *reduced bearing* (R.B.). Similarly, if reduced bearings of the line are given they can be converted into W.C.B.

4.16 FORE AND BACK BEARINGS   (W-07, 08, 10)

- The bearing observed in the direction of progress of survey is called *Fore Bearing* (F.B.) and the bearing observed in the opposite direction is called *Back Bearing* (B.B.).

- Every survey line has two bearings, one observed at each end of the line.

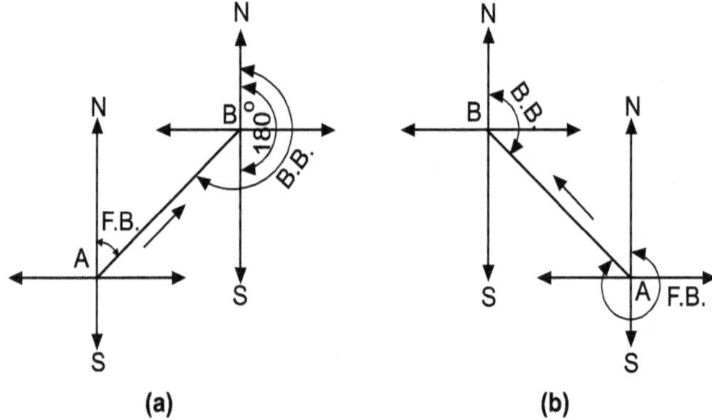

Fig 4.5 : Fore Bearing and Back Bearing

- Thus, in Fig. 4.5 above bearing of line AB is observed at A towards B, is called fore bearing of the line AB and the bearing observed at B towards A is called as back bearing of the line AB. It is also called as fore bearing of BA.

- The bearing is always measured from North direction in clockwise direction.

- It is seen from the figure that the fore and back bearing of a line differ exactly by 180°. Therefore, in W.C.B. system.

    Back bearing = Fore bearing ± 180°   **(S-12)**

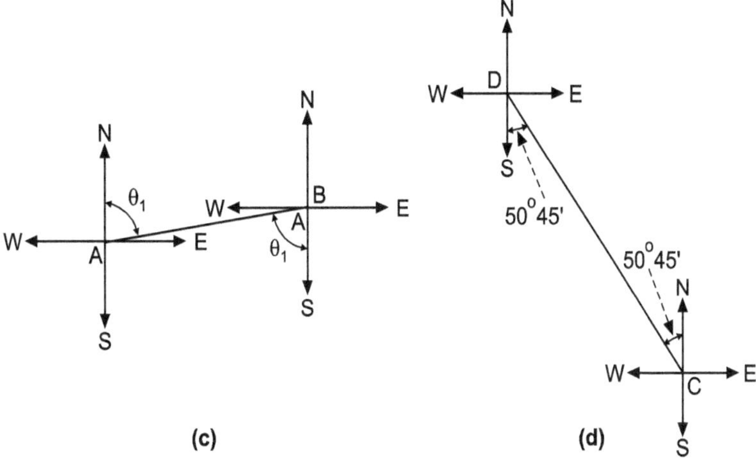

Fig. 4.5 : Fore Bearing and Back Bearing

- Use (+) sign when fore bearing is less than 180° and (−) sign if it exceeds 180°. In the quadrantal system, the fore and back bearing are exactly equal but with opposite signs.

- For example : If the fore bearing of a line AB is $N\theta_1°E$ as shown in Fig 4.5 (c), its back bearing will be $S\theta_1°$ W. Similarly, if the fore bearing of line CD is N 50° 45' W then its back bearing will be S 50° 45' E.

- Thus, it is obtained simply by substituting N for S or S for N and E for W or W for E.

4.17 CALCULATION OF ANGLES FROM BEARINGS

- By using compass, the angle between the two lines cannot be read. However, knowing the bearing of two lines, the angle between them can be calculated.
- The angle between two consecutive lines is called *included angle.*
- It may be interior or exterior angle.
- To avoid confusion about the value of the angle a sketch should be drawn.
- The following rules may be applied to find out the included angles between the two lines whose bearings are known.

4.17.1 Given the Whole Circle Bearing of Lines.

(a) *When the bearings of two lines as measured from the point of intersection are given.*

Rule : Subtract the smaller from the greater. The difference will give the interior angle, if it is less than 180°. If it is more than 180°, it is the exterior angle. Obtain the interior angle by deducting the difference from 360°. Sometimes the interior angle may also be more than 180°. In such cases to avoid confusion a sketch should be drawn to decide whether it is less than 180° or more than 180°.

For example,

(i)   Let lines AB and BC meet at B as shown in Fig. 4.6 (a).

Then included angle ABC = Difference of bearings BA and BC.

Suppose, bearing of BA = 30° 15' and that of BC = 105° 30',

Then included angle ABC = 105° 30' – 30° 15' = 75° 15'

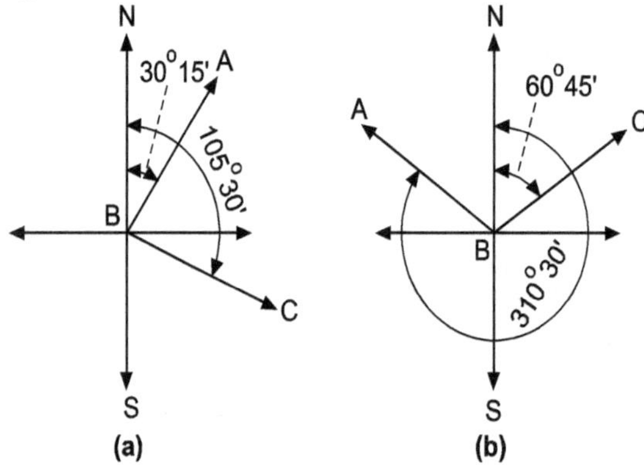

Fig. 4.6

(ii)   Similarly, in Fig. 4.6 (b)

Let bearing of BC = 60° 45'

and bearing of BA = 310° 30'.

Then included angle ABC = 310° 30' – 60° 45' = 249° 45'

This being greater than 180° , **is an exterior angle.**

∴   Included angle = 360° – 249° 45' = 110° 15'

(b) *When the bearings of two lines are given.*

The bearings are first expressed as if measured from the point where the lines meet and then the rule is applied.

Refer Fig. 4.6 (c).

Let the bearing of AC = 230° 30' and that of BC is 110° 45'

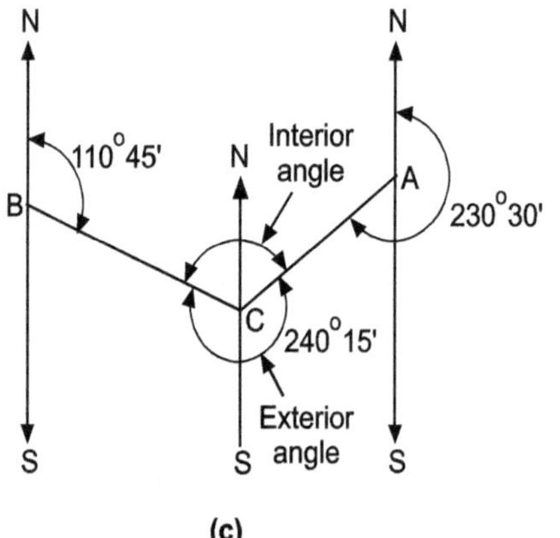

Fig. 4.6

To calculate the included angle ABC

$$\text{Bearing of AC} = 230° 30'$$

$$\text{Bearing of CA} = 230° 30' - 180° = 50°30'$$

$$\text{Bearing of BC} = 110° 45'$$

$$\text{Bearing of CB} = 110° 45' + 180° = 290° 45'$$

Now, applying the Rule for included angle –

$$\text{Included angle ACB} = 290° 45' - 50° 30'$$

$$= 240° 15' \text{ (Exterior angle)}$$

$$\text{Interior angle, } \angle ACB = 360° - 240° 15' = 119° 45'$$

4.17.2 Given the Reduced Bearing of Lines

Rule : (a) If the lines are all on the same side of the same meridian as in Fig. 4.7 (a).

$$\text{Included angle} = \text{Difference of the two R.B.'s}$$

$$\therefore \qquad \angle ABC = \text{Difference of bearing of BA and BC}$$

(b) If the lines are on the same side of the different meridian, as in Fig. 4.7 (b).

$$\text{Included angle} = 180° - \text{Sum of the two R.B.'s.}$$

$$\therefore \qquad \angle ABC = 180° - \text{Sum of bearings of AB and BC.}$$

(c) If the lines are on different sides of the different meridian, as in Fig 4.7 (c)

$$\text{Included angle} = 180° - \text{Difference of two R.B.'s}$$

$$\angle CBA = 180° - \text{Difference of the bearings of BA and BC.}$$

(d) If the lines are on opposite sides of the same meridian, as in Fig. 4.7 (d).

$$\text{Included angle} = \text{Sum of the two R.B.'s}$$

$$\angle CBA = \text{Sum of bearings of BC and BA}$$

To avoid confusion a sketch should always be drawn to show the direction of lines.

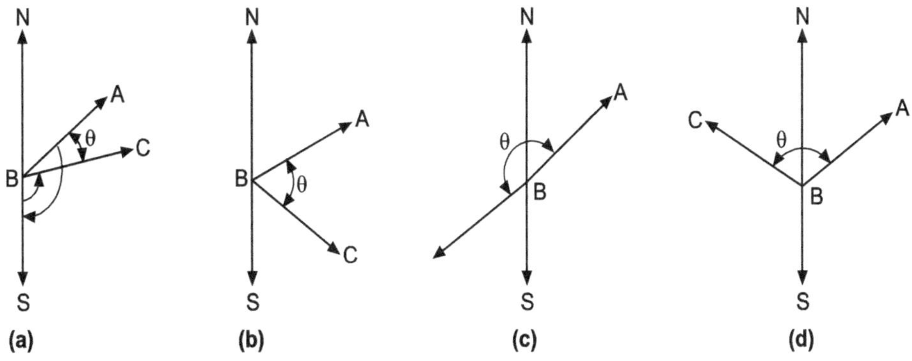

Fig. 4.7

4.18 CALCULATION OF BEARINGS FROM ANGLES

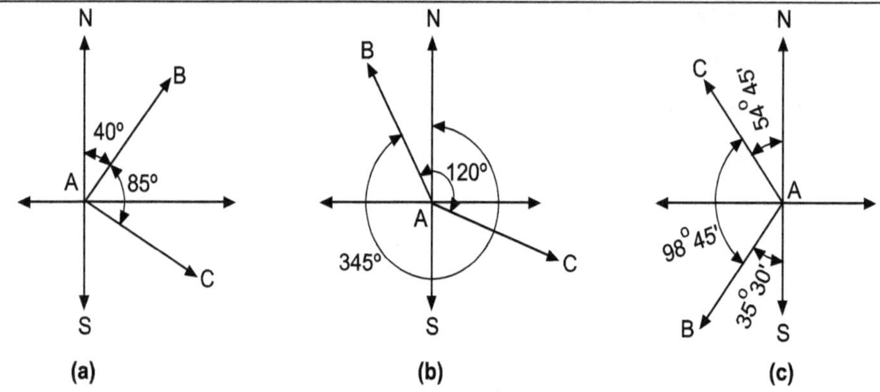

Fig. 4.8

The bearings of survey lines may be either directly observed or calculated from given bearing and included angle measured clockwise between the various lines.

Case I : When two lines AB and AC meet at a point 'A' and included angle and fore bearing of a line are given :

Here, Bearing of a line = Given bearing + Included angle [Fig. 4.8 (a)]

Given : Bearing of AB = 40°, $\angle$ BAC = 85° (Interior angle)

$\therefore$ The bearing of AC = 40° + 85° = 125°

Similarly, in Fig. 4.8 (b) bearing of line, AB = 345° – 0' and included angle BAC = 120° 0'

Bearing of line AC = 120° – (360° – 345°) = 105°

Case II : When bearing of line AB and included angle $\angle$ BAC are given.

In Fig. 4.8 (c).

    Let bearing of AB = S 35° 30' W

and   bearing of AC = θ

Included angle,   BAC = 98° 45'

$\therefore$ Included angle BAC = 180° – Sum of the bearings (using the given rule.)

$$98° 45' = 180° – (35° 30' + \theta)$$

$$98° 45' = 180° – 35° 30' – \theta = 144° 30' – \theta$$

$$\theta = 144° 30' – 98° 45' = N 45° 45 ' W$$

4.19 LOCAL ATTRACTION   (S-09; W-05, 07, 08, 09, S-12)

- The compass needle does not point to magnetic meridian or magnetic north when it is under the influence of the external attractive forces. It is seriously deviated from its normal position (North direction) when placed in the vicinity of iron or steel objects, iron ore, electricity current. The deviation arising from such external or local sources is called *local attraction*.

- In certain localities, particularly in cities, its effect is more.

- It is not likely to be the same at one point as at another, even though the points are a short distance apart.

- Compass needle is even affected by objects such as steel tape, chain, arrows, axe, bunch of keys etc.

4.19.1 Causes of Local Attraction

(1) Electric wires.

(2) Steel tape.

(3) Chain, arrows.

(4) Buches of key.

(5) Area affected by magnetic field.

4.20 DETECTION OF LOCAL ATTRACTION   (S-08; W-09)

- The local attraction can usually be detected by observing the bearing (F.B. and B.B.) of a line at two or more points on the same line.

- If the difference between fore and back bearing of the line is exactly 180°, there is no local attraction at either point. If not, local attraction is suspected at either station or both. Care should be taken that there are no observational or instrumental errors.

4.21 EFFECT OF LOCAL ATTRACTION ON INCLUDED ANGLE (S-12)

- The amount of local attraction is the same for each of the bearing observed at the affected station.

- Hence, the difference between the bearings of the lines observed at the station will give the correct included angles between the lines even though the station is affected by local attraction.

- The only thing is to observe the bearing at the same time with the same compass.

- When we plot the close traverse from observed F.B. and B.B. readings due to error caused by local attraction the total sum of internal included angles of the traverse is not equal to $(2n - 4) \times 90°$, where n = number of sides of traverse.

Illustration : The bearings observed at point A of the lines AB and AC are θ_1^0 and θ_2^0 respectively.

Included angle BAC = $(\theta_2^0 - \theta_1^0)$

Let, the local attraction of $\alpha°$ be at station A.

Then bearing of the lines AB = $\theta_1^0 + \alpha°$

Bearing of the line AC = $\theta_2^0 + \alpha°$

Included angle BAC = $(\theta_2^0 + \alpha°) - (\theta_1^0 + \alpha°)$

$$= (\theta_2^0 - \theta_1^0)$$

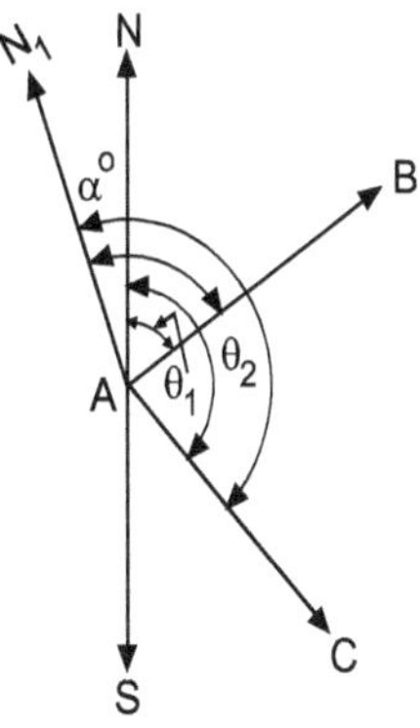

Fig. 4.9

4.22 CORRECTION OF BEARING AFFECTED BY LOCAL ATTRACTION 

There are two methods of correcting bearings of lines affected by local attraction.

Method 1 :

- In this method, bearings of the lines are first examined and the line having a difference between fore and back bearings exactly equal to 180° is selected.

- The bearings of this line are correct. Starting from this line, bearings of the successive lines are corrected by applying corrections to the observed bearings.

- The error will be negative when the observed bearing is less than the corrected bearing and the correction will be positive and vice versa.

- If there is no line whose bearing differ by 180°, the correction should be done from the mean value of the bearing of that line whose fore and back bearing differ minimum.

Method 2 :

- In this method, included angles are calculated from the observed fore and back bearings of the lines.

- These are true included angles since the amount of error due to local attraction is the same for all the bearings measured at the station.

- In a closed traverse, the sum of the included angles must be $(2n - 4) \times 90°$.

- If there is any discrepancy in it, observational or instrumental errors exist. Such error is distributed equally to all angles to make the sum total equal to the theoretical one.

How to select method of correction ?

(1) We can use method 1 as well as method 2 : When summation of all included angles of closed traverse is equal to $(2n - 4) \times 90°$ and the difference between F.B. and B.B. of atleast one survey line is 180°.

(2) We can use method 2 in the following cases :

(i) When summation of all included angles of closed traverse is not equal to $(2n - 4) \times 90°$ and the difference between F.B. and B.B. of atleast one survey line is 180°.

(ii) When summation of all included angles of closed traverse is not equal to $(2n - 4) \times 90°$ and there is no single survey line having difference between F.B. and B.B. as 180°.

Note : The quadrantal bearings for convenience, may be converted to W.C.B. and the same procedure is adopted for correction.

4.23 CORRECTION FOR BEARING WHEN ALL THE STATIONS ARE AFFECTED

In case when all the stations are affected by local attraction, the observed bearing of no line will differ by 180°.

Such a problem can be solved by the following steps :

(1) Examine the bearings and select a line whose fore and back bearing differ very nearly equal to 180° · Calculate the corrected bearings of this line by distributing half the error to each of the readings i.e. Difference is 180° 20'. Distribute 10' to each reading of that line. In one bearing the error will be + ve and in the other, it will be – ve.

(2) Compute the included angles of the traverse and check the sum with theoretical sum i.e. (2n – 4) × 90°. If the total differs, distribute the error equally at all angles and make it exactly equal to theoretical sum.

(3) From the calculated correct included angles and correct bearing of the above line, find out the bearings of other lines.

4.24 DIP OF THE NEEDLE   (S-11)

- The inclination of the magnetic needle with the horizontal is called *magnetic dip of the needle.*

- Ordinary needle if perfectly balanced on pivot, remains in horizontal position. But when the needle is magnetized, it may not always remain in horizontal plane due to the magnetic influence of the earth.

- In the northern hemisphere the north end of the needle is deflected downwards and in southern hemisphere the south end of the needle points upwards.

- The dip is not constant but varies in different zones of the earth. It will be zero at the equator and 90° at the poles.

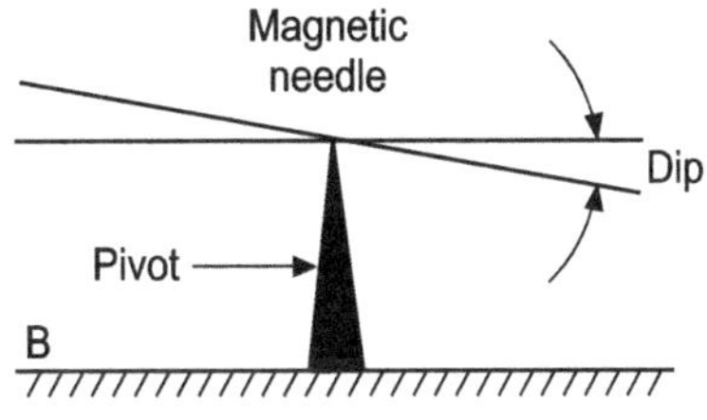

Fig. 4.10

- To keep the needle in horizontal position a brass coil or aluminium strip as sliding weight is attached on the side of the needle which is at higher position.

4.25 MAGNETIC DECLINATION   (S-11)

- The magnetic meridian at a place does not coincide with the true meridian at that place.

- In some cases the magnetic meridian is deflected to the East side of the true meridian called as 'East declination' while in others it points to the west of the true meridian called as 'West declination'.

- The horizontal angle made by the magnetic meridian with the true meridian is called 'magnetic declination'.

- The magnetic meridian varies from place to place and also from time to time on the surface of the earth and hence, the declination is also different at different places.

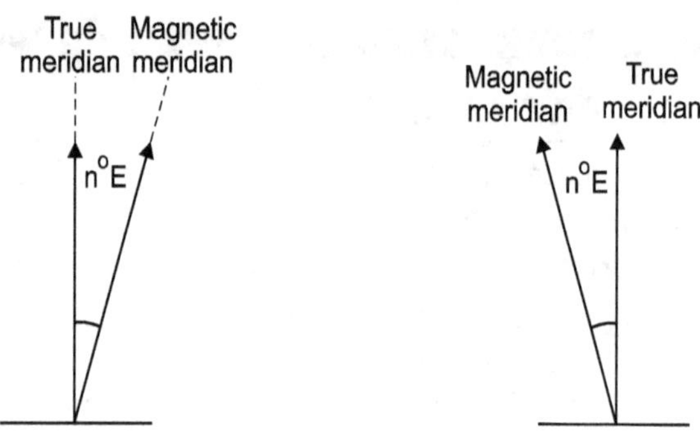

(a) East declination (+) (b) West declination (–)

Fig. 4.11

Noting of declination of plan :

- On account of variations in declinations it is necessary to note on the plan or map the date of survey and the amount of declination. It will be helpful in retracing the survey lines of an old survey if required on latter date.

4.26 VARIATIONS IN DECLINATION   (S-11)

- The declination at any place is not constant. It changes from time to time as the magnetic needle does not constantly point in one direction.

- The declination is of four types :

  (i)   Secular   (iii) Daily or diurnal and

  (ii) Annual   (iv) Irregular.

(i) Secular variation : The magnetic meridian swings like a pendulum. It swings in one direction of the true north for many years even 100 to 150 years, comes to rest gradually coinciding with true north and again swings in the opposite side of it.

(ii) Annual variation : If observations are taken for the whole year. We see that the magnetic declination varies due to the rotation of the earth in an elliptical path around the sun is known as 'annual variation'. The variations will be from 1 to 2 minutes with respect to the true north.

(iii) Daily variation : Due to the rotation of the earth about its own axis in 24 hours there is a variation in magnetic declination, known as 'daily variation'. The needle varies 3 to 12 minutes at the place from its mean position during the day. This variation is more in summer than in winter and it is more in high altitudes and less near the equator.

(iv) Irregular variation : Variations in magnetic declination caused due to natural disturbances for example, storms, earthquakes, volcanic eruptions etc. are called 'irregular variations', which may occur at any time. They are not certain and cannot be predicted. The amount of variation may be 1° to 2°.

4.27 DETERMINATION OF TRUE BEARINGS

- All the important survey maps such as revenue map, topographical maps etc. are plotted with reference to the true meridian.

- Knowing the magnetic declination at a place, at the time of observations, the true bearing may be determined by the following rule.

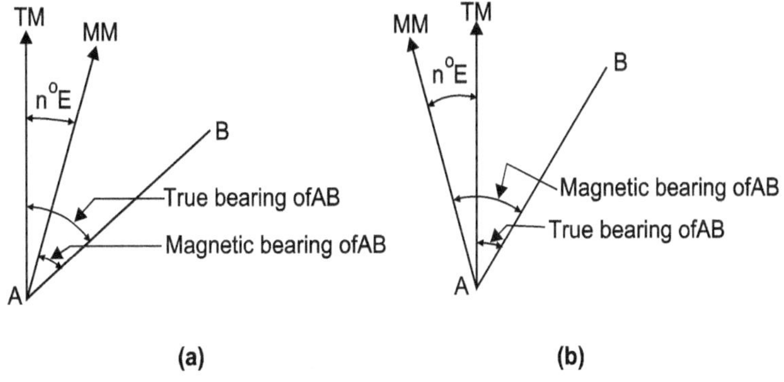

Fig. 4.12

- **Rule 1 :** True bearing of a line = Magnetic bearing of the line $\pm$ Magnetic Declination.

    Use (+) sign when the declination is towards east and

    (–) sign when the declination is towards west.

- **Rule 2 :** Magnetic bearing of a line = True bearing of the line + Magnetic declination.

    Use (–) sign when the declination is towards east and

    (+) sign when the declination is towards west.

- The above rules are applicable to W.C.B.

- In case of quadrantal bearings, to avoid confusion, first convert them to W.C.B. and apply these rules.

- Alternatively, draw the sketch showing the magnetic bearings and declination at each station to find true bearings.

- The old survey line can be relaid on the ground with a compass if the present magnetic declination is known, applying Rule No. 2.

4.28 TRAVERSING WITH CHAIN AND COMPASS

- In traversing with chain and compass the distance between the stations are measured by a chain and the directions of chain lines are determined by taking bearing by compass.

- The free or loose needle method is usually adopted. The compass is set up at each of the successive station, and fore bearing and back bearing of each of the lines are observed independently of others.

Closed traverse and Unclosed traverse :

A traverse is classified as (a) Closed traverse and, (b) Unclosed traverse or Open traverse.

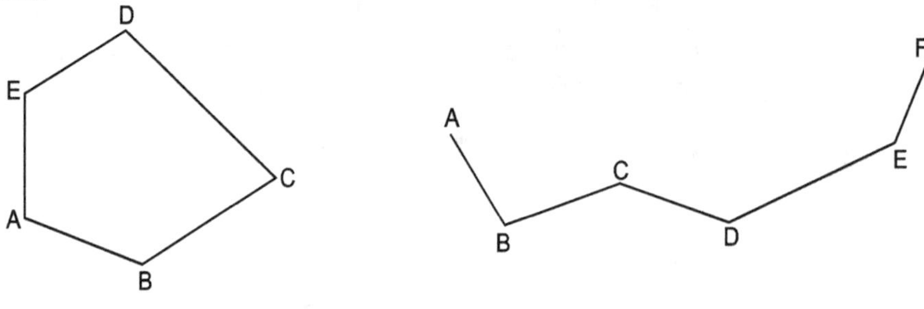

(a) Closed Traverse　　　　**(b) Unclosed (Open) Traverse**

Fig. 4.13

(a) Closed traverse :

- A traverse is said to be a closed traverse when it forms a closed polygon as shown in Figure 4.13 (a). It begins and ends at the same point.
- It is suitable for locating boundaries of ponds, forest, and for survey of moderately large area.

(b) Unclosed or Open traverse :

- A traverse is said to be unclosed or open when it does not form a closed polygon as shown in Fig. 4.13 (b).
- In this traverse, the series of line extend in the same direction and do not return to the starting point. It is suitable for the survey of long narrow strip of ground i.e. river valley, coast line, railway line, road etc.

Distinguish between Open traverse and Closed traverse　　　　**(W-05, 07; S-11)**

Closed Traverse	Open Traverse
1. When a traverse forms closed polygon it is called 'closed traverse'.	1. When a traverse does not form a closed polygon it is called as 'open traverse'.
2. It is a series of lines which begins and ends at the same point.	2. It is a series of lines which extend in the same direction but not returns to the starting point.
3. It is suitable for locating boundaries like ponds, forest etc.	3. It is suitable for long narrow strips of ground like river, valley, road etc.
4.　　　**Fig. 4.14 (a)**	4.　　　**Fig. 4.14 (b)**

It mainly consists of -

(a) Reconnaissance

(b) Marking and referencing stations.

(c) Running of survey lines.

(d) Picking up of details.

(e) Booking of field notes.

The survey stations should be so selected that :

(1) They are mutually visible.

(2) Obstacles between two chain stations should be minimum so that chaining between them is easy.

(3) The survey lines joining the stations are as near the boundaries and objects to be located as possible, and should run through ground as far as possible.

(4) They are as long as possible.

(5) There should not be sources of local attraction, for example, electric pole near to the survey stations.

Procedure of Chain and Compass Survey :

- Before survey of any place, detailed inspection of that place should be done. The main stations should be selected first by considering the above given conditions.

- At each station pegs are driven to fix its position. Ranging rods are also erected at each station, such that they are visible from far of distance.

- Suppose, for example, it is required to run a traverse ABCDE as shown in Fig. 4.15. The compass is centered over station A, and is levelled.

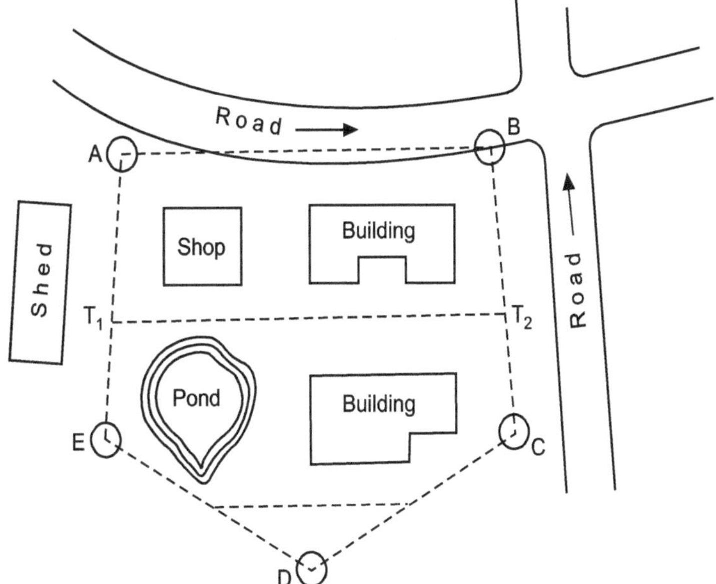

Fig. 4.15 : Compass Traverse

- The fore bearing of the line AB and back bearing of line EA are taken by sighting the ranging rods at B and E respectively.

- The line AB is chained and offsets to the object on either side of line AB are taken.

- The compass is then shifted and set up at station B and is levelled. At station B, the back bearing of the line AB and the fore bearing of the line BC are taken by sighting ranging rods at A and C respectively.

- The line BC is then chained and the offsets are taken in usual way. Such operations are repeated at each of the remaining station C, D, E.

- This method is known as *"Free or loose needle method"*.

- The fore bearing and back bearing of the line should differ exactly by 180°. If the error between the fore and back bearings of a line exceeds the permissible error of reading (15'), the fore and back bearing should be observed again.

- In case, the error still persists, and there is no other error, it may be considered that local attraction exists at one or both stations.

- The bearings affected by local attraction are corrected as by any one method. The traverse may be run clockwise or anticlockwise direction.

- After the observations are taken and recorded in the field book plotting is started.

4.29 PLOTTING A COMPASS TRAVERSE　　　(S-05, 08, W-11)

- Before plotting of a traverse survey on the drawing sheet. It is advisable to draw a rough sketch on a separate paper in order to ascertain the size and shape of the plan to know the best position of it on drawing the sheet.

- The observed bearing must be corrected before plotting. The most common methods of plotting a traverse, are discussed below.

4.29.1 By Parallel Meridian through each Station

- The position of starting station A is fixed suitably on the paper.

- A direction of magnetic meridian is drawn through it.

- The fore bearing of line AB is marked with an ordinary protractor, and with a scale its length is marked to fix the position of B.

- Through a point B, a meridian is drawn parallel to previously drawn meridian at A and bearing of BC is marked.

- The distance BC is set off and its length is measured with the same scale.

- This process is then repeated at each station until all the lines of the traverse are drawn.

- In case of closed traverse, the last line will end on the starting station A, otherwise the discrepancy is referred to as the closing error.

4.29.2 By Included Angle Method

- In this method first fix the position of starting station A.
- Then the magnetic meridian is drawn through the station A on the paper.
- The bearing of line AB is marked and length of line AB is plotted to some scale.
- Thus, position of B is fixed. At B the included angle ABC is plotted with a protractor and the length of BC is marked with scale.
- This operation is repeated at each of the successive stations till all the lines of traverse are drawn. Fig. 4.16 (b)

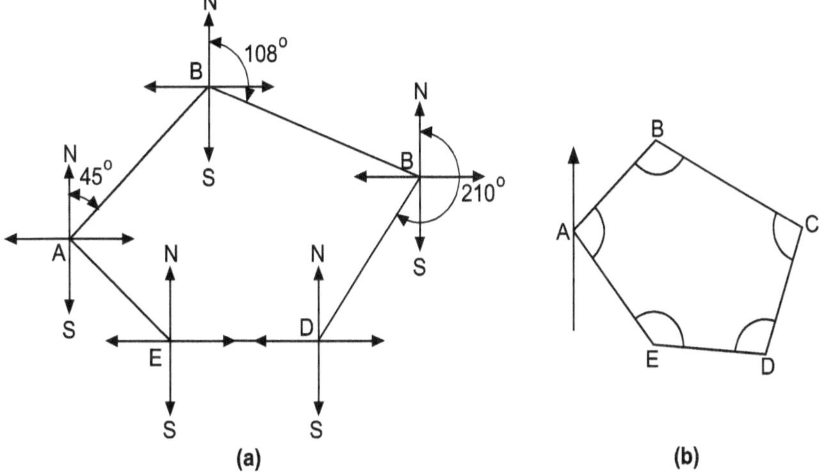

(a)   (b)

Fig. 4.16 : Closed traverse

4.30 CLOSING ERROR IN COMPASS SURVEYING   (S-09, S-12)

- While plotting a closed traverse from the field measurements the end point of the traverse sometimes does not coincide with the starting point as shown in figure.
- The traverse ABCDE is plotted. The last point does not coincide with the starting point A. It is then marked as A_1.

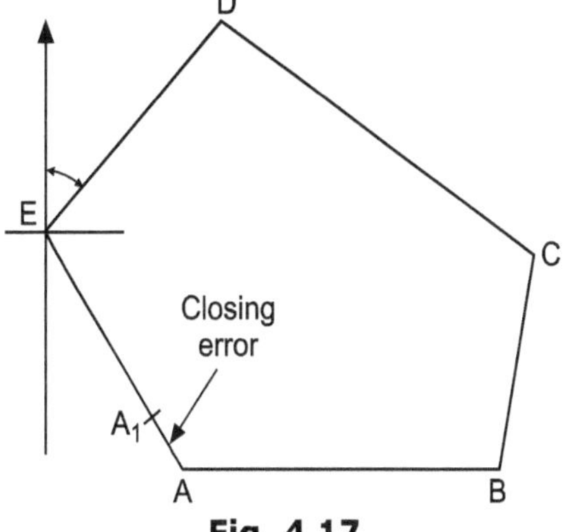

Fig. 4.17

- The actual distance by which the traverse fails to close is known as *closing error* or *error of closure* (AA_1).
- If the closing error is large, it shows that an error has been made in chaining.
- The lines then should be remeasured. If closing error is small, it may be eliminated and the traverse is made to close by slightly modifying the shape of it i.e. it can be measured by graphical method.

4.31 GRAPHICAL ADJUSTMENT OF CLOSING ERROR (S-09; W-05)

- In this method correction is applied both to the lengths and bearings of the lines in proportion to their lengths. This is known as *proportional method*.
- This method is graphical application of Bowditch's Rule.

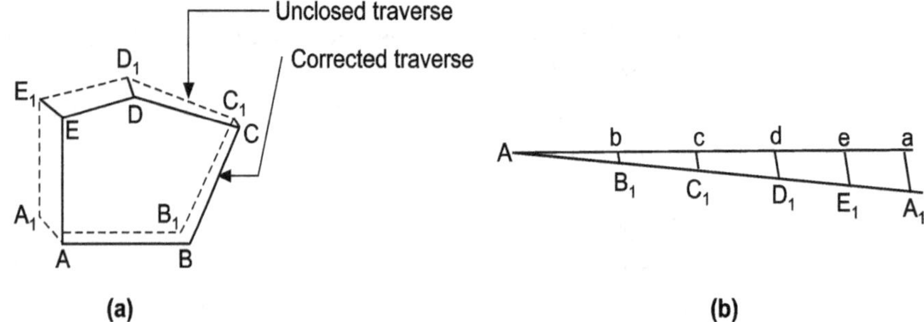

Fig. 4.18 : Graphical Method of Adjustment

- Let the plotted traverse be represented by the Fig. 4.18 (a). AA_1 is the closing error, which is to be adjusted so that the traverse will close.
- Draw a horizontal line equal to the length of the perimeter of the traverse, set of distances, AB_1, B_1C_1, C_1D_1, D_1E_1 and E_1A_1 equal to the lengths of the sides to any convenient scale. It is usually much smaller than that used for plotting the traverse.
- At A, draw a line A_1a parallel and equal to the closing error AA_1. Join A_1a. Draw lines B_1b, C_1c and E_1e, parallel to A_1a as shown in Fig. 4.18 (b). Thus, the intercepts B_1b, C_1c, D_1d, E_1e and A_1a are corresponding errors both in magnitude and direction through which stations, A_1, B_1 C_1, D_1, E_1 have to be shifted.
- In the present case it will be noticed that the whole traverse has to be shifted downwards. To do this draw short lines parallel through the station B_1, C_1, D_1, and D_1 and E_1 corresponding to the intercepts B_1b, C_1c, D_1d and E_1e, ABCDEA then represents the adjusted traverse.

4.32 CHECKS ON CLOSED AND OPEN TRAVERSE

- The error is caused in traversing due to :
  (i) linear measurements and
  (ii) angular measurements.
- To check the linear measurement, every chain line should be measured twice For example : chain the line AB from A to B then from B to A.
- The angular measurements are checked as follows :

(i) Close traverse : (a) The sum of the measured included angles should be equal to the theoretical sum $(2n - 4) \times 90°$, where 'n' is the number of sides of traverse.

(b) The fore bearing of the last line of traverse should tally with its back bearing $\pm 180°$.

(ii) Open traverse : There is no direct check on angular measurements. However, indirect checks can be applied. In open traverse ABCDEF as shown in figure, the bearings of AB, BC, CD etc. are taken. As a check, fore bearing of line AD is observed from station A and on reaching to station D, back bearing of the line AD is observed. The two bearings of this line should differ by 180° exactly. If the error is small, it can be suitably adjusted and the work is continued. Otherwise, the whole traverse is repeated.

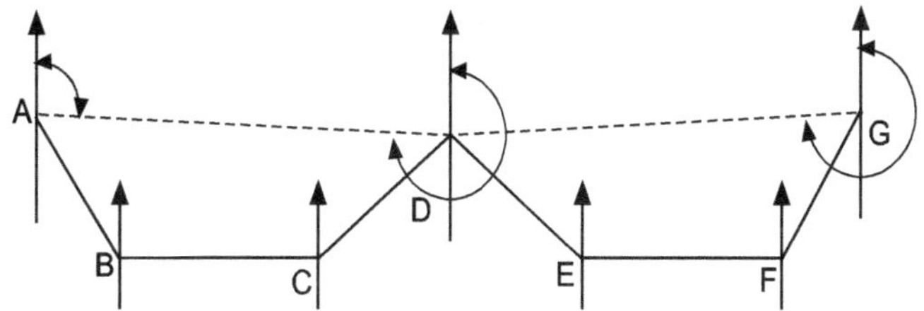

Fig. 4.19 : An Open Traverse

4.33 ADVANTAGES AND DISADVANTAGES OF COMPASS TRAVERSING

The following are the advantages and disadvantages of compass traversing survey.

Advantages :

(1)   It is a quick survey in which the bearings are observed quickly.

(2)   The bearing of lines can be observed from any intermediate point on it.

(3)   Each bearing is observed independently and hence there is no accumulation of error.

(4)   The compass traversing is suitable for areas where chain surveying is not convenient.

(5)   The instrument is light and compact. It can be easily carried.

Disadvantages :

(1)   It is mainly a rough type of survey and cannot be relied upon where great accuracy is required.

(2)   It is unsuitable in areas having local attraction.

SOLVED EXAMPLES

TYPE-I : CONVERT WCB TO RB OR RB TO WCB

Example 4.1 : *Convert the following whole circle bearings to quadrantal bearings.*

(i) 65° 45' **[W-11]** *(ii) 143° 30'* **[W-11]** *(iii) 232° 15' (iv) 341° 0'*

Solution : Using the Rule for R.B. (Table 4.1) ;

(i)   W.C.B. = 65° 45'

Quadrantal bearing = N 65° 45' E ... **Ans.**

(ii) W.C.B. = 143° 30'

Quadrantal bearing = 180° – W.C.B. = 180° – 143° 30' = S 36° 30' E **... Ans.**

(iii) W.C.B. = 232° 15'

 Quadrantal bearing = W.C.B. – 180° = 232° 15' – 180° = S 52° 15' W **... Ans.**

(iv) W.C.B. = 341° 0'

Quadrantal bearing = 360° – W.C.B. = 360° – 341° = N 19° 0' W **... Ans.**

Example 4.2 : *Convert the following reduced bearing to whole circle bearings (i) N 28° 33' E (ii) S 41° 45' E* **(W-11)** *(iii) S 58° 0' W (iv) N 12° 15' W* **(W-11)**

Solution : Using the rule for W.C.B. (Table 4.2)

(i) R.B. = N 28° 30' E

  W.C.B. = 28° 30' **... Ans.**

(ii) R.B = S 41° 45' E

  W.C.B = 180° – R.B. = 180° – 41° 45' = 138° 15' **... Ans.**

(iii) R.B. = S 58° 0' W

  W.C.B. = 180° + 58° 0' = 238° 0' **... Ans.**

(iv) R.B. = N 12° 15' W

  W.C.B. = 360° – R.B. = 360° – 12° 15' = 347° 45' **... Ans.**

Example 4.3 : *Find the reduced bearing of a line having W.C.B. 280° 30'.*

Solution : W.C.B. = 280° 30'

Here W.C.B. lies between 270° and 360° i.e. IVth quadrant.

∴   R.B. = 360° – W.C.B.

     = 360° – 280° 30'

     = N 79° 30' W **... Ans.**

Example 4.4 : *Convert the following R.B. to W.C.B.*

(i) N 40° 15' W, (ii) S 36° 30' W, (iii) S 43° 30' E, (iv) N 26° 45' E

Solution : (i) R.B. = N 40° 15' W

∴   W.C.B. = 360° – 40° 15'

∴   W.C.B. = 319° 45' **... Ans.**

(ii) R.B. = S 36° 30' W

∴   W.C.B. = R.B. + 180°

     = 36° 30' + 180°

     = 216° 30' **... Ans.**

(iii) R.B. = S 43° 30' E

∴   W.C.B. = 180° – R.B.

     = 180° – 43° 30'

     = 136° 30' **... Ans.**

(iv) R.B. = N 26° 45' E

∴   W.C.B. = R.B.

     = 26° 45' **... Ans.**

Example 4.5 : *Convert the following W.C.B. to R.B.*

(i) 70°40', (ii) 289°45', (iii) 348°15', (iv) 178°0'.

Solution : (i) W.C.B. = 70° 40'

∴   R.B. = W.C.B.

       = N 70° 40' E   **... Ans.**

(ii)   W.C.B. = 289° 45'

∴   R.B. = 360° – W.C.B.

       = 360° – 289° 45'

       = N 70° 15' W   **... Ans.**

(iii)   W.C.B. = 348° 15'

       = 360° – W.C.B.

∴   R.B. = 360° – 348° 15'

       = N 11° 45' W   **... Ans.**

(iv)   W.C.B. = 178° 0'

      R.B. = 180° – 178° 0'

       = S2° 0' E   **... Ans.**

Example 4.6 : *Convert the following bearings into other relevant system.*

(i) 140°40', (ii) 230°30', (iii) S 40°40' E, (iv) N 65°30' W.

Solution : (i) W.C.B. = 140° 40'

∴   R.B. = 180° – W.C.B.

       = 180° – 140° 40'

       = S 30° 20' E

(ii)   W.C.B. = 230° 30'

∴   R.B. = W.C.B. – 180°

       = 230° 30' – 180°

       = S 50° 3' W   **... Ans.**

(iii)   R.B. = S 40° 40' E

∴   W.C.B. = 180° – R.B.

       = 180° – 40° 40'

       = 139° 20'   **... Ans.**

(iv)   R.B. = N 65° 30' W

∴   W.C.B. = 360° – R.B.

       = 360° – 65° 30' = 294° 30'   **... Ans.**

Example 4.7 : *(i) Convert following R.B. to W.C.B.*

  (A) N 15° 15' E

  (B) N 67° 48' W

 (ii) Convert following W.C.B. to R.B.

  (A) 236° 37'

  (B) 132° 12'　　　　**(W-07)**

Solution : (i) (A) R.B.　$=$　N 15° 15' E

    W.C.B.　$=$　15° 15'　　　**... Ans.**

(B)　　　　R.B.　$=$　N 67° 48' W

    W.C.B.　$=$　360° – 67° 48'

      $=$　292° 12'　　　**... Ans.**

(ii) (A)　　W.C.B.　$=$　236° 37'

    R.B.　$=$　S (236° 37' – 180°) W

      $=$　S 56° 37' W　　　**... Ans.**

(B)　　　　W.C.B.　$=$　132° 12'

    R.B.　$=$　S (180° – 132° 12') E

      $=$　S 47° 48' E　　　**... Ans.**

Example 4.8 : *Convert the following bearings into relevant bearings :*

(i) 129°45' (ii) 215°30', (iii) S 42°30' E, (iv) N 79°15' W.　　　**(W-08)**

Solution : (i) W.C.B.　$=$　129° 45'

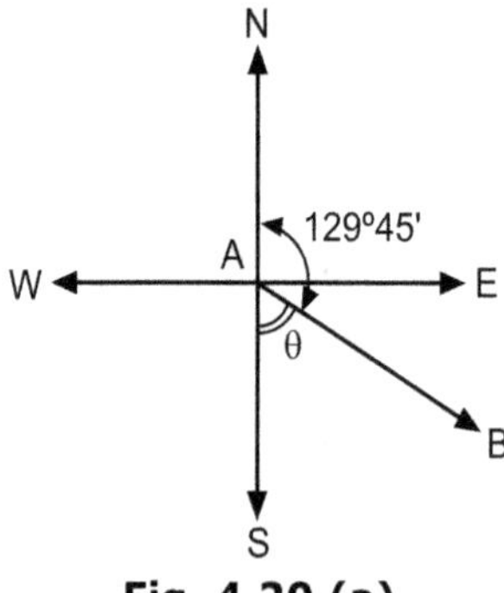

Fig. 4.20 (a)

∴　　　　R.B.　$=$　180° – W.C.B.

   R.B.　$=$　S (180° – 129° 45') E

    $=$　S 50° 15' E　　　**... Ans.**

(ii) W.C.B. = 215° 30'

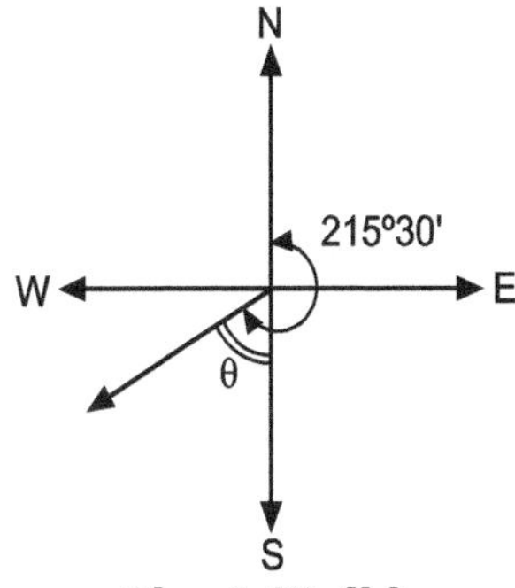

Fig. 4.20 (b)

∴   R.B.   = W.C.B. − 180°

                        R.B.   = S (215° 30' − 180°) W

                               = S 35° 30' W   ... **Ans.**

(iii) R.B. = S 42° 30' E

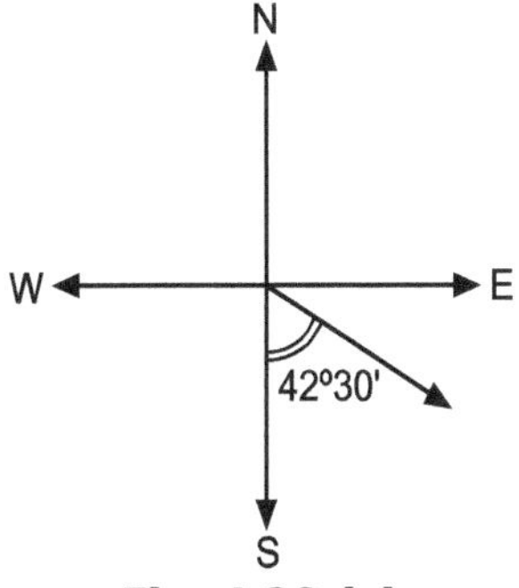

Fig. 4.20 (c)

∴   W.C.B. = 180° − R.B.

                W.C.B. = 180° − 42° 30'

                        = 137° 30'   ... **Ans.**

(iv) R.B. = N 79° 15' W

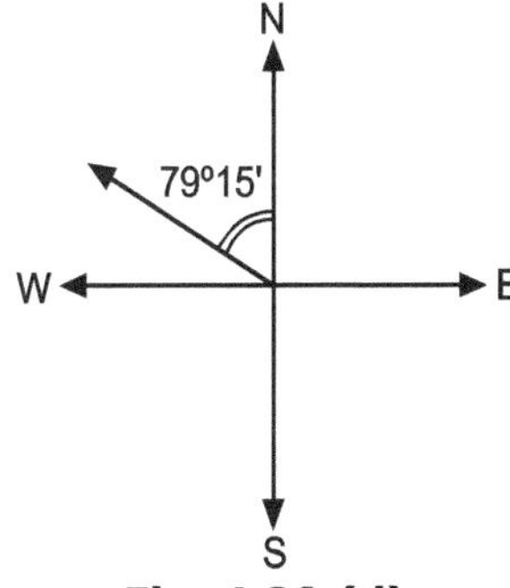

Fig. 4.20 (d)

∴   W.C.B. = 360° − R.B.

                W.C.B. = 360 − 79° 15'

                        = 280° 45'   ... **Ans.**

Example 4.9 : *Convert the following W.C.B. to R.B.*

(i) 93° 7', (ii) 285° 10'.　　　　　　　　　(W-09)

Solution : (i)　　W.C.B.　= 93° 7'

　　　　　　　　R.B.　= S (180° – 93° 7') E

　　　　　　　　　　= S 86° 53' E　　　　　　... **Ans.**

(ii)　　　　　W.C.B.　= 285° 10'

　　　　　　　　R.B.　= N (360° – 285° 10') W

　　　　　　　　　　= N · 74° 50' W　　　　　... **Ans.**

TYPE-II : CONVERSION OF F.B. AND B.B.

Example 4.10 : *The following are the observed fore bearings of the lines.*

(i) AB 42° 30' (ii) BC 146° 15' (iii) CD 215° 45' and (iv) DE 327° 30'. Find their back bearings.

Solution : Rule : Back bearing of line in W.C.B. system = Fore bearing ± 180°.

Use '+' Sign if fore bearing is less than 180° and use '–' sign if it is more than 180°

(i)　Fore bearing of line AB　=　42° 30'

　　Back bearing of line AB　=　42° 30' + 180° = 222° 30'　　... **Ans.**

(ii)　Fore bearing of line BC　=　146° 15'

　　Back bearing of line BC　=　146° 15' + 180° = 326° 15'　　... **Ans.**

(iii)　Fore bearing of line CD　=　215° 45'

　　Back bearing of line CD　=　215° 45' – 180° = 35° 45'　　... **Ans.**

(iv)　Fore bearing of line DE　=　327° 30'

　　Back bearing of line DE　=　327° 30' – 180° = 147° 30'　　... **Ans.**

Example 4.11 : *(i) Fore bearing of a line is 149° 45'. Find its back bearing.*

(ii) Convert W.C.B. in to reduced bearing : (1) 299° 50' and (2) 141° 18'.　(S-08)

Solution : (i) Fore bearing of line = 149° 45'

　　Back bearing of line = 149° 45' + 180°

　　　　　　　　　　= 329° 45'　　　　　　... **Ans.**

(ii) (1) W.C.B. = 299° 50'

∴　　　　　　R.B. = N (360° – 299° 50') W = N 60° 10' W　　... **Ans.**

　　(2) W.C.B. = 141° 18'

∴　　　　　　R.B. = N (180° – 141° 18') E = N 38° 42' E　　... **Ans.**

Example 4.12 : *The following are the observed fore bearings of line of quadrantal system.*

AB N 47° 15' E, BC S 24°30' E, CD S 51° 45' W, DE N 68° 15' W. Find their back bearings.

Solution : In quadrantal system the back bearing of the line is numerically equal to its fore bearing but with opposite direction.

(i)	F.B. of AB	=	N 47° 15 ' E	
	B.B. of AB	=	S 47° 15' W	... **Ans.**
(ii)	F.B. of BC	=	S 24° 30' E	
	B.B. of BC	=	N 24° 30' W	... **Ans.**
(iii)	F.B of CD	=	S 51° 45' W	
	B.B. of CD	=	N 51° 45' E	... **Ans.**
(iv)	F.B. of DE	=	N 68° 15' W	
	B.B. of DE	=	S 68° 15' E	... **Ans.**

TYPE-III : TO CALCULATE INCLUDED ANGLE FOR GIVEN BEARINGS OF LINES

Example 4.13 : *The bearing of a line PR is 148° 20' and the angle PRQ is 122° 35'. What is the bearing of RQ ?*

Solution : Bearing of PR = 148° 20'

Bearing of RP = 148° 20' + 180° 0' = 328° 20'

Now, Bearing of RQ = 122° 35' – (360 – 328° 20')

         = 90° 55'   ... **Ans.**

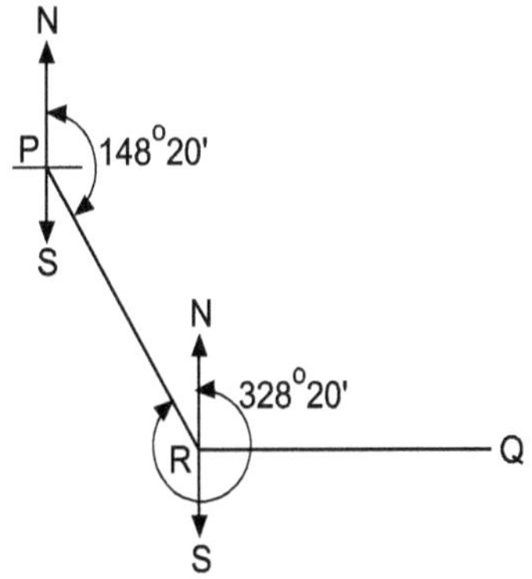

Fig. 4.21

Example 4.14 : *Find the included angles between the following lines :*
(a) N 32° 10' E and S 67° 38' E
(b) 52° 30' and 328° 45'

Solution :

(a) N 32° 10' E and S 67° 38' E

    ∠BAC = (90° 0' – 32° 10') + (90° 0' – 67° 38')

       = 57°50' + 22° 22' = 80° 12'

(b) Refer Fig. 4.22 (b)

Bearing of AB = 52° 30' and bearing of AC = 328° 45'

∴   ∠BAC = 328° 45' – 52° 30' = 276° 15'

        [Ext. angle, from the geometry of the figure.]

Hence, Included angle $= 360° 0' - 276° 15'$

$\qquad\qquad\qquad = 83° 45'$ **... Ans.**

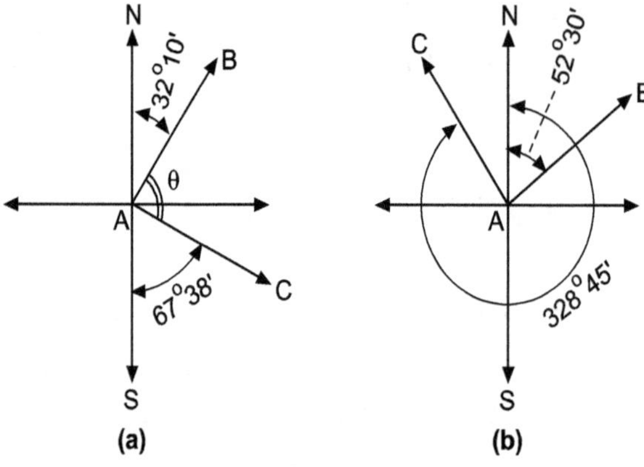

Fig. 4.22

Example 4.15 : *The bearing of a line PQ is 160° 20' and the angle PQR is 130° 40'. Find bearing of QR ? (clockwise with PQ).*

Solution : Given :

$\qquad$ Forward bearing of line PQ $= 160° 20'$

and $\qquad\qquad\qquad\qquad \angle\, PQR = 130° 40'$

Now, Backward bearing of line PQ $=$ F.B. of PQ $+ 180°$

$\qquad\qquad\qquad\qquad\qquad = 160° 20' + 180°$

$\qquad\qquad\qquad\qquad\qquad = 340° 20'$

And,$\quad$ Forward bearing of line QR $=$ B.B. of PQ $- \angle\, PQR$

$\qquad\qquad\qquad\qquad\qquad = 340° 20' - 130° 40'$

$\qquad\qquad\qquad\qquad\qquad = 209° 40'$

$\therefore\quad$ Bearing of line QR is $209° 40'$. **... Ans.**

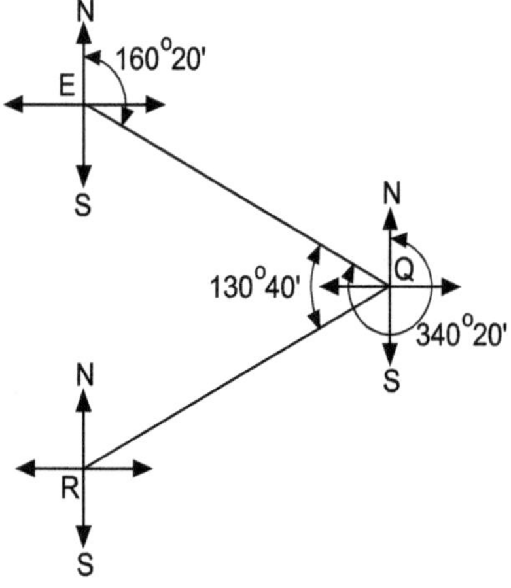

Fig. 4.23

Example 4.16 : *The bearing of a line AB is 153° 30' and the angle ABC is 135° 40'. What is the bearing of BC.* (W-06)

Solution :

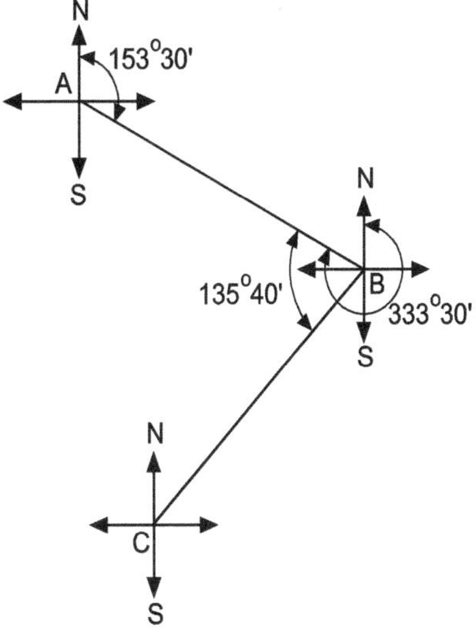

Fig. 4.24

Forward bearing of line AB $= 153° 30'$

Backward bearing of line AB $=$ F.B. $+ 180°$

$\qquad = 153° 30' + 180°$

$\therefore$ Backward bearing of line AB $= 333° 30'$

Now, Bearing of line BC $=$ B.B. of AB $- \angle$ ABC

$\qquad = 333° 30' - 135° 40'$

$\qquad = 197° 50'$

$\therefore$ Bearing of line BC is $197° 50'$. **... Ans.**

Example 4.17 : *The following bearings were recorded in running a closed compass traverse ABCDE. Calculate the included angles of the traverse.*

Line	Observed	
	F.B.	**B.B**
AB	110° 0'	290° 0'
BC	30° 15'	210° 15'
CD	244° 45'	64° 45'
DE	310° 0'	130° 0'
EA	193° 0'	13° 0'

Solution : Draw a rough sketch of the traverse from the given fore bearings of the lines as shown in Fig. 4.25.

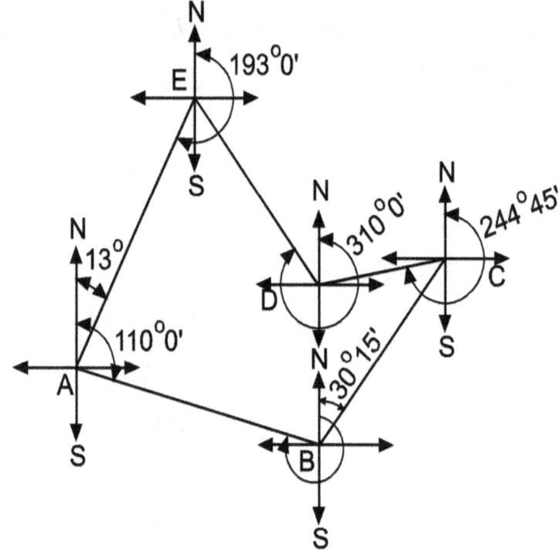

Fig. 4.25 : Included angles

$\angle$ A = F.B. of AB – B.B. of EA

= 110° 0' – 13° 0' = 97° 0'

$\angle$ B = B.B. of AB – F.B. of BC

= 290° 0' – 30° 15' = 259° 45' (Exterior angle)

∴   Interior angle = 360° – 259° 45'

= 100° 15'

$\angle$ C = F.B. of CD – B.B. of BC

= 244° 45' – 210° 15'

= 34° 30'

and $\angle$ D = F.B. of DE – B.B. of CD

= 310° 0' – 64° 45'

= 245° 15'

From the geometry of the figure, though the angle is greater than 180°, it is included angle.

$\angle$ E = F.B. of EA – B.B. of DE

= 193° 0' – 130° 45'

= 63° 0'   ... **Ans.**

Check : Sum of all the included angles = (2n – 4) × 90°

= (2 × 5 – 4) × 90° = 540°

'n' being the number of sides sum of all angles is,

$\angle$ A = 97° 0'

+ $\angle$ B = 100° 15'

+ $\angle$ C = 34° 30'

+ $\angle$ D = 245° 15'

+ $\angle$ E = 63° 0'

Sum = 540° 0'

Hence the proof.

Example 4.18 : *The bearing of one side of plot in the shape of a regular pentagon is 80°. Find the bearings of remaining sides taken in clockwise order the same way round.* **(W-07)**

Solution :

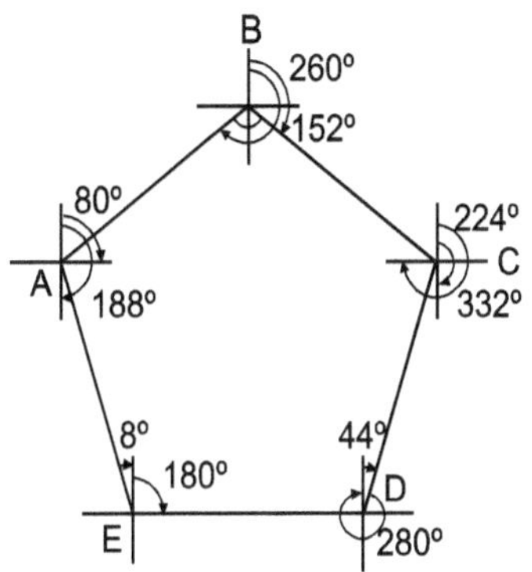

Fig. 4.26

Sum of included angles of pentagon = 540°

∴   Each angle of pentagon $= \dfrac{540°}{5} = 108°\ 00'$

Included angle of pentagon is 108°.

$$
\begin{aligned}
\text{Bearing of line AB} &= 80° \\
\text{Bearing of line BA} &= 80° + 180° = 260° \\
\text{Bearing of line BC} &= 260° - 108° \\
&= 152° \\
\text{Bearing of line CB} &= 180° + 152° \\
&= 332° \\
\text{Bearing of line CD} &= 332° - 108° \\
&= 224° \\
\text{Bearing of line DC} &= 224° - 180° \\
&= 44° \\
\text{Bearing of line DE} &= 360° - (108° - 44°) \\
&= 296° \\
\text{Bearing of line ED} &= 296° - 180° = 116° \\
\text{Bearing of line EA} &= 116° - 108° \\
&= 08° \\
\text{Bearing of line AE} &= 180° + 8° = 188° \\
\text{Bearing of line AD} &= 188° - 108° \\
&= 80°
\end{aligned}
$$

Example 4.19 : *Following are the bearings of the lines of a closed traverse ABCD :*

Line	Fore Bearing
AB	N 45° 10' E
BC	S 60° 40' E
CD	S 9° 50' W
DA	N 80° 40' W

Calculate the interior angles of traverse. **(W-08)**

Solution :

Line	R.B.	W.C.B.
AB	N 45° 10' E	45° 10'
BA	S 45° 10' W	225° 10'
BC	S 60° 40' E	119° 20'
CB	N 60° 40' W	299° 20'
CD	S 9° 50' W	189° 50'
DC	N 9° 50' E	9° 50'
DA	N 80° 40' W	279° 20'
AD	S 80° 40' W	99° 20'

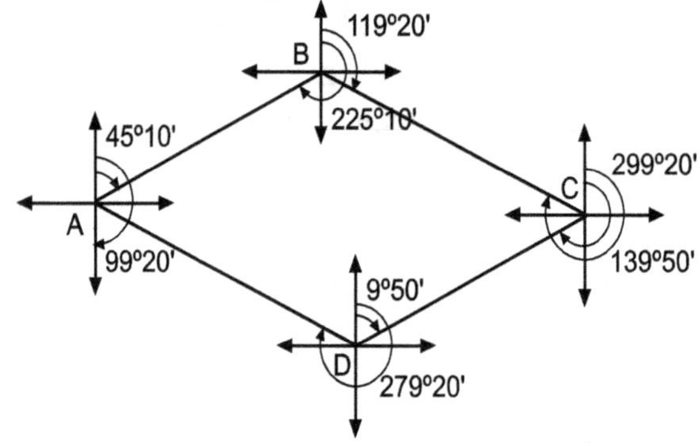

Fig. 4.27

$$\angle A = \text{W.C.B. AD} - \text{W.C.B. AB}$$

$$= 99° \; 20' - 45° \; 10' = 54° \; 10' \qquad \text{... Ans.}$$

$$\angle B = \text{W.C.B. BA} - \text{W.C.B. BC}$$

$$= 225° \; 10' - 119° \; 20' = 105° \; 50' \qquad \text{... Ans.}$$

$$\angle C = \text{W.C.B. CB} - \text{W.C.B. CD}$$

$$= 229° \; 20' - 189° \; 50' = 109° \; 30' \qquad \text{... Ans.}$$

$$\angle D = (360° - \text{W.C.B. DA}) + \text{W.C.B. DC}$$

$$= (360° - 279° \; 20') + 99° \; 20' = 180° \qquad \text{... Ans.}$$

Example 4.20 : *The whole circle bearings of lines of a closed traverse are as given below :*

290° 30', 250° 30', 196° 0', 175° 30', 112° and 30° 0'. Determine included angles of the traverse. Apply check. (S-08)

Solution :

Line	F.B.	B.B.	Angle calculation
AB	290° 30'	110° 30'	∠ A = F.B. of AB – B.B. of FA = 290° 30' – 210° = 80° 30'
BC	250° 30'	70° 30'	∠ B = F.B. of BC – B.B. of AB = 250° 30' – 110° 30' = 140°
CD	196° 0'	16°	∠ C = F.B. of CD – B.B. of BC = 196° – 70° 30' = 125° 30'
DE	175° 30'	355° 30'	∠ D = F.B. of DE – B.B. of CD = 175° 30' – 16° = 150° 30'
EF	112°	292°	∠ E = (360° – B.B. of DE) + F.B. of EF = (360° – 355° 30') + 112° = 116° 30'
FA	30° 0'	210°	∠ F = (360° – B.B. of EF) + F.B. of FA = (360° – 292) + 30° = 98°

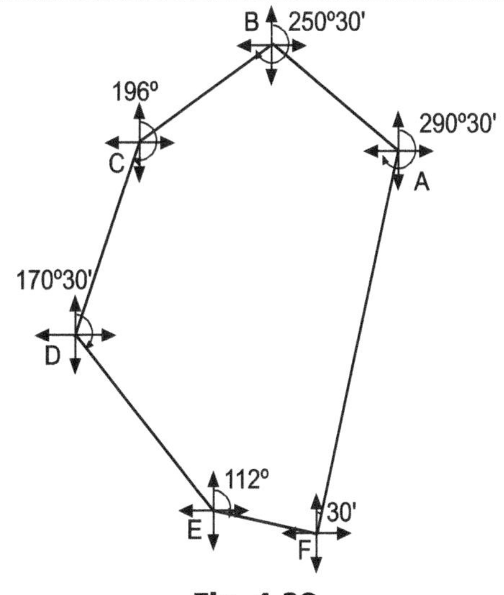

Fig. 4.28

Example 4.21 : *The following fore bearings were observed in running a compass traverse. Find the back bearings and interior angles of the traverse. Apply check.*

(S-09)

Line	F.B.
AB	50° 30'
BC	120° 15'
CD	183° 00'
DA	292° 45'

Solution :

Line	F.B.	B.B.
AB	50° 30'	230° 30'
BC	120° 15'	300° 15'
CD	183° 00'	3°
DA	292° 45'	112° 45'

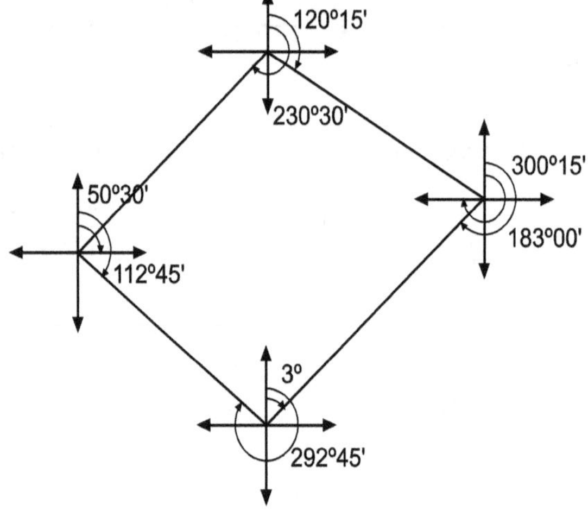

Fig. 4.29

Interior Angles :

$\angle A = 230°\ 30' - 120°\ 15' = 110°\ 15'$

$\angle B = 330°\ 15' - 183· = 117·\ 15'$

$\angle C = 360° - 292°\ 45' + 3° = 70°\ 15'$

$\angle D = 112°\ 45' - 50°\ 30' = 62°\ 15'$

Total = 360°   [Check]

TYPE-IV : CALCULATION OF CORRECTED BEARING

Example 4.22 : *Calculate the included angle for a closed traverse survey and apply usual check.* (W-09)

Line	F.B.	B.B.
AB	46° 10'	226° 10'
BC	119° 20'	298° 40'
CD	169° 30'	351° 10'
DA	280° 20'	99° 20'

Solution :

Line	Observed bearing	Correction	Corrected bearing
AB	46° 10'	0	46° 10'
BA	226° 10'	0	226° 10'
BC	119° 20'	0	119° 20'
CB	298° 40'	0° 40'	299° 20'
CD	169° 30'	0° 40'	170° 10'
DC	351° 10'	– 1°	350° 10'
DA	280° 20'	– 1°	279° 20'
AD	99° 20'	0	99° 20'

For line AB, 226° 10' – 46° 10' = 180°.

Stations A and B are free from local attraction.

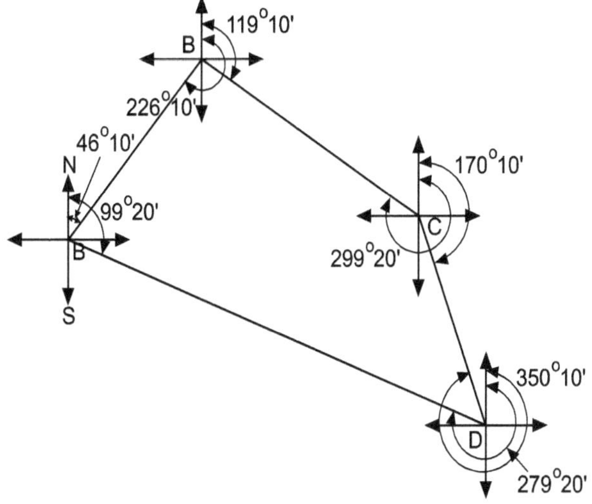

Fig. 4.30

Calculation for Interior Angles :

$$\angle A = 99° 21' - 46° 10' = 53° 10'$$

$$\angle B = 226° 10' - 119° 20' = 106° 50'$$

$$\angle C = 299° 20' - 170° 10' = 129° 10'$$

$$\angle D = 350° 10' - 279° 20' = 70° 50'$$

Check : Total $\angle A + \angle B + \angle C + \angle D = 360°$

Example 4.23 : *The followings fore and back bearings were observed in running a close compass traverse :*   (W-07)

(a) *Find the stations free from local attraction.*

(b) *Workout corrected fore and back bearings of the lines.*

Line	Fore Bearing	Back Bearing
AB	44° 30'	226° 30'
BC	124° 30'	303° 15'
CD	181° 0'	1° 0'
DA	289° 30'	108° 45'

Solution : The difference between F.B. and B.B. of the line CD is exactly equal to 180°. Hence, stations C and D are free from local attraction, and the bearings observed from C and D are correct.

Thus, commencing from Line CD.

The F.B. and B.B. of CD i.e. 181° 0' and 1° 0'.

Observed F.B. of line, DA = 289° 30' is correct,

and hence corrected B.B. of line DA = 289° 30' – 180° = 109° 30';

but the observed B.B. of DA is 108° 45'.

The error is 109° 30' – 108° 45' = 0° 45', the correction at A is therefore + 0° 45'.

The observed F.B. of line AB = 44° 30'

Applying correction of 0° 45' (+ve) at A –

Corrected fore bearing of AB = 44° 30' + 0° 45'

$\qquad\qquad\qquad\qquad$ = 45° 15'

Now,   Required B.B. of AB   = 45° 15' + 180° = 225° 15'

But the observed B.B. of AB = 226° 30'

Hence, the error is 226° 30' – 225° 15' = 1° 15' (+ ve), and the correction is 1° 15' (–ve) at station B.

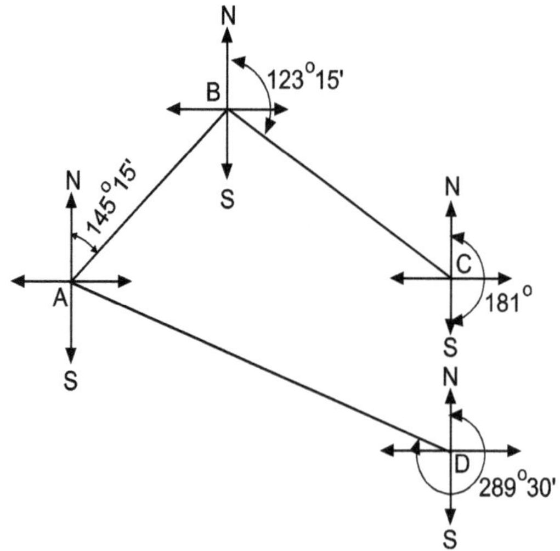

Fig. 4.31

Observed F.B. of BC = 124° 30'

Corrected F.B. of BC = 124° 30' – 1° 15' = 123° 15'

Required B.B. of BC = 123° 15 + 180° = 303° 15'

Check : The observed bearing is also 303° 15' which tallies, since the station C is free from local attraction.

The results are tabulated as under :

Line	Observed		Correction	Corrected		Remarks
	F.B.	**B.B.**		**F.B.**	**B.B.**	
AB	44° 30'	226° 30'	+ 45' at A	45° 15'	225° 15'	Stations
BC	124° 30'	303° 15'	– 1° 15' at B	123° 15'	303° 15'	C and D
CD	181° 0'	1° 0'	0' at C	181° 0'	1° 0'	are free
DA	289° 30'	108° 45'	0' at D	289° 30'	109° 30'	from local attraction

Example 4.24 : *Following bearings were taken in running a closed traverse :*

Line	F.B.	B.B.
AB	124°30'	304°30'
BC	68°15'	246°0'
CD	310°30'	135°15'
DA	200°15'	17°45'

At what station do you suspect local attraction ? Find the correct bearings of lines.

(W-08)

Solution :

At line AB

$$\text{W.C.B. of BA} - \text{W.C.B. of AB} = 304° 30' - 124° 30' = 180°$$

∴ Station A and B are free from local attraction

$$\text{Corrected W.C.B. of CB} = 68° 15' + 180° = 248° 15'$$

$$\text{Corrected at C} = 248° 15' - 246°$$
$$= 2° 15'$$

$$\text{Corrected W.C.B. of CD} = \text{W.C.B. of CD} + \text{correction at C}$$
$$= 310° 30' + 2° 15'$$
$$= 312° 45'$$

$$\text{Corrected W.C.B. of DC} = 312° 45' - 180°$$
$$= 132° 45'$$

$$\text{Corrected at D} = 132° 45' - 135° 15'$$
$$= - 2° 30'$$

$$\text{Corrected W.C.B. of DA} = 200° \, 15' - 2° \, 30'$$
$$= 197° \, 45'$$
$$\text{Corrected W.C.B. of AB} = 197° \, 45' - 180°$$
$$= 17° \, 45' \qquad \text{(Check)}$$

Line	W.C.B.	Correction	Corrected W.C.B.
AB	124° 30'	0	124° 30'
BA	304° 30'	0	304° 30'
BC	68° 15'	0	68° 15'
CB	246° 0'	2° 15'	248° 15'
CD	310° 30'	2° 15'	312° 45'
DC	135° 15'	– 2° 30'	132° 45'
DA	200° 15'	– 2° 30'	197° 45'
AD	17° 45'	0	17° 45' (check)

Example 4.25 : *Following are the bearings of the sides of a closed compass traverse. At what stations is local attraction suspected ? Compute the correct bearings of the sides of the traverse.* **(S-09)**

Line	F.B.	B.B.
AB	325° 30'	145° 30'
BA	67° 00'	243° 00'
CD	195° 15'	20° 15'
DC	219° 00'	37° 00'

Solution :

Line	Observed bearings	Correction	Corrected bearing
AB	325° 30'	0	325° 30'
BA	145° 30'	0	145° 30'
BC	67° 00'	0	67° 0'
CB	243° 00'	4°	247°
CD	194° 15'	0	198° 15'
DC	20° 15'	– 2°	18° 15'
DA	219° 0'	– 2°	217° 0'
AD	37° 00'	0	37° 0'

Example 4.26 : *The following bearings were taken in running a closed compass traverse.*

Line	F.B.	B.B.
AB	80° 10'	259° 0'
BC	120° 20'	301° 50'
CD	170° 50'	350° 50'
DE	230° 10'	49° 30'
EA	310° 20'	130° 15'

Compute the interior angles and correct them for observational errors. Assuming the bearing of the line CD to be correct, adjust the bearings of the remaining sides.

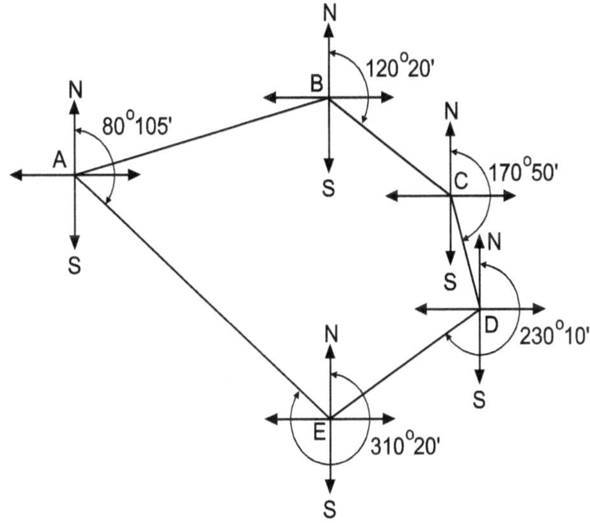

Fig. 4.32

Solution : Included angles

$$\angle A = \text{B.B. of EA} - \text{F.B. of AB}$$
$$= 130° \ 15' - 80° \ 10' = 50° \ 05'$$

$$\angle B = \text{B.B. of AB} - \text{F.B. of BC}$$
$$= 259° \ 0' - 120° \ 20' = 138° \ 40'$$

$$\angle C = \text{B.B. of BC} - \text{F.B. of CD}$$
$$= 301° \ 50' - 170° \ 50' = 131° \ 0'$$

$$\angle D = \text{B.B. of CD} - \text{F.B. of DE}$$
$$= 350° \ 50' - 230° \ 10' = 120° \ 40'$$

$$\angle E = \text{F.B. of EA} - \text{B.B. of DE}$$
$$= 310° \ 20' - 49° \ 30' = 260° \ 50' \ \text{(Exterior angle)}$$
$$= 360° - 260° \ 50' = 99° \ 10' \ \text{(Interior angle)}$$

Sum of all included angles

$$\angle A + \angle B + \angle C + \angle D + \angle E = 50^\circ\ 05' + 138^\circ\ 40' + 131^\circ\ 0' + 120^\circ\ 40' + 99^\circ\ 10'$$

$$= 538^\circ\ 95' = 539^\circ\ 35'$$

Theoretical sum $= (2n - 4) \times 90^\circ = 540^\circ$

∴　　　　　　　Error $= 540^\circ - 539^\circ\ 35' = 0^\circ\ 25'$

It is equally divided among 5 stations i.e. + 05' at each angle station.

Hence, corrected included angles are :

$\angle A = 50^\circ\ 10'$, $\angle B = 138^\circ\ 45'$, $\angle C = 131^\circ\ 05'$, $\angle D = 120^\circ\ 45'$, $\angle E = 99^\circ\ 15'$.

∴　　　　　Sum total $= 540^\circ$

For correction of bearings :

Commencing from the bearings of unaffected line CD

$$\text{Bearing of CB} = \text{Bearing of CD} + \angle C$$
$$= 170^\circ\ 50' + 131^\circ\ 05' = 301^\circ\ 55'$$
$$\text{Bearing of BC} = 301^\circ\ 55' - 180^\circ = 121^\circ\ 55'$$
$$\text{Bearing of BA} = \text{Bearing of BC} + \angle B$$
$$= 121^\circ\ 55' + 138^\circ\ 45' = 260^\circ\ 40'$$
$$\text{Bearing of AB} = 260^\circ\ 40' - 180^\circ = 80^\circ\ 40'$$
$$\text{Bearing of AE} = \text{Bearing of AB} + \angle A$$
$$= 80^\circ\ 40' + 50^\circ\ 10' = 130^\circ\ 50'$$
$$\text{Bearing of EA} = 130^\circ\ 50' + 180^\circ = 310^\circ\ 50'$$
$$\text{Bearing of ED} = \text{Bearing of EA} + \angle E$$
$$= 310^\circ\ 50' + 99^\circ\ 15' = 410^\circ\ 05'$$
$$\text{Bearing of DE} = 410^\circ\ 05' - 180^\circ = 230^\circ\ 05'$$
$$\text{Bearing of DC} = \text{Bearing of DE} + \angle D$$
$$= 230^\circ\ 05' + 120^\circ\ 45' = 350^\circ\ 50'$$
$$\text{Bearing of CD} = 350^\circ\ 50' - 180^\circ = 170^\circ\ 50' \qquad \text{(Check)}$$

TYPE-V : PROBLEMS ON MAGNETIC DICLINATION

Example 4.27 : *The magnetic bearing of a line AB is 207° 30'. Find its true bearing, if the magnetic declination is 5° 45' W.*

Solution : The magnetic needle is deflected to the West of True meridian by an amount 5° 45'.

Hence, True bearing of AB = Magnetic bearing of AB − Declination

$$= 207^\circ\ 30' - 5^\circ\ 45'$$

$$= 201^\circ\ 45' \qquad \qquad \textbf{... Ans.}$$

Example 4.28 : *The magnetic bearing of a line AB is S 41° 30' E and the magnetic declination is 6° 15' E . Find the true bearing of the line.*

Solution : The magnetic north is deflected by 6° 15' from the true north towards East.

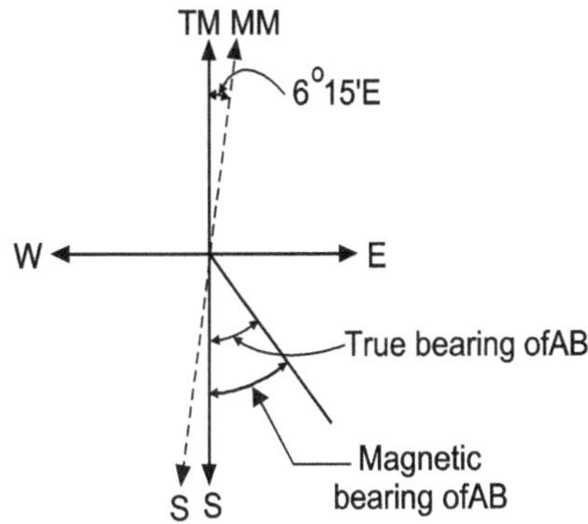

Fig. 4.33

Convert S 41° 30' E to W.C.B.

∴   W.C.B. = 180 − 41° 30' = 138° 30'

Now, applying Rule No. 1.

True bearing of AB = Magnetic bearing + Declination

= 138° 30' + 6° 15' = 144° 45'

∴   Converting to R.B. = 180° − 144° 45'

= S 35° 15' E   ... **Ans.** [Check]

Example 4.29 : *A line was drawn to magnetic bearing of 192° on an old map when the magnetic declination was 5° 30' East. To what bearing it should be set now if the magnetic declination of the line at present is 3° 15' West ?*

Solution :

True bearing of the line = Magnetic bearing ± Declination

= 192° + 5° 30' (declination + ve, being East)

= 197° 30'

Now, the declination is 3° 15' West.

To set the line now,

Magnetic bearing = True bearing ± Declination

= 197° 30' + 3° 15'

= 200° 45' (declination +ve, being West)   ... **Ans.**

Example 4.30 : *A line was drawn to magnetic bearing of 238° 20' on an old map when magnetic declination was 5° 40' E. To what bearing it should be set now, if present magnetic declination is 3° 10' W ?*

Solution : True bearing of the line

$$= \text{Magnetic bearing} \pm \text{Delination}$$

$$= 238° \ 20' + 5° \ 40' \qquad \text{(Declination +ve, being East)}$$

$$= 244° \ 0'$$

Now, the declination is 3° 10' West.

To set the line now,

$$\text{Magnetic bearing} = \text{True bearing} \pm \text{Declination}$$

$$= 244° \ 0' + 3° \ 10' \qquad \text{(Declination +ve, being West)}$$

$$= 247° \ 10'$$

The magnetic bearing of a line AB is 176°.   **... Ans.**

Example 4.31 : *Find the magnetic declination if the magnetic bearing of the sun at noon is (i) 188° (ii) 355° 38'.*   **(S-11)**

Solution : (1) The sun is exactly on the geographical meridian at noon. Hence, its bearing is either 0° or 180°.

Since the magnetic bearing of the sun is 188°. It is at the south pole.

Magnetic bearing of the south pole is 188°, and that of North pole is 8°.

∴   Declination is 188° – 180° = 8° W.

               ... Ans.

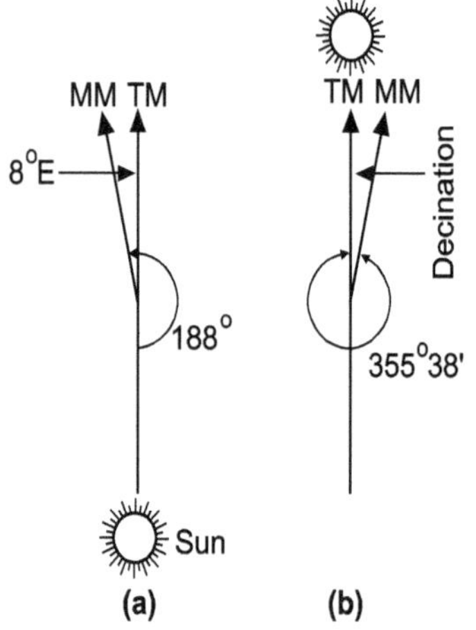

Fig. 4.34

(ii) The magnetic bearing of the sun at noon is 355° 38'.

The true bearing of the sun is 360°. The sun is now at North pole.

∴   Declination is 360° – 355° 38' = 4° 22' E

Hence, magnetic meridian is 4°22' to the East of true meridian.

∴   Magnetic declination is 4° 22' E   **... Ans.**

Example 4.32 : *The value of magnetic declination at a place is 7° 20' W. Convert the following compass direction to true bearings.*

(i) S 45° 40' E (ii) S 85° 15' W

Solution : (i) The given R.B. = S 45° 40' E.

$$\text{W.C.B.} = 180° - 45° 40' = 134° 20'$$

True bearing = Magnetic bearing ± Declination

= 134°20' – 7° 20' (∵ Declination is to West)

= 127° 0'

Converting to the R.B. –

180° – 127° 0' = S 53° 0' E   ... **Ans.**

(ii)   The given R.B. = S 85° 15' W

∴   W.C.B. = 180° + 85° 15'

= 265° 15'

True Bearing = Magnetic bearing ± Declination

= 265° 15' – 7° 20' (∵ Declination is to West)

= 257° 40'

Converting to the R.B. –

360° – 257° 40' = S 120° 20' W   ... **Ans.**

Example 4.33 : The true bearing of tower as observed from a station is 350° 30' and the magnetic bearing of a tower is 2° 30'. The back bearing of the line AB when measured with a prismatic compass was found to be 330° 30'. What is the true bearing of the line AB ?

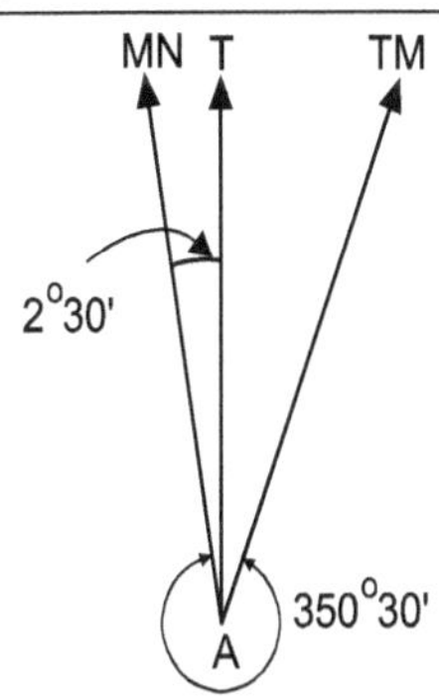

Fig. 4.35

Solution : Magnetic declination = 360° – 350° 30' + 2° 30' = 9° 30' + 2° 30' = 12° 0' W.

Magnetic fore bearing of AB = 330° 30' – 180° = 150° 30'

True bearing of AB = 150° 30' – 12°0' = 138° 30'   ... **Ans.**

Important Points

- The principle of compass survey is Traversing, which involves a series of connected survey lines (may be open or closed) whose lengths and bearings are measured by linear and angular measuring instruments.
- The true or geographical meridian passing through a point on the earth's surface is the line in which the plane passing through the given point and the north and south poles intersects the surface of the earth.
- The direction indicated by a freely suspended and properly balanced magnetic needle unaffected by local attractive force is called the magnetic meridian.
- Arbitrary meridian may be a direction from a survey station to some well-defined permanent object or the first survey line.

- The angle made by the survey line with the magnetic meridian i.e. north-south line is called magnetic bearing.
- The horizontal angle between the line and true meridian is called true bearing of line.
- The angle made by the survey line with the arbitrary meridian is called arbitrary bearing.
- The bearing of a survey line is measured in clockwise direction from the north is called Whole circle Bearing.
- Quadrantal or Reduced bearing of a line is measured clockwise or anticlockwise from the north or south pole whichever is nearer the line and towards east or west.
- The bearing observed in the direction of progress of survey is called *Fore Bearing* (F.B.) and the bearing observed in the opposite direction is called *Back Bearing* (B.B.).
- The compass needle does not point to magnetic meridian or magnetic north when it is under the influence of the external attractive forces. It is seriously deviated from its normal position (North direction) when placed in the vicinity of iron or steel objects, iron ore, electricity current. The deviation arising from such external or local sources is called *local attraction*.
- The local attraction can usually be detected by observing thedifference between F.B. and B.B. of a line .If the difference is 180^0 then there is no LA. Otherwise there is LA.
- The inclination of the magnetic needle with the horizontal is called *magnetic dip of the needle.*
- The horizontal angle made by the magnetic meridian with the true meridian is called 'magnetic declination'.
- True bearing of a line = Magnetic bearing of the line ± Magnetic Declination.

  Use (+) sign when the declination is towards east and

  (–) sign when the declination is towards west.
- A traverse is said to be a closed traverse when it forms a closed polygon. It begins and ends at the same point.
- A traverse is said to be unclosed or open when it does not form a closed polygon. The end point does not coincide with the starting point.

Practice Questions

1. Draw a neat sectional elevation of a prismatic compass and name all the important component parts.

2. How does the chain and compass surveying differ from chain surveying. Explain briefly the method of compass surveying.

3. Give reasons for the following -

   (a) A prison is provided in a prismatic compass.

   (b) Hinged sun glasses are attached to the eye vane.

   (c) Adjustable mirror is provided with object vane.

   (d) A pivot should be exactly at the centre of the pointed sharp.

(e) A ball and socket arrangement is provided on tripod stand of compass.

(f) A compass traversing is not reliable.

4. State the conditions under which traversing by compass is preferable to chain surveying.

5. Describe the field procedure of compass traverse.

6. Define magnetic meridian.

7. Define the following terms used in compass surveying :

(i)   Meridian   (iv)   Dip of the needle

(ii) Magnetic declination   (v)   Local attraction

(iii) True meridian

8. What is meant by local attraction ? How is it detected ? How are the observed bearings corrected for local attraction ? State any two causes of local attraction ?

9. Write short notes on :

(i)   Dip of the needle.

(ii) Graphical adjustment by Bowditch's rule.

(iii) Errors in compass surveying.

(iv) Testing of compass.

(v)   Precautions in using the compass.

(vi) Limits of precision in compass surveying.

10. Describe temporary adjustment of prismatic compass.

11. Convert the following R.B. to W.C.B.

(i)   N 47° W   (ii)   S 38° 45' W

(iii) N 47° 10' E   (iv)   S 35° 15' E

[**Ans.** (i) 313° (ii) 218° 45' (iii) 47° 10' (iv) 144° 45']

12. A line was drawn to a magnetic bearing of 234° 40' on an old map when the magnetic declination was 4° 16' E. To what bearing should it be set now, if the present magnetic declination is 2° 20' W ?

[**Ans.** 241° 16']

13. In 1900, a certain line had a magnetic bearing of S 67° 30' E and the magnetic declination at that place was 8° E. In 1962, the magnetic declination was 4° W. Determine the magnetic bearing of the line in 1962.

[**Ans.** S 53° 03']

14. Find the angle between the lines AO and OB, if their respective bearings are :

(i)   132° 10' and 60° 20' (ii) N 65° 20' E and S 50° 30' E

[**Ans.** (i) 108° 10' (ii) 115° 50'.]

15. Below are the bearings observed in a traverse survey conducted with a prismatic compass at a place where local attraction was suspected.

Line	Fore bearing	Back bearing
PQ	124° 30'	304° 30'
QR	68° 15'	246° 0'
RS	310° 30'	135° 15'
SP	200° 15'	17° 45'

At what stations do you suspect local attraction ? Find the corrected bearing of the lines and also calculate the included angles.

[**Ans.** Stations R and S are affected by local attraction.

North is deflected 2° 15' at R towards West and 2° 30' at S towards east.

Line	Fore bearing	Back bearing
PQ	124° 30'	304° 30'
QR	68° 15'	248° 15'
RS	312° 45'	132° 25'
SP	197° 45'	17° 45'

Included angles : ∠P =106° 45', ∠Q = 123° 45'. ∠R = 64° 30', ∠S = 65° 0']

16. The following bearings were taken in traversing with a compass in a place, where local attraction was suspected.

Line	Fore bearing	Back bearing
AB	S 45° 30' E	N 45° 30' W
BC	S 60° 0' E	N 60° 40' W
CD	S 5° 30' E	N 3° 20' W
DA	N 4° 30' W	S 6° 0' E

At what stations do you suspect local attraction ? determine the corrected fore and back bearing of each of the lines.

[**Ans.** Stations C and D are affected by local attraction.]

Line	Correction	Corrected	
		F.B.	**B.B.**
AB	0 at A	S 45° 30' E	N 45° 30' W
BC	0 at B	S 60° 0' E	N 60° 0' W
CD	+ 40' at C	S 4° 50' E	N 4° 50' W
DA	+ 1° 30' at D	N 6° 0' W	S 6° 0' E

17. Mention the value of magnetic declination if the magnetic bearing of the sun at noon is

(a) 184°

(b) 345°

[**Ans.** (a) 4° W; (b) 6° E.]

MSBTE Questions & Answers

Summer 2010

1. Define :

   (i)　Magnetic bearing

   (ii)　True bearing.

2. What is local attraction and how it is detected in a compare traverse ?

Ans. Refer Section 4.19.

3. Convert following W.C.B. to R.B.

   (i)　$100° \cdot 45'$

   (ii)　$303° \cdot 15'$

Ans. (i)　S 79° 15' E

   (ii)　N 56° 45' W

4. Convert following R.B. to W.C.B. :

   (i)　S 35° · 45' E

   (ii)　N 31° · 15' E

Ans. (i)　144° 15'

   (ii)　31° 15'

5. Explain the following of a lifting level in a prismatic compare with a neat sketch.

Ans. Refer Section 4.6.

6. The following bearings were taken in running a compass traverse :

Line	Fore bearing	Back bearing
AB	124° 30'	304° 30'
BC	68° 15'	246° 0'
CD	310° 30'	135° 15'
DA	200° 15'	17° 45'

At what stations do you suspect local attraction ? Find the correct bearings of the lines.

Ans. Refer Section 4.24.

7. ABCD is a closed polygon $\angle A = 125°$, $\angle B = 110°$, $\angle C = 55°$, $\angle D = 70°$ F.B. of line AB is 135° · 30'. Find out fore and back bearings of all the lines.

8. Explain the graphical method of adjustment of closing error in a closed traverse.

Ans. Refer Section 4.30.

Winter 2010

1. Following are observed bearings of lines using a compass at a place where local attraction was suspected.

Line	Fore bearing	Back bearing
AB	191° 45'	13° 0'
BC	39° 30'	222° 30'
CD	22° 15'	200° 30'
DE	242° 45'	62° 45'
EA	330° 15'	147° 45'

Find :

(i)   Stations affected by local attraction and

(ii) Corrected bearings of the lines.

Ans. Same as Problem No. 4.24.

2. Define 'magnetic meridian' and 'arbitrary meridian'.

Ans. Refer Section 4.13.

3. Define fore bearing' and 'back bearing' of a line.

Ans. Refer Section 4.16.

4. Convert the following bearings to the other system

(i)   S 41° 15' W

(ii)   41° 15'

(iii) N 10° 40' W

(iv)   118° 10'

Ans. (i)   221° 15'

(ii)   N 41° 15' E

(iii) 349° 20'

(iv) S 61° 50' E

5. State any four components of a prismatic compass and give their, uses.

Ans. Refer Section 4.4.

6. Explain with figure the graphical adjustment of closing error. The bearings of the sides of a traverse ABCDE are as follows :

Line	Fore bearing	Back bearing
AB	107° 15'	287° 15'
BC	22° 0'	202° 0'
CD	281° 30'	101° 30'
DE	189° 15'	9° 15'
EA	124° 45'	304° 45'

Compute the interior angles of the traverse. Apply check.

Summer 2011

1. What is true meridian ?

Ans. Refer Section 4.13.

2. Find angle between lines OA and OB if their respective bearings are 16° 30' and 332° 18'.

3. Convert the following whole circle bearing to reduced bearing :
   (i) 232° 15'
   (ii) 341°

Ans. (i) S 52° 15' W
  (ii) N 19° W

4. Convert the following quadrantal bearing to whole circle bearing :
   (i) N 32° 15' E
   (ii) S 30° 30' W

Ans. (i) 32° 15'
  (ii) 210° 30'

5. Define meridian and write different types of meridians.

Ans. Refer Section 4.13.

6. Give the difference between close traverse and open traverse in compass survey.

Ans. Refer Section 4.28.

7. What is meant by dip of magnetic needle ?

Ans. Refer Section 4.25.

8. Define magnetic declination and give the various types of declinations.

Ans. Refer Section 4.25.

9. Find the magnetic declination if the magnetic bearing of the sun at noon is :
   (i) 188°
   (ii) 355° 38'

Ans. Refer Example 4.31.

Winter 2011

1. Write difference between whole circle bearing and quadrantal bearing.

Ans. Refer Section 4.14.1.

2. Find the angle between lines OA and OB if their respective whole circle bearings are 32° 45' and 148° 15'.

3. Convert following whole circle bearing to quadrantal bearings
   (i) 65° 45'
   (ii) 143° 30'

Ans. (i) N 65° 45' E
  (ii) S 36° 30' E

4. Convert reduced bearing to whole circle bearing
   (i) S 41° 45' E
   (ii) N 12° 15' W

Ans. (i) 138° 15'
  (ii) 347° 45'

5. Write the precautions taken while compass observations.

Ans. Refer Section 4.11.

Give the reasons :

(i) The zero is marked at south in prismatic compass.

Ans. Refer Section 4.5.

(ii) A prism is provided in prismatic compass.

Ans. Refer Section 4.5.

6. Below are the bearings observed in traverse survey conducted with a prismatic compass at place where local attraction was suspected.

Line	Fore bearing	Back bearing
PQ	124° 30'	304° 30'
QR	68° 15'	246° 0'
RS	310° 30'	135° 15'
SP	200° 15'	17° 45'

At what stations do you suspect local attraction ? Find the corrected bearing of the lines.

Give the field procedure of compass traverse.

Ans. Refer Example 4.24.

7. The following are the bearings of the lines of a closed traverse ABCD :

Line	Fore bearing
AB	N 45° 10' E
BC	S 60° 40' E
CD	S 9° 50' W
DA	N 80° 40' W

Calculate the interior angles of the traverse.

Ans. Refer Example 4.19.

8. Write the different component parts with its functions of prismatic compass (any eight).

Ans. Refer Section 4.3.

Summer 2012

1. State the principle of compass surveying.

2. Differentiate between true meridian and magnetic meridian.

Ans. Refer Section 4.13.1.

3. State the formula to find back bearing of a line from its fore bearing.

Ans. Refer Section 4.16.

4. Define "local attraction".

Ans. Refer Section 4.19.

5. How would you determine included angles from bearings ? Explain with neat sketch.

Ans. Refer Section 4.29.2.

6. Differentiate between whole circle bearing and quadrantal bearing system of measuring bearing.

7. Describe graphical adjustment of closing error by Bowditch's rule.

Ans. Refer Section 4.31.

8. Convert following W.C.B. in to quadrantal bearing and quadrantial bearing in to W.C.B.

   (i)   119° 45' (ii) 289° 50' (iii) N 42° 30' W (iv) S 31° 48' E

Ans. (i)   S 60° 15' E, (ii) N 70° 10' W, (iii) 327° 30', (iv) 148° 12'.

9. Following are bearings observed in a closed compass traverse

	Line	**Fore bearing**	**Back bearing**
	PQ	124° 30'	304° 30'
PQRS	QR	68° 15'	246°
	RS	310° 30'	135° 15'
	SP	200° 15'	17° 45'

At what stations do you suspect local attraction ? Find corrected bearings of the lines.

10. The whole circle bearings of sides of a closed traverse are : 290° 30', 250° 30', 196° 30', 175° 30', 112° and 30°. Calculate included angles and angular error for the traverse.

Ans. Refer Ex. 4.24.

Winter 2012

1. State different types of meridians.

Ans. Refer Section 4.12.

2. Define for bearing and back bearing of line.

Ans. Refer Section 4.16.

3. Convert the following reduced bearing to whole circle bearing :

   (i)   N 70° 30' E

   (ii)   S 48° 30' W

Ans. (i)   70° 30'

   (ii)   228° 30'

4. State any two causes of local attraction.

Ans. Refer Section 4.19.1.

5. Draw a neat labelled sketch of prismatic compass.

Ans. Refer Section 4.4.

6. The following observations were recorded in running a closed compass traverse.

Line	Fore bearing	Back bearing
AB	120° 30'	300° 30'
BC	240° 30'	62° 00'
CA	32° 00'	210° 30'

Mention the station/s affected by local attraction workout corrected bearing of all lines. Calculate included angles.

7. Convert following whole circle bearing into reduced bearing :
   - (i) 175° 30'
   - (ii) 38° 30'
   - (iii) 232° 30'
   - (iv) 341° 00'

Ans. (i) S 4° 30' E, (ii) N 38° 30' E, (iii) S 52° 30' W, (iv) N 19 W.

8. Differentiate between reduced bearing and whole circle bearing.

Ans. Refer Section 4.14.1.

9. What is meant by closing error ? Explain graphical method of adjustment of closing error.

Ans. Refer Section 4.30.

Summer 2013

1. State the principle of compass surveying.

Ans. Refer Section 4.2.

2. State the formula to find back bearing of a line from its fore bearing.

Ans. Refer Section 4.16.

3. Define "local attraction".

Ans. Refer Section 4.19.

4. Differentiate between whole circle bearing and quadrantal bearing system of measuring bearing.

Ans. Refer Section 4.14.1 and 4.14.2.

5. Describe graphical adjustment of closing error by Bowditch's rule.

Ans. Refer Section 4.31.

6. Following are bearings observed in a closed compass traverse.

PQRS	Line	Fore bearing	Back bearing
	PQ	124° 30'	304° 30'
	QR	68° 15'	246°
	RS	310° 30'	135° 15'
	SP	200° 15'	17° 45'

Ans. Refer Section 4.24.

7. The whole circle bearings of sides of a closed traverse are : 290° 30', 250° 30', 196° 30', 175° 30' 112° and 30°. Calculate included angles and angular error for the traverse.

Ans. Refer Section 4.17.

5...

Plane Table Surveying

Contents

5.1 INTRODUCTION

- Plane tabling is a peculiar method of surveying in which the field work and plotting are carried out simultaneously.

- It is particularly suitable for the preparation of small scale maps medium scale maps and filling in the details between theodolite stations.

- It is extensively used for recording topography in engineering surveys. The plane table and the various ways in which it is used in surveying are dealt with in this chapter.

5.2 THE PLANE TABLE

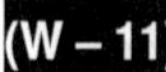

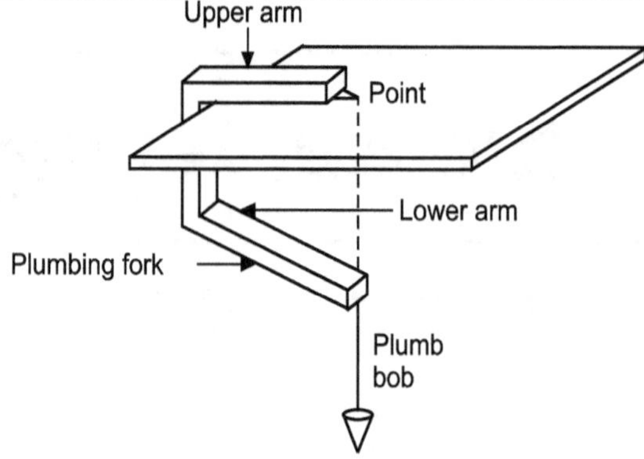

Fig. 5.1 : Plane Table with Plumbing Fork and Plumb Bob

It consists of two parts :

1. The table or board mounted on a tripod and

2. A straight edge called the 'alidade'

1. The table or board is made-up of well seasoned wood of good quality such as teak or pine, and of size varying from 40 cm × 30 cm to 75 cm × 60 cm. It is mounted on tripod in such a way that it can be levelled and rotated about a vertical axis and clamped in any position.

2. ***The alidade*** : It is made of brass or gunmetal or it is simply a straight edge carrying a line of sight. The alidade is used for sighting the objects to be located.

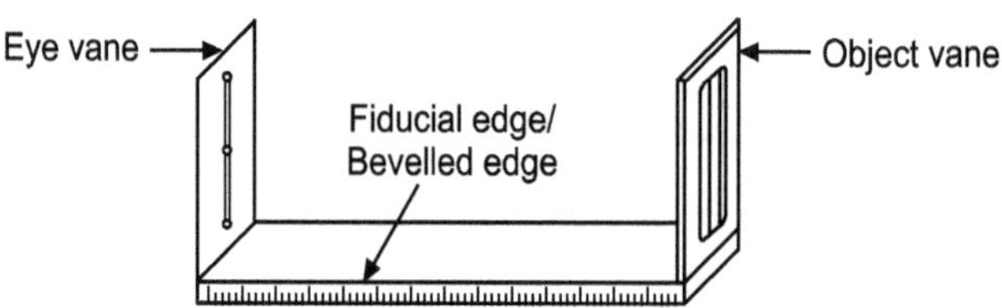

Fig. 5.2 : The Alidade

The ruling edge of alidade is called a *fiducial edge*.

There are two kinds of alidade :

(a) Simple alidade and

(b) Telescopic alidade.

- The simple alidade is fitted with sight vanes at both ends. One of the sight vanes is provided with a central hair.

- In case of telescopic alidade a telescope is attached to it. The edge of the alidade and the axis of the telescope are parallel. In both the alidades, the line of sight is the same vertical plane as the fiducial edge is parallel to it. The fiducial edge is graduated so that it can be used as a scale for plotting. The telescope is provided with a vertical circle, a bubble and also stadia hairs.

(For details of telescopic alidade see appendix.)

5.3 ACCESSORIES TO THE PLANE TABLE

(W - 05, 08, 09, 10; S - 06, 09, 10, 11, 12)

The remaining features of the instrument are :

(i) A *trough compass* or *circular box compass,* for marking North direction on the drawing sheet (Fig. 5.3).

- The trough compass is a rectangular box made of non-magnetic metal containing a magnetic needle provided at the centre.
- The compass consists of a '0' mark at both ends to locate the N-S direction.
- The circular box compass carries a pivoted magnetic needle at the centre.
- The circular box is fitted on a square base plate.
- Sometimes two bubble tubes are fixed at right angles to each other on the base plate.

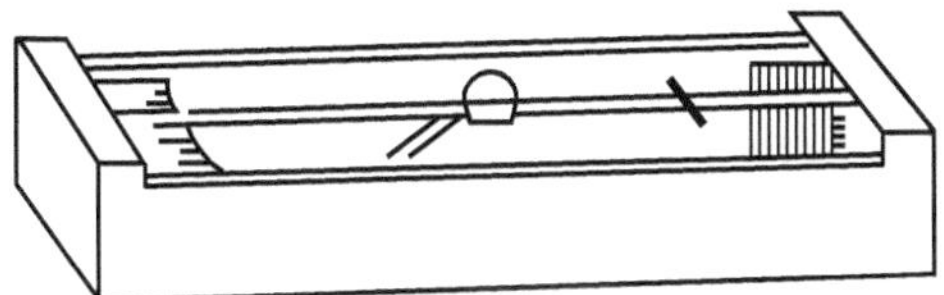

Fig. 5.3 : Trough compass

(ii) A *plumbing* or *U fork* (Fig. 5.4) for centering the table i.e. to indicate when the point on a plan is vertically over the station point on the ground.

- The U-frame consists of a hairpin shaped light metal frame having legs of equal length.
- The lower leg carries a hook in which a plumb-bob is suspended.
- It is used for centering the table.
- It is placed horizontally round the table, so that the extremity of one leg coincides with the point on the paper, while exactly below it, from the extremity of the other leg, is suspended the plumb-bob, which other leg, is suspended the plum-bob, which should coincide with the corresponding point on the ground.   **(S - 08)**

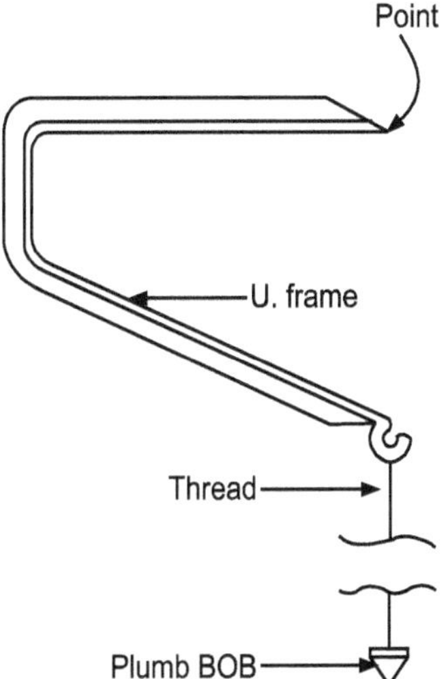

Fig. 5.4 : Plumbing or U-fork

(iii) A *spirit level* (if not fitted to the alidade) may be used for ascertaining if the table is properly levelled.

- The level may be either of the tubular variety or of the circular type, essentially with a flat base so that it can be laid on the table and is truly level when the bubble is central.

- The table is levelled by placing the level on the board in two positions at right angles and getting the bubble central in both positions.

(iv) A *Water-proof cover*, to protect the sheet from rain.

(v) *Drawing paper :* The quality of paper used for plane tabling, should be good.

- It should never be folded or rolled but should be carried flat. Faint coloured drawing paper may be used to reduce the strain on the eyes.

- Zinc or celluloid sheets should be used for plane tabling in damp climates. The paper should be properly stretched on the drawing board by suitable clips or pasting the edges.

- Other drawing materials required : pins, pencil, eraser, scales etc.

5.4 PRINCIPLE OF PLANE TABLE SURVEYING   (S - 09, 12)

- Plane table surveying is based on the principle that lines drawn during plotting always lie parallel to the corresponding lines actually present on the ground if plane table is in properly oriented position.

- The principle of plane table surveying is that the rays drawn from different points should pass through a single point i.e. a position of station point.

- And the position of the table at any station should be the same as that at previous station, i.e., the table should be accurately oriented at all subsequent stations.

5.5 USING THE PLANE TABLE (FIELD WORK)   (S - 05, 06, 11)

While using the plane table the following operations are needed.

(i) Fixing : Fixing the table on the tripod.

(ii) Setting : Setting can be divided into two parts :   (S - 07)

(a) The table should be set-up at a convenient height for working say at about 1 m. The legs of the tripod should be spread well apart, and firmly fixed into the ground.

(b) *Centreing* : The table should be so placed over the station on the ground that the point plotted on the sheet corresponds to the station occupied and it should be exactly over the station on the ground. The operation is known as *centering of the table*. It is done by using a plumbing fork or U frame.   (S-05)

Procedure of Centering :

- Place the pointed end of upper leg of plumbing fork coinciding with the point on drawing paper and suspend a plumb bob from the other leg of it.
- Adjust the table until the plumb bob hangs exactly over the station peg.
- In absence of plumb bob, centreing may be done by dropping a small piece of stone from the point on the underside of the table.
- The degree of accuracy required depends upon the scale of the map. In small scale maps the centreing may be done approximately as the error of 20 to 30 cm would not show on the map. But, in large scale maps, accurate centreing is necessary.
- *(c) Levelling* : The table is levelled by placing the level on the board in two positions at right angles. It is adjusted by leg adjustment till the bubble remains in centre in both the directions. If the table is provided with levelling screws, or ball and socket arrangement the process of levelling is expedited.
- **(iii) Orientation (W - 06, S - 12)** : The system of keeping the table, at each of the successive stations, parallel to the position which it occupied at the first station is called orientation. **(W - 04, 08, 09, 11; S - 05, 06, 08, 09)**

Necessity :

- It is necessary when the table has to be set-up at more than one station. Orientation if properly done, the lines on the paper will be parallel to the respective lines on the ground.
- If orientation is not done, different meridians will be used at each of the successive stations which is incorrect.

  There are two methods of orientation :

  (a) Magnetic meridian method.

  (b) Backsighting method.

(a) Magnetic meridian method :

- The magnetic meridian is drawn at the first station on the paper by trough compass.
- When the table is shifted to the successive station, the trough compass is placed along the above meridian and the board is then turned until the zeros of the needle points the meridian exactly.
- The board is then clamped in position. This method is suitable for rough, small scale plotting. It is not reliable, in areas where local attraction exists.

(b) Backsighting method : **(S - 05, 06, 10; W - 06, 07)**

- Suppose the table is set-up over the station B on the line AB which has been previously marked as 'ab' from the station A. To orient the table at station B the alidade is placed along the line 'ba'. The board is then rotated until the line of sight bisects the ranging rod at A.
- It is then properly clamped without disturbing the centreing. This is most accurate method of orientation and is always preferred.

(iv) Sighting the Objects :

- After setting the table i.e. after centreing, levelling and orientation has been done, the points to be located are sighted through the alidade.
- The following points should be kept in mind while sighting :

    (a) The fiducial edge of the alidade should be centred on the plotted station point.

    (b) The table remains clamped in position while the objects are being sighted.

    (c) The board is turned only for orientation.

    (d) The small letters a, b, c, denote the points plotted on the paper to represent points A, B, C etc. on the ground respectively.

5.6 METHODS OF PLANE TABLING   (W - 05, 08, 11; S - 08, 11)

There are four methods of surveying with the plane table :

1. Radiation   2. Intersection

3. Traversing and 4. Resection

5.6.1 Radiation   (W - 04, 09; S - 05, 09, 12)

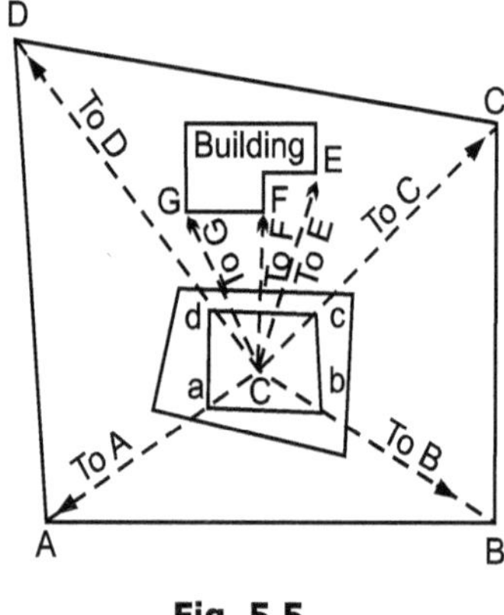

Fig. 5.5

Procedure :

1. Select an instrument station O from which all the points to be surveyed are visible.

2. Set-up and level the table and clamp it.

3. Select a point O, on the sheet to represent the instrument station.

4. With alidade touching, O, sight the various points A, B, C etc. to be located, drawing radial lines towards them.

5. Measure the distances OA, OB, OC etc. and plot them to some scale, and join the points a, b, so obtained.

Note :

- The method is suitable for survey of small areas which can be commanded from a single station.
- This method is employed chiefly in combination with some other methods otherwise its use would be restricted to a comparatively small area i.e. ground which can be covered from a single set-up.

5.6.2 Intersection   (S - 03, 07, 09, 12; W - 03, 05)

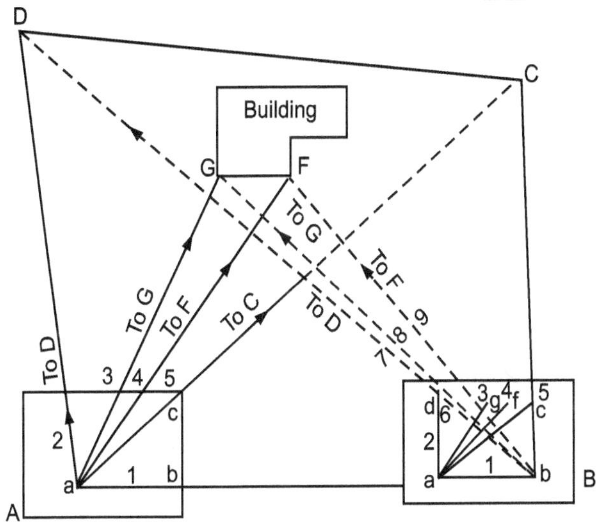

Fig. 5.6

This method is largely used for :

(i)   Mapping details.

(ii) For locating the distant and inaccessible points, broken boundaries, banks of rivers, edges of woods, and for plotting the positions of points to be used subsequently as the instrument stations. The only linear measurement required is that of a base line. The ease with which points may be located by intersection is the greatest advantage of this method.

Procedure :

1. Lay out a base line AB and measure it.

2. Plot the distance 'ab' on the sheet using convenient scale.

3. Set-up the instrument at A with 'a' over A.

4. Orient the table by placing alidade along 'ab' and turn the table, until the ranging rod at B is bisected, clamp the table.

5. With the alidade touching point 'a' draw rays 1, 2, 3, 4 and 5 of indefinite length as shown in the figure.

6. The table is then moved to station B, oriented it by backsighting on A i.e. keeping the alidade along 'ba' until ranging rod at A is bisected. Through 'b' draw rays towards the point previously sighted i.e. line 6, 7, 8 and 9 are drawn to determine the points on intersection d, g, f and c.

5.6.3 Traversing

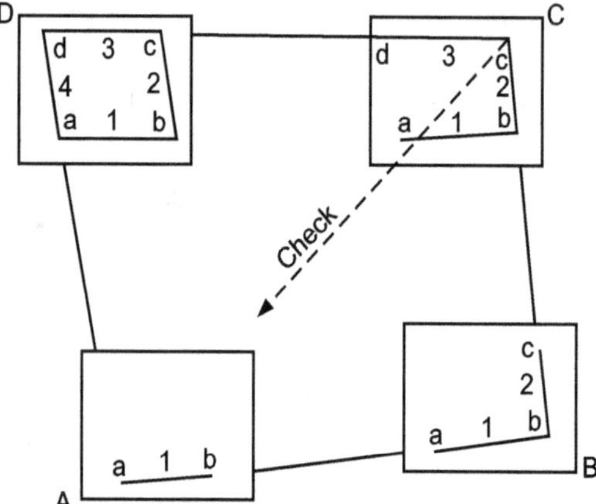

Fig. 5.7 : Traversing Chosen at the Bends

- In this method, the plane table is moved from one station to another. After setting-up over one station, it is necessary to orient the table.

- It is used for running survey lines between the stations previously fixed by theodolite or other methods, to locate the topographical details and also for survey of roads, rivers etc. the stations being chosen at the bends.

Procedure :

Suppose it is required to plot boundary lines ABCD :

1. Set-up the plane table at A. Choose a corresponding point 'a' on the sheet. Centre and level the table carefully.

2. Mark the direction of magnetic meridian on the sheet, and draw ray 'ab' with the alidade bisecting the ranging rod at B.

3. Measure the distance AB with the chain or tape and lay it off to scale on the ray drawn towards B, thus fixing the position of 'b' on the sheet.

4. Locate the surrounding details by radiation or by offsets taken by usual method, and distant objects by intersection.

5. Shift the table and set-up at B, orient it by mangnetic meridian or by backsighting on A with the alidade along 'ba' and then clamp the table.

6. With the alidade touching 'b', sight the station C and draw a ray.

7. Measure the distance BC and lay it off to scale on the ray drawn towards C to fix the point 'c' on the sheet. The nearby details are located as usual.

8. Proceed in this manner untill all the remaining stations, in each case orienting the table before taking the foresight.

Note :

1. This method requires all stations to be visible.

2. The transversing work can be checked by taking sights to two or more preceeding stations visible from the station occupied. If no station is visible any well-defined points such as corner of building, gate etc. may be sighted.

3. In case of a closed traverse, the work can be checked by plotting the starting point from the last station of the traverse finding the error of closure. The error may be adjusted graphically as in compass traversing.

5.6.4 Resection

- This method is a modification of intersection. The chief characteristic is that point determined by the intersecting line is the station occupied by the plane table.

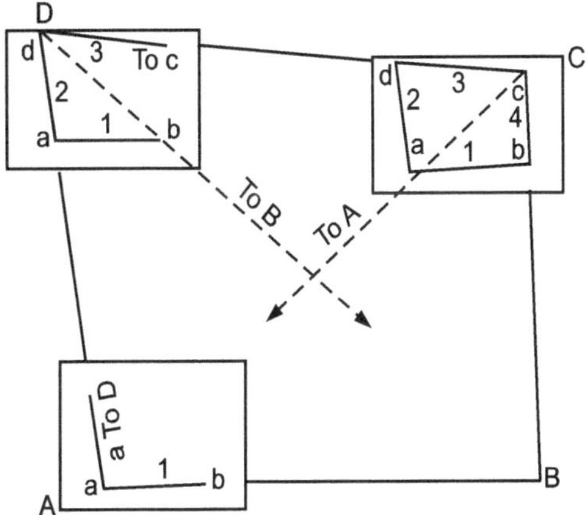

Fig. 5.8 : Resection

- This means that a plane table can be set-up anywhere and the corresponding point on the map can be found by resection, provided these points already plotted are visible from the plane table station.

- This method requires one linear measurement of a base line.

Procedure :

1. Set-up the plane table at A and centre it so that a is over A.

2. Bisect the ranging rod at B, measure AB and lay-off ab to the scale adopted and draw a ray 2 towards point D.

3. Set-up the table at D, with the estimated position of d over D and orient by backsighting on A.

4. Place the alidade against b, and sight B where the edge of alidade cuts (resects) the line 2 will be the point d.

5. From d draw a ray towards C, set-up at C with the estimated position of c over C and orient by backsighting on D.

6. Place the alidade against b and sight B, obtain the intersection c, check C by sighting A with the alidade touching a.

Note :

1. This method is also called a *back ray method* as it is necessary to draw a ray from the preceeding station to the station to be occupied by the plane table. Errors of centreing are inevitable but once resection is usually used for small scale work, it will not affect the accuracy of the work.

2. Avoid too oblique intersections.

3. Details are best located by radiation or intersection. The well-known three point problem and the two point problem are problems in resection.

5.7 SUITABLITY OF DIFFERENT METHODS 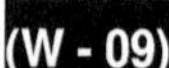

1. **Radiation :** It is suitable for the survey of small area which can be commanded from a single station. It is accurate but slow and requires linear measurements to be taken to every object. It is used in combination with other methods.

2. **Intersection :** This method requires no linear measurements except that of base line. It is useful for locating inaccessible points, broken boundaries, rivers and instrument stations which can be used in the future. It is also used for checking objects.

3. **Traversing :** This method requires every station to be accessible. It is used for locating stations, running survey lines between them. The method is suitable for survey of roads, rivers etc.

4. **Resection :** It is used for locating instrument station. It requires some liner measurements. Two point and three point problems are important case of resection.

5.8 FIELD PARTY

- The field party comprises of one surveyor with two men to perform chaining, marking of stations etc.

- The number of men required depends on the nature of ground and the method adopted.

- In large survey work experienced persons as assistant to the surveyor may be employed to expedite the work.

Equipment : The equipment to be carried depends upon the nature and magnitude of survey work.

It mainly consists of

(a) Plane table, tripod, alldade, drawing sheet.

(b) Spirit level, trough compass, U fork, plumb bob, water-proof cover, field glass, ranging rods and flags.

(c) Scales, one or two set squares, pencils, rubber, sand paper, small note book.

(d) In addition.

For tacheometry-staff and stadia reduction tables for traversing etc., chain or band and tape.

5.9 VERTICAL CONTROL

- The plane table surveying is widely used in the preparation of contour maps on account of the great advantage that the Surveyor (Topographer) has the terrain in view while plotting it in the field.

- The vertical control is effected.

   1. With telescopic alidade.

   2. With plain alidade and level. The plain alidade can be used for horizontal control only. The elevations are determined by ordinary level, hand level or tangent clinometer.

- In the field work of plane tabling the horizontal and vertical control depend on the following factors.

   (a) Scale of plotting.

   (b) Degree of accuracy required.

   (d) Character of ground.

   (e) Time available for the work.

5.10 GENERAL SUGGESTIONS FOR PLOTTING

1. The pencil used should be hard and sharpened. The lines must be drawn as fine as possible.

2. Draw all lines close to the straight edge.

3. Unnecessary complication of rays should be avoided.

4. Erase unwanted rays and reference points with soft rubber.

5. The drawing sheet should be kept as clean as possible.

5.11 ERRORS IN PLANETABLING　　　　(W - 04, S - 06, 08, 11)

The sources of errors in plane tabling may be classified as :

1. Instrumental errors.

2. Errors of manipulation and sighting.

3. Errors of plotting.

(1) Instrumental Errors :

(i)　The surface of the plane table not being perfectly levelled and even.

(ii)　The working edge of the alidade not being straight.

(iii)　The fitting of the table and tripod may be loose.

(iv) Defective trough compass which affects the orientation.

(v) Sight vanes of alidade not being perpendicular to the base of ruler.

(vi) Line of sight not being exactly over the ruling edge.

(2) Errors of Manipulation and Sighting :

Errors of manipulation and sighting may be due to :

 (i) The board not being horizontal - This error affects chiefly the measurement of vertical angles.

(ii) The table not being accurately centred. The plotted position of the occupied station not being exactly over the station on the ground.

(iii) The table not being correctly oriented. To prevent this error, the orientation of the table should be checked at as many stations as possible by backsighting or by magnetic meridian.

(iv) The table being displaced from its initial position. There is likely to be slight rotation or other displacement of the table. Frequent check-sights should be taken to detect and correct any displacement.

(v) The defective sighting - The objects not being correctly sighted. The resulting errors, however, will tend to compensate and are relatively unimportant.

(3) Errors of Plotting :

These include

(i)   Drawing too thick lines and drawing a line which does not coincide with the edge of the alidade or not parallel to it.

(ii) Careless pricking of points of intersection.

(iii) Mistakes in laying-off distances to scale. Such errors can only be minimised by constant care in drawing and in use of scales.

(iv) Errors due to contraction and expansion of drawing paper. It can be eliminated by using good quality paper.

5.12 TESTING AND ADJUSTING THE PLANE TABLE　　(S - 07)

The Board :

1. The upper surface of the board should be perfectly plane.

Test : Apply the fiducial edge of alidade in several directions.

Adjustment : If the surface is not perfectly plane, remove high spots by planning or sand papering.

2. The upper surface of the board should be perpendicular to the vertical axis of the instrument.

Test : Place the spirit level on table and centre the bubble. Turn the table through 180°. Place the level at 90° to its original position and repeat. If the bubble remains central in both the directions the adjustment is correct.

Adjustment : If not, correct half the apparent error by inserting a packing between underside of the board and its support. Repeat the test until correct.

The Alidade :

1. The fiducial edge of the alidade should be a straight line.

Test : Draw a fine line along its edge. Reverse the alidade end for end and place it against the ends of the line. If the two lines coincide, the edge of the alidade is true or straight.

Adjustment : If not, make the edge true by repeated rubbing (filing) and testing.

2. The axes of the spirit level mounted on the alidade should be parallel to the base of the alidade.

Test : Place the alidade (in this case it is a telescopic alidade fitted with spirit level) on the table and bring the bubble to the centre of its run by the levelling screws of the table.

Draw a line against the edge of the alidade. Lift and reverse the alidade end for end and replace it against the above line. If the bubble remains central the adjustment is correct.

Adjustment : If not, eliminate half the error by means of the level tube adjusting screws and remaining half by the levelling screws. The second level tube may be examined and adjusted in the same way.

3. The sight vanes of the alidade should be perpendicular to the base of the rules.

Test : Level the table (suspend a plumb line in front of the instrument). Observe whether the sighting slit and horse hair appear parallel to the plumb line.

Adjustment : If not, adjust by filing or packing the base of sights.

The Telescope :

In case of telescopic alidade, the essential requirements are :

1. The line of collimation should be perpendicular to the horizontal axis of the telescope.

2. The horizontal axis should be parallel to the base of the alidade ruler.

3. The axis of telescope level should be parallel to the line of sights.

4. The fiducial edge of the alidade should be coincident with or parallel to the plane of collimation.

5. The vertical circle should read zero when the line of sight is horizontal.

5.13 ADVANTAGES AND DISADVANTAGES OF PLANE TABLING

(S-05, 06, 07, 12)

Advantages : (W - 08, 09; S - 09, 10)

1. It is most rapid and suitable for small scale maps.
2. Since the map is plotted in the field, there is no danger of omitting necessary measurements.
3. The Surveyor can compare the plotted work with the actual features of the area.
4. Booking is seldom required and hence, there are no chances of committing mistakes in booking.
5. It is most suitable for the localities where the compass survey is unreliable due to local attraction.
6. No greater skill is required to prepare satisfactory map.
7. Errors of measurement and plotting can be readily detected by check-lines.
8. Contours and irregular objects may be represented accurately since the tract is in view.
9. It is less costly.
10. The office work consists of only finishing of drawings. Disadvantages :

Disadvantages : (S - 03, 04, 05)

1. The plane table is essentially a tropical instrument. It is unsuitable for work in wet climate and is awkward in high wind.
2. It is inferior to the compass in densely wooded country and is only suitable in open country.
3. In absence of the field notes, it is inconvenient to replot the survey to different scale and to compute the quantities.
4. It is not intended for greater accuracy.
5. The instrument is heavy and cumbersome. It is awkward to carry.
6. Number of accessories are to be carried and being loose may get lost.
7. Plotting becomes difficult in bright sun due to the strain on eyes.

Important Points

- Plane tabling is a special method of surveying in which the field work and plotting are carried out simultaneously.

Principle of plane table surveying :

- Plane table surveying is based on the principle that lines drawn during plotting always lie parallel to the corresponding lines actually present on the ground if plane table is in properly oriented position.

- **Accessories to the plane table**
  1. A *trough compass* or *circular box compass*, for marking North direction on the drawing sheet
  2. A *plumbing* or *U fork* for centering the table i.e. to indicate when the point on a plan is vertically over the station point on the ground.
  3. A *spirit level* may be used for ascertaining if the table is properly levelled
  4. ***The alidade*** : It is made of brass or gunmetal or it is simply a straight edge carrying a line of sight. The alidade is used for sighting the objects to be located.
  5. A *Water-proof cover*, to protect the sheet from rain.
  6. *Drawing paper :* The quality of paper used for plane tabling, should be good. It should never be folded or rolled but should be carried flat.
- **Orientation :** The system of keeping the table, at each of the successive stations, parallel to the position which it occupied at the first station is called orientation.
- There are two methods of orientation :

  (a) Magnetic meridian method.

  (b) Backsighting method.
- There are four methods of surveying with the plane table :
  1. Radiation
  2. Intersection
  3. Traversing and
  4. Resection

1. **Radiation :** It is suitable for the survey of small area which can be commanded from a single station. It is accurate but slow and requires linear measurements to be taken to every object. It is used in combination with other methods.

2. **Intersection :** This method requires no linear measurements except that of base line. It is useful for locating inaccessible points, broken boundaries, rivers and instrument stations which can be used in the future. It is also used for checking objects.

3. **Traversing :** This method requires every station to be accessible. It is used for locating stations, running survey lines between them. The method is suitable for survey of roads, rivers etc.

4. **Resection :** It is used for locating instrument station. It requires some liner measurements. Two point and three point problems are important case of resection.

Practice Questions

1. What is plane table ? What is meant by plane tabling ? Under what circumstances you would recommend it ? **(W - 09)**

2. Explain the principle of plane table surveying and describe the temporary adjustments of a plane table.

3. Describe concisely the components of a plane table out fit.

4. State the advantages and disadvantages of plane table surveying over chain and compass surveying ?

5. What are the methods of plane tabling ? Describe each of them with neat sketches.

6. Which method of plane tabling you will select for locating the distance and inaccessible objects ? Explain it.

7. What do you understand by orientation ? What are the different methods of orientation ? Discuss the relative merits and demerits of each.

8. State the importance of orientation in plane table surveying.

9. Describe the traversing method of plane tabling.

10. Describe the intersection method of plane tabling.   **(S - 09)**

11. What precautions must a surveyor take to maximize accuracy of field work in plane table surveying ?

12. Enlist the sources of errors in plane tabling. How are they eliminated ?

13. A map of a polytechnic campus is required to be drawn by conducting a plane table survey using methods of radiation, intersection and traversing. Explain the procedure with reference to the following points :
    (i)   Field party,
    (ii) Equipment required,
    (iii) Running a traverse assuming imaginary campus.

14. Write explanatory notes on :
    (a) Plane table and its accessories.
    (b) Orientation by backsighting method.
    (c) Testing and adjusting the plane table.
    (d) Essential requirements of telescope alidade.

MSBTE Questions & Answers

Summer 2009

1. What is the principle of plane tabling ?

Ans. Refer to Page No. 1.3.

2. What is orientation ? State the methods of orientation and explain any one of the method.

Ans. Refer to Page No. 1.4.

3. Discuss the merits and demerits of plane table surveying.

Ans. Refer to Page No. 1.12.

4. Explain intersection method of plane table surveying.

Ans. Refer to Page No. 1.6.

5. Enlist the accessories with their functions, used in plane table survey.

Ans. Refer to Page No. 1.2.

6. Explain radiation method of plane table survey with sketch.

Ans. Refer to Page No. 1.5.

Winter 2009

1. State the situations where plane table is suitable.

Ans. Refer to Page No. 1.9.

2. State accessories required for plane table survey along with their use.

Ans. Refer to Page No. 1.2.

3. What is meant by orientation of plane table ? State its method. Which method is the best ? Why ?

Ans. Refer to Page No. 1.4.

4. State advantages of plane table survey.

Ans. Refer to Page No. 1.12.

5. Explain the radiation method of plane table with neat sketch.

Ans. Refer to Page No. 1.5.

6. State the disadvantages of plane table survey.

Ans. Refer to Page No. 1.12.

Summer 2010

1. Enlist : Accessories in plane table surveying.

Ans. Refer to Page No. 1.2.

2. Explain orientation by method of Back sighting.

Ans. Refer to Page No. 1.5.

3. What are the advantages and disadvantages of plane table survey.

Ans. Refer to Page No. 1.12.

4. Explain 'Traversing' method of plane Table Surveying.

Ans. Refer to Page No. 1.7.

Summer 2011

1. Enlist the accessories of plane table.

Ans. Refer to Page No. 1.2.

2. Describe the method of orientation by backsighting of plane table with a neat sketch.

Ans. Refer to Page No. 1.4.

3. Explain the method of traversing of plane table surveying with sketch.

Ans. Refer to Page No. 1.7.

4. What are the errors that may occur in plane tabling ?

Ans. Refer to Page No. 1.10.

5. Explain in brief radiation method of plane tabling and state its advantages over other methods.

Ans. Refer to Page No. 1.5.

Winter 2011

1. What is the principle of plane table survey ?

Ans. Refer to Page No. 1.1.

2. Define orientation and explain any one method of orientation in detail.

Ans. Refer to Page No. 1.4.

3. Explain the intersection method of plane tabling.

Ans. Refer to Page No. 1.5.

Summer 2012

1. State the principle of plane table survey.

Ans. Refer Page No. 1.3.

2. State the procedure of radiation method with neat sketch.

Ans. Refer Page No. 1.5.

3. State any four accessories of plane table with their use.

Ans. Refer Page No. 1.2.

4. State any four advantages and four disadvantages of plane table survey.

Ans. Refer Page No. 1.12.

5. State the procedure of intersection method of plane tabling with neat sketch.

Ans. Refer Page No. 1.6.

6. What is meant by orientation of plane table ? Explain any one method of it.

Ans. Refer Page No. 1.4.

6...

Levelling

Contents

6.1 LEVELLING

- Levelling is 'an art of determining relative heights or elevations of different points on the earth's surface so that the same may be represented on a plan or map'. It is essentially a process dealing with the measurements in vertical plane.

Principle of Levelling :

- The principle of levelling is to obtain a horizontal line of sight with respect to which vertical distances of the points above or below this line are found.

The Object of Levelling :

Following are the objects of levelling

(i)   To find the elevations of given points with respect to some assumed reference line called Datum.

(ii) To establish points at required elevation with respect to datum.

Necessity of Levelling :

(i)   Levelling is an operation of prime importance to the engineer.

(ii) Levelling is used for acquiring data for the design of all classes of works such as roads, canals, railways, dams, bridges, buildings, water-supply and sanitary schemes etc.

(iii) Levelling is also necessary for setting out grades for sewers, roads, railways track and pipelines and the estimation of reservoir capacities.

Important Terms in levelling :

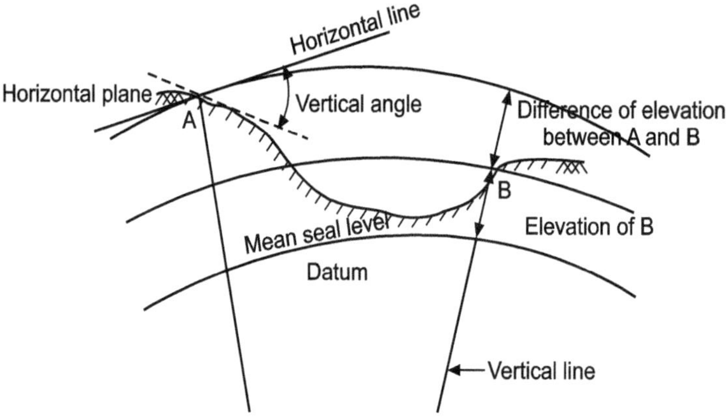

Fig. 6.1 : Terms used in Levelling

6.2 DEFINITIONS OR MEANINGS OF TERMS USED IN LEVELLING

(1) **Level surface (W-07, 09, 10) :** It is a surface parallel to the mean spheroidal surface of the earth. It is normal to the direction of plumb line at all points. Owing to the form of the earth, a level surface is not a plane but of irregular form. The surface of still water is an example of level surface.

(2) Level line (W-07, S-12) : It is a line lying in a level surface. It is, therefore, normal to the plumb line at all points.

(3) Horizontal plane or surface (W-09) : Horizontal plane through a point is a plane tangential to the level surface at that point. It is, therefore, perpendicular to the plumb line.

(4) Horizontal line (W-09, S-12) : It is a straight line tangential to the level line at a point. It is also perpendicular to the plumb line.

(5) Datum surface or line (W-06, 08, 10) : It is an arbitrary level surface (line) from which elevations of points may be referred. In India, mean sea level at Karachi is considered as datum of elevation zero. Vertical distances (elevations) of the points are measured with respect to this datum.

(6) Mean sea level (W-09) : Mean sea level is the average height of the sea for all the stages of tides. It is derived by averaging the hourly tide heights over a long period of 19 years at a place.

(7) Elevation or Reduced level : It is the height or depth of any point above or below any datum. It is known as reduced level (R.L.) or elevations of a point.

6.3 BENCH MARKS   (S-08, 09; W-08, 10; S-11, W-11, S-12)

Bench mark (B.M.) : It is a fixed reference point of known or assumed elevation. It is used either as a starting point for levelling or as a check while closing.

There are four kinds of bench marks.

(i)   Great Trigonometrical Survey (G. T. S.) bench mark

(ii)   Permanent bench mark.

(iii) Arbitrary bench mark.

(iv) Temporary bench mark.

(i) G.T.S. Bench Marks (S-12) :

- These are the bench marks established with very high precision at regular intervals by the survey of India Department all over the country.

- Their positions and bench mark values (R.L.s) with respect to the mean sea level at Karachi are given in catalogue formed by the department. They are also known as G.T.S. maps.

(ii) Permanent Bench Marks :

- Permanent bench marks are fixed in between the G.T.S. bench marks by the government such as PWD and/or CPWD.

- The bench marks are fixed on permanent objects such as culvert, parapet wall of a bridge, plinth of a building, a gate pillar, a kilometre stone etc.

- Their values are clearly written and their positions are recorded on the top of respective object for future reference.

(iii) Arbitrary Bench Marks :

- These are used in small levelling work or practices.

- Their elevations do not refer to any fixed datam when there is no any permanent bench mark nearby the place of survey.

- These are used when elevation difference is important rather than elevation. Such a B.M. may be assumed as 100.000 or 50.000 m etc.

(iv) Temporary Bench Marks :

- They are the reference points established during the levelling operations when there is a break in work, or at the end of day's work or to leave some check points.

- The values of reduced levels are marked on some permanent objects such as guard stones, boundary stones, at the roots of trees or on curb of well etc.

- The levelling work when resumed is continued from such points.

6.4 INSTRUMENTS FOR LEVELLING

The following instruments are essentially required for levelling :

1. Level, 2. Levelling staff.

Other equipments required are chain, tape, pegs, ranging rods, level field book etc.

(1) Level : The instrument used to furnish horizontal line of sight for observing staff readings by means of which the elevations (R.L.s) of the points are determined.

A level essentially consists of the following parts :

(i)   Levelling head - to bring the bubble in its centre of run.

(ii)   The limb - to support the telescope.

(iii)   Telescope - to provide line of sight.

(iv)   Level or bubble tube - to make the line of sight horizontal.

(v)   Tripod stand - to support the instrument.

6.5 TYPES OF LEVELS   (S-11, S-12)

There are various types of levels viz.

1. Dumpy level   4. The cushing's level

2. Wye level   5. Tilting level (Modern tilting or I.O.P. Level)

3. Cooke's reversible level 6. Automatic levels.

The two types of levels viz. (i) dumpy levels and (ii) tilting levels are commonly used in Civil Engineering practice. Automatic level or self aligning level is a recent development.

The scope of the syllabus is limited to the study of dumpy level and auto level.

6.6 DUMPY LEVEL

- The dumpy level is simple, compact and stable instrument consists of levelling lead and telescope.

- The levelling head consists of two parallel plates with three foot screws, which bring the instrument in a proper level by bringing the bubble in its center of its run.

- The telescope is rigidly fixed to its supports. Hence, it cannot be rotated about its longitudinal axis or cannot be removed from its supports.

- The telescope consists of a movable eye piece and an object glass.

- There is a diaphragm consisting a circular glass with cross-wires fixed infront of the eye piece. Before observing, cross-wires of diaphragm are made clear and distinct by rotating eye piece clockwise or anti-clockwise.

- The name dumpy is because of its compact and stable construction.

- The axis of telescope is perpendicular to the vertical axis of the level.

- The level tube is permanently placed so that its axis lies in the same vertical plane of telescope but it is adjustable by means of capstan headed nuts at one end.

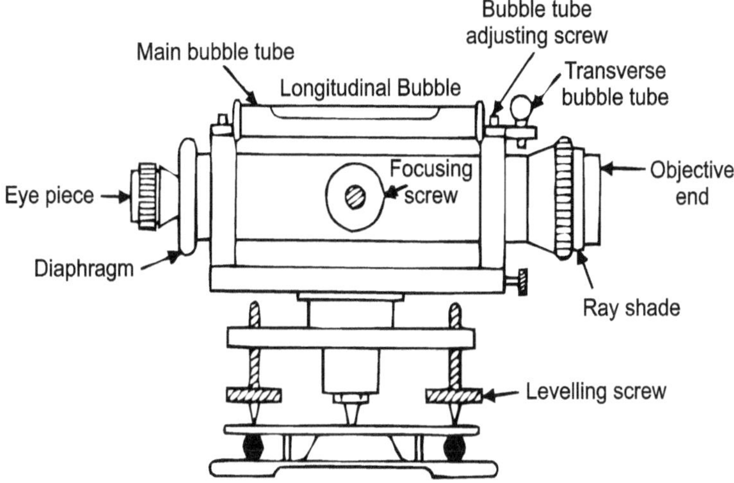

Fig. 6.2 : Dumpy level

1. Levelling head	2. Telescope
3. Eye piece	4. Diaphragm
5. Focussing screw	6. Ray shade
7. Bubble tube	8. Capstan headed nut
9. Cross bubble tube	10. Level compass

- There is a focussing screw provided on the telescope. It makes the images of the object clear and distinct. It can also helps to bring image in the plane of the cross-hairs.
- A ray shade is provided to protect the object glass.
- A clamp and slow motion screw are provided in modern levels to control the movement of spindle, about the vertical axis.
- The telescope has a magnifying power of about thirty diameters.
- The level tube is graduated to 2 mm divisions and it has normally a sensitiveness of 20 seconds of arc per graduation.
- The telescope may be internal focussing or external type.

Objectives of Dumpy Level :

(1) To obtain the level difference between two respective points.

(2) To find the reduced level of points with respective to mean sea level.

(3) To obtain the R.L. with respect to arbitrary bench mark.

6.6.1 Important Terms Related to Dumpy Level

(i) **Axis of Telescope** (W-07) **:** It is a line joining the optical centre of the object of glass to the centre of eye piece.

(ii) **Line of collimation** (W-07, 08, S-11) **:** It is a line joining the intersection of the cross hairs of diaphragm to the optical centre of the object glass and its continuation. It is also known as *line of sight.* The RL of line of collimation is called as height of instrument.

(iii) **Axis of bubble tube :** An imaginary line tangential to the longitudinal curve of the bubble tube at its middle point is known as axis of bubble tube. It is horizontal when the bubble is in centre of its run.

(iv) **Vertical axis :** It is the axis about which the telescope of level rotates in horizontal plane.

6.6.2 Desired Relations in the Axes of Dumpy Level

For a dumpy level in perfect adjustment, the following relations should exist.

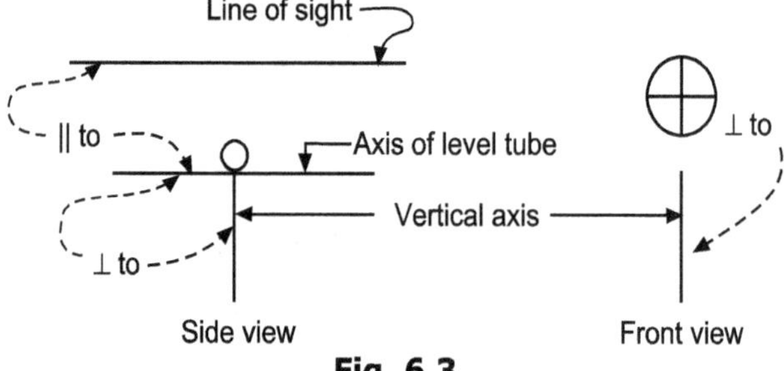

Fig. 6.3

(1) The axis of the level tube should be perpendicular to the vertical axis.

(2) The line of collimation should be parallel to the axis of the bubble (level) tube.

(3) Axis of telescope and line of collimation should coincide.

6.7 ADJUSTMENT OF THE DUMPY LEVEL

The level needs two types of adjustments :

1. Temporary adjustments and

2. Permanent adjustments.

The permanent adjustment will be described later.

6.7.1 Temporary Adjustments of Dumpy Level　(S-08, 09; W-08, 10)

These adjustments are performed at each set-up of the level before taking any observation.

(a) Setting-up of the level.

(b) Levelling of the level.

(c) Focussing the eye piece.

(d) Focusing the object glass to remove the parallax.

(a) Setting-up the level : This includes (1) fixing the instrument on tripod and (2) levelling the instrument approximately by leg adjustment.

Procedure :

(i) **Fixing the instrument on the tripod :** The tripod legs are well spread on the ground with tripod head nearly level and at convenient height. Fix-up the level on the tripod.

(ii) **Leg adjustments :** Bring all the foot screws of the level in the centre of their run. Fix any two legs firmly into the ground by pressing them with hand and move the third leg to the right or left until the main bubble is roughly in the centre. Finally the leg is fixed after centering approximately both bubbles. This operation will save the time required for levelling.

(b) Levelling : Levelling is done with the help of foot screws and bubbles. The purpose of levelling is to make the vertical axis truly vertical. The method of levelling the instrument depends upon whether there are three foot screws or four foot screws. In all modern instruments three foot screws are provided and this method only is described.

Procedure :

(i) Place the telescope parallel to a pair of foot screws.

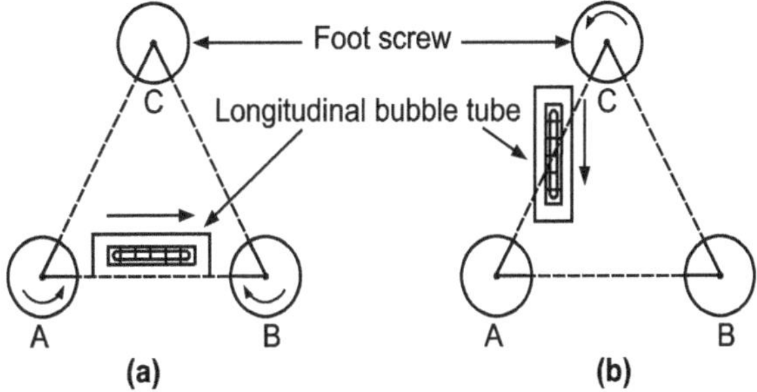

Fig. 6.4 : Levelling-up With Three Foot Screws

(ii)　Hold these two foot screws between the thumb and first finger of each hand and turn them uniformly so that the thumbs move either towards each other or away from each other until the bubble is in centre.

NOTE : The bubble will move in the direction of movement of the left thumb.

(iii)　Turn the telescope through 90° so that it lies over the third foot screw.

(iv)　Turn this foot screw only until the bubble is centred.

(v)　Bring the telescope back to its original position without reversing the eye piece and object glass ends.

(vi)　Again bring the bubble to the centre of its run and repeat these operations until the bubble remains in the centre of its run in both positions which are at right angle to each other.

(vii)　Now, rotate the instrument through 360° in any position, the bubble should remain in centre provided the instrument is in accurate levelling and the telescope is now ready for further work.

Note that, if the bubble do not remain in the centre even after repetition of procedure the instrument needs ready permanent adjustment.

(c) Focussing the eye piece : To focus the eye piece, hold a white paper in front of the object glass, and move the eye piece in or out till the cross hairs are distinctly seen. Care should be taken that the eye piece is not wholly taken out. Sometimes graduations are provided at the eye piece and that one can always remember the particular graduation position to suit his eyes. This will save much time of focussing the eye piece.

(d) Focussing the object glass : Direct the telescope to the levelling staff and on looking through the telescope, turn the focussing screw until the image appears clear and sharp. The image is thus formed inside the plane of cross hairs. Parallax, if any is removed by exact focussing. It may be noted that parallax is completely eliminated when there is no change in staff reading after moving the eye up and down.

NOTE : Centering is not done in levelling as we are interested in the measurement in the vertical plane only.

6.7.2 Permanent Adjustments of Level

The purpose of the permanent adjustment is to establish the fixed relationships between the fundamental lines or fundamental axes.

6.8 THE FUNDAMENTAL AXES OF THE INSTRUMENT　(S-09, W-10)

There are four principal axis of a dumpy level.

(i)　The vertical axis.

(ii)　The axis of the bubble tube (level tube).

(iii)　The line of collimation.

(iv)　The axis of the telescope.

6.9 PERMANENT ADJUSTMENT OF DUMPY LEVEL　(S-11, W-11)

The parts requiring adjustments are (i) Level tube and (ii) Cross hairs. Basis for adjustments is the vertical axis.

I.　To make the Axis of level tube perpendicular to the vertical axis.

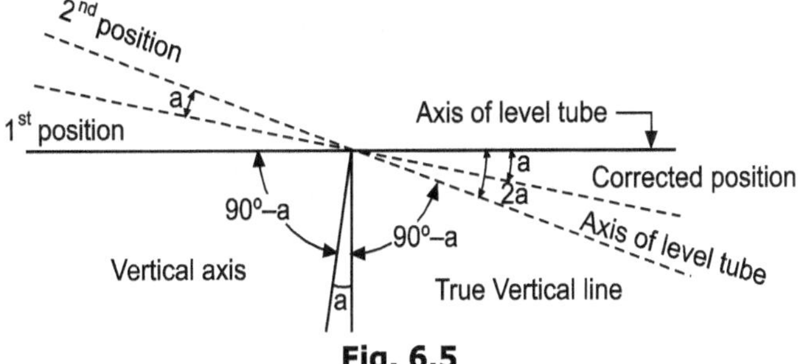

Fig. 6.5

Necessity : This adjustment is made for convenience only.

Test :

(1)　Set-up the level on firm ground and level it carefully in the usual way.

　　The bubble will now be central in two positions at right angles to each other one parallel to the pair of foot screws and the other over the third foot screw.

(2)　Bring the telescope over the third foot screw or a pair of foot screws and turn it through 180° in azimuth. If the bubble remains in centre, the adjustment is correct.

Adjustment :

(1)　If the bubble does not remain in centre, measure the deviation, say 2 divisions.

(2)　Bring the bubble halfway back (1 division) by raising or lowering one end of the tube by means of adjusting nuts and the remaining half with the foot screw beneath the telescope or pair of foot screws.

(3)　Rotate the telescope and see if the bubble remains in centre, if not repeat the above process until correct.

Note : The apparent error of deviation is twice the actual error, hence the actual error is half the deviation (1 division) of the bubble.

II.　To make the line of collimation parallel to the axis of the level tube.

Necessity : This condition is very important. It is the basis of spirit levelling. If this relation is established the line of collimation becomes horizontal when the bubble is centred.

Test : Two peg method is used to verify the relationship.

Procedure (The two peg method) :

(1)　Fix two pegs A and B at a distance D = 60 to 100 m apart third peg at O exactly midway between A and B.

(2) Set-up the level at O and level it accurately. Take staff readings on A and on B, with the bubble in centre. For each staff reading the bubble should be brought to the centre if necessary, let the readings be a and b respectively.

(3) Transfer the level and set it up over O_1, d metres away from A or B as shown in the Fig 6.7.

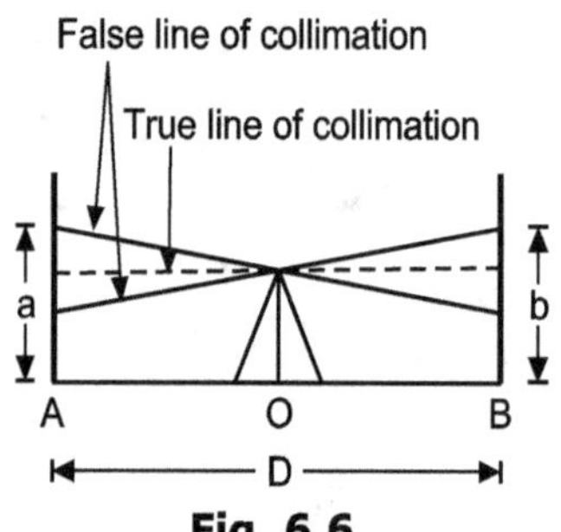

Fig. 6.6

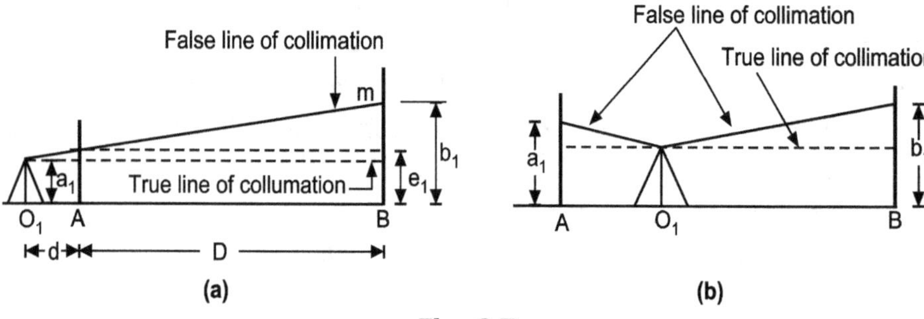

Fig. 6.7

(4) With the bubble exactly centered, take readings again on staff held vertically at A and B. Let these readings be a_1 and b_1 respectively.

(5) Find the difference of a and b (a ~ b) gives the true difference between the level of A and B. $(a_1 - b_1)$ gives the apparent difference between the level of A and B. If (a b) = (a_1 ~ b_1), the line of collimation is in adjustment, if not, it is inclined.

Adjustment : The adjustment is made on diaphragm, with adjusting screws.

(1) See whether the true difference is a rise or fall.

(2) Add the true difference to the reading on the peg A near the instrument, if it is fall from A to B or vice versa. Let the reading be e_1 . e_1 and b_1 is compared.

(3) If b_1 is greater than e_1 the line of collimation is inclined upwards. And if is less than e_1 it is inclined downwards.

(4) (b_1 ~ e_1) = Collimation error in distance D.

(5) Find the correction to be applied to the reading on A and B, using the following equations.

Correction to the reading on far peg (B)

$$c_1 = \frac{D+d}{D} (b_1 - e_1) \qquad \qquad \text{... (1)}$$

and for near peg (A)

$$c_2 = \frac{d}{D}(b_1 - e_1) \qquad \ldots (2)$$

The corrections are +ve or –ve according as the line of collimation is inclined downward or upwards.

The correct reading on the peg (B) = $b_1 \pm c_1$

The correct reading on the peg (A) = $a_1 \pm c_2$

(6) The adjustment is made on far peg and checked on near peg. Looking through the telescope, observe the correct reading on the far peg.

Adjust the horizontal hair of diaphragm to the correct reading by means of diaphragm adjustment screws, loosening one and tightening the other. To increase the staff reading, loosen the upper screw of diaphragm and tighten the lower and vice versa. The diaphragm moves towards the screw tightened.

6.10 ALTERNATIVE METHOD OF ADJUSTING THE LINE OF COLLIMATION

1. The level is set-up exactly midway between the points A and B.

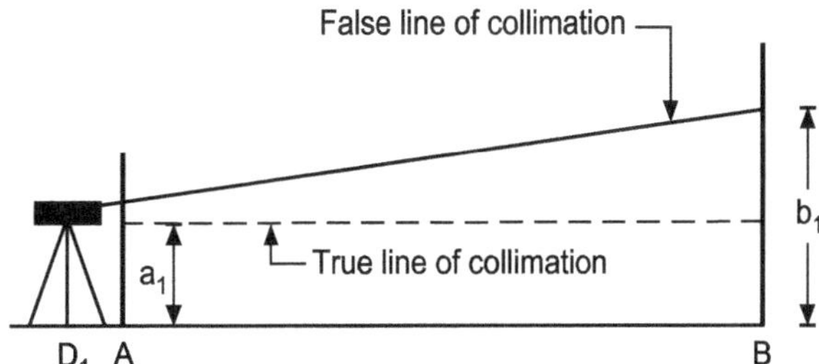

Fig. 6.8

2. With the bubbles in centre of its run, take readings on staff held vertically at A and B.

3. Find the true difference in elevation (a ~ b) between A and B. If a is greater than b, there is a rise from A to B and if b is greater than a, there is a fall from A to B.

4. Shift the level and set-up very near to A or B and level it accurately. Take staff reading on A and B.

   The reading on near staff is taken through the object glass; let the reading be a_1 and b_1 respectively.

5. If there is rise from A to B.

   Correct staff reading on B = Observed staff reading on A – True Difference.

   or if it is fall from A to B.

   Correct reading on B = Observed reading on A + True difference.

6. If the reading (b_1) differs from the required reading on B, the line of collimation is not in adjustment. If b_1 is greater than the required reading the line of collimation is inclined upwards, but if it is less, it is inclined downwards. The required reading on far peg B is obtained by moving the diaphragm screws as described above.

6.11 AUTOMATIC LEVEL   (S-09)

- It is of recent development. The fundamental difference between this auto level and other levels is that the levelling is not done manually using a tubular spirit level but is levelled automatically.

- Automatic levels have two principal adjustments (1) Circular bubble and (2) Line of sight. It should be checked that the compensator is functioning properly.

- It is achieved by an inclination compensating device called till compensator suspended like a pendulum.

- It is inserted in the path of light rays through the telescope. When a parallel plate micrometre is fitted in it, it becomes a precision level. One form of self levelling is shown in the Fig. 6.9.

  (Self aligning level) or (Self levelling level)

Fig. 6.9 : Automatic Level

The Advantages of Auto level :   (S-12)

The following are the advantages of auto level over the ordinary levels.

(1) Operational comfort : Use of auto level is not fatiguing. There is no strain on eyes, nerves and hands of the observer. It does not require any protection from sun.

(2) High precision : Mean elevation error on invar staff with a least count of 5 mm varies from ± 0.5 to 0.8 mm in one km for forward and backward levelling.

(3) High speed : Time required for levelling is 50% of that required with ordinary dumpy level.

(4) Freedom from errors : Due to erect telescope image, the levelling staves are read with erect figures. In automatic levelling there is no possibility of forgetting to centre the bubble.

(5) Freedom from external influences : The external influences like rain, clouds, magnetic fields, vibrations have no influence on the levelling work.

(6) Range of application : The level can be used for medium and large size projects. It can also be used for getting bench mark accurately established.

6.12 THE LEVELLING STAFF

Vertical distances are measured below the line of collimation of the level. The levelling staff is a scale on which these distances are measured.

Levelling staves are of two types :

(i) Self reading staff and (ii) Target staff.

6.12.1 Self Reading Staff

The self reading staff can be read directly by the level man looking through the telescope.

Common forms of levelling staves :

(1) Ordinary staff.

(2) Sopwith telescopic staff.

(3) Folding staff.

1. Ordinary staff :

- Ordinary staff is merely a simple long flat piece of wood about 7.5 cm wide and 2.5 cm thick, with a metal shoe on the bottom and carrying graduations on one face.

- Greatest accuracy is achieved by means of a staff in one length, not exceeding 3 m but progress is expedited by using a longer staves and for convenience of transportation. It consists of two or three joints in the form of sopwith telescopic staff, folding staff etc.

2. Sopwith Telescopic Staff :

- It is made of well seasoned timber, such as mahogany and is protected with brass mountings. They are usually available in 4 m vertical length. It consists of two hollow slides and one solid top piece.

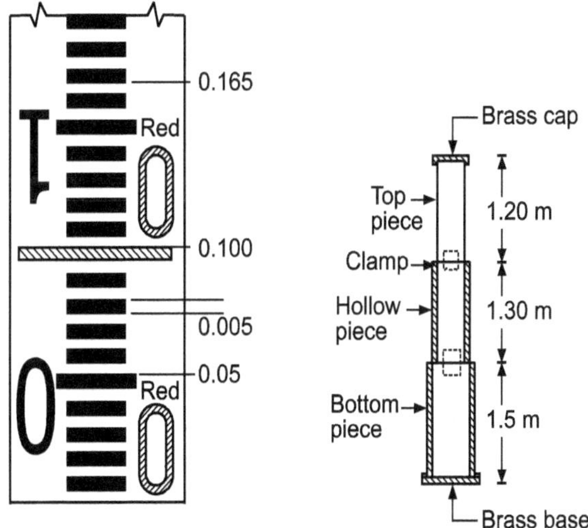

Fig. 6.10 : Levelling Staff Telescopic Metric Staff

- When extended, the lengths are held by brass spring catches. The length of top piece is 1.25 m, the middle one is 1.25 m, and the lower one is of 1.5 m. It is thus 4 m in length when fully extended.
- The graduations are marked erect. The staff appears upside down when viewed through the telescope so that the readings are taken from top to bottom. As required, the staff is extended.
- The pieces are held at inner side with the help of metal spring clamps.

3. Folding Staff :

- The staff is made of well seasoned timber such as cypruses blue pine or deodar.
- It consists of two 2 m long and 75 mm wide wooden or aluminium pieces with the joint assembly.
- Each joint is of detachable type with a locking device at the back as shown in (Fig 6.11).
- The staff is joined together in such a way that when locked together, become straight and rigid.

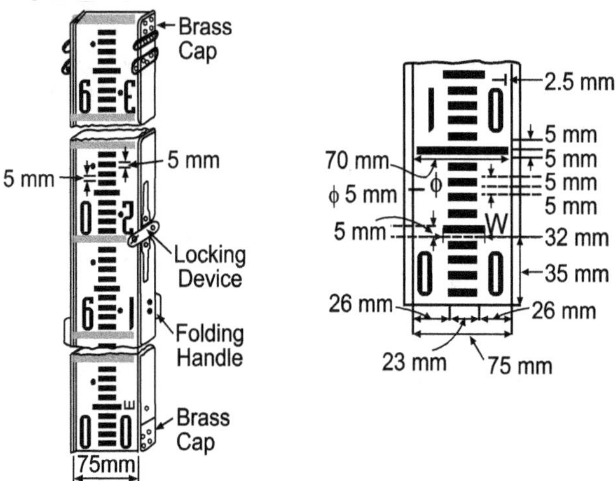

Fig. 6.11 : Folding Staff

- It is generally provided with a pill bubble of 25 minute sensitivity at the back to facilitate holding the staff in plumb.
- Each metre is subdivided into 200 divisions, to read to the accuracy of 5 mm.
- Every decimetre length is figured with the corresponding numerals.
- This metre numeral is marked in red and the decimetre numeral in black.
- The gradutions are marked inverted so as to look them erect while looking through the telescope.

6.12.2　Target Staff

- For very precise works and sights target staff is used.
- A movable target is provided in this staff.
- It consists of a circular disc of about 12.5 cm in diameter with horizontal and vertical lines formed by the junction of alternate quadrants of red and white rectangular opening infront of the target exposed a portion of the rod to view so that the reading can be seen.

- A vernier is also provided on target.

- The level man directs the staff man to slide the target up or down until it is bisceted by the line of sight. With the target clamped in this position, the staff man or both observe the reading.

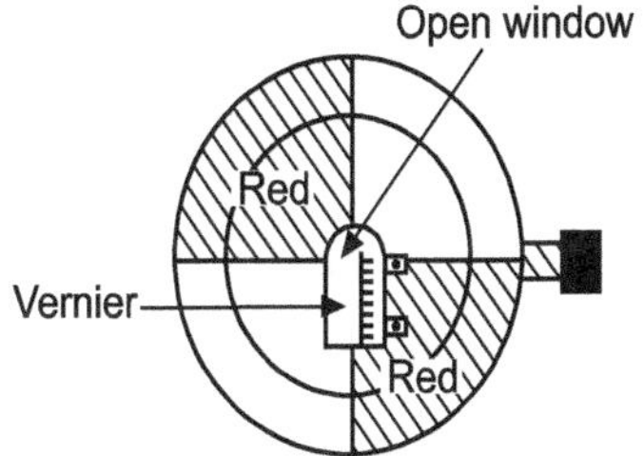

Fig. 6.12 : Target Staff

6.12.3 Comparision of Self Reading and Target staff

(i)   The readings can be taken quicker with the self-reading staff.

(ii)   In case of target staff, more trained staffman is required as compared to the self reading staff.

(iii)   The reading with the target staff can be taken with greater fineness than self reading.

6.13 HOLDING THE STAFF

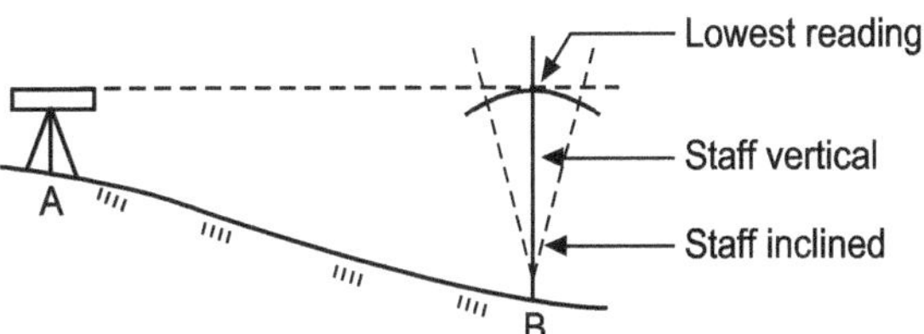

Fig. 6.13 : Holding the Staff

- It is very important to held the staff truly vertical while taking the reading during the levelling work.

- It should be fully extended when required and the spring clips are secured.

- A staffman should be trained for holding the staff.

- He should stand behind the staff and should hold it between the palms of his hands at the height of his face.

- In precise levelling, the staff is equipped with a circular bubble at its back to hold it exactly in plumb.

- In ordinary levelling, the staff is waved slowly forward and backward as shown in the Fig. 6.13, and the minimum reading is taken to avoid the errors.

- The staff is held inverted when the point is above the line of sight.

6.14 READING THE STAFF

The staff reading is taken in the following manner :

(i)　After level is set-up and levelled accuralely, direct the telescope towards the staff held in plumb on the staff station and focus it.

(ii)　Bring the staff between the two vertical hairs of diaphragm. If only one vertical hair is provided on diaphragm, bisect the staff with it. Always take the reading on staff at the horizontal hair.

(iii)　Observe if the bubble is in centre. If not, bring it to the centre using one of the foot screws most nearly in line with the telescope. Note the reading at which the horizontal hair appears to cut the staff.

- In taking reading on staff, first note the red figures of metres, then the black figures of decimetres and finally count the spaces (each space being 5 mm thick).

- Then record the reading in the field book.

- When the graduations on the staff are erect, they are seen inverted, such a staff should be read from above downwards and not upwards.

- When the graduations on the staff are inverted they are seen erect through the telescope, such a staff should be read upwards. In case of target staff, the target is set by the staff-man as directed by the level-man and then the reading is taken and recorded by the staff-man.

6.15 THE SURVEYING TELESCOPE

There are two types of telescopes used in levels and theodolites (1) External focussing and (2) Internal focussing.

6.15.1 External Focussing Telescope

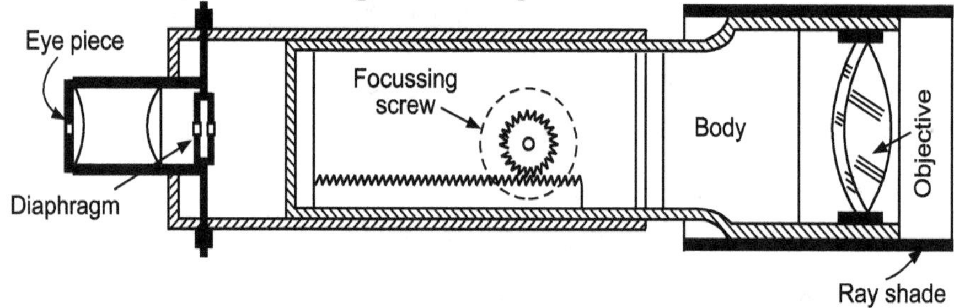

Fig. 6.14 (a) : External Focussing Telescope

The principle parts of the telescope are :

(i)　the body (ii) the object glass (iii) the eye piece (iv) the diaphragm.

The subsidiary parts are :

(a)　ray shade or dust cap.

(b)　rack and pinion arrangement operated by focussing screw.

(c)　diaphragm screws to support the diaphragm.

(d)　the stops for cutting-off extra light.

The body of the telescope is formed of two tubes capable of sliding axially within the other means of rack and pinion attached to the focussing screw for a given power. The main disadvantage of this type is the longer length of telescope.

6.15.2 Internal Focussing Telescope

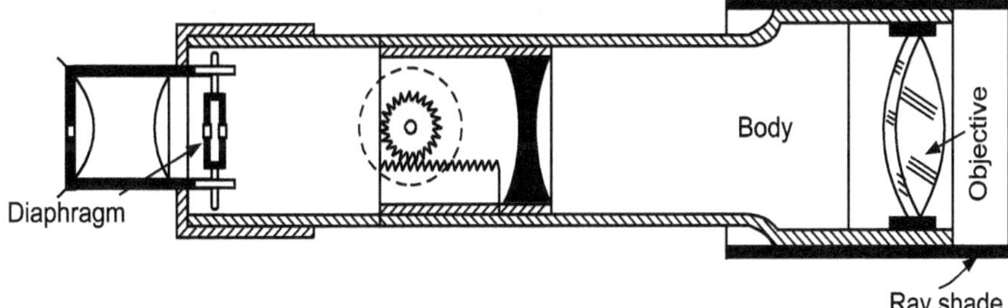

Fig. 6.14 (b) : Internal Focussing Telescope

- In this telescope the objective and eye piece are fixed in position. A double concave lens is mounted in a short tube which is moved by the rack and pinion and external focussing screw between the diaphragm and the object.
- The main advantages of internal focussing telescope are :
  - (a) The interior of the telescope is free from dust and moisture.
  - (b) It is well balanced.
  - (c) The line of collimation is less likely to be affected by focussing.
  - (d) The overall length of telescope is short and fixed as compared to external focussing telescope.
- The main disadvantage is that the internal lens reduces the brilliancy of the image.

Different Parts of Telescope :

1. Object glass or Objective

- The objective is invariably a compound lens consisting of (i) an outer double convex lens made of crown glass, and (ii) an inner concave convex lens made of dense flint glass. Such a compound lens is known as **Achromatic lens**.
- The two serious defects viz. spherical aberation and chromatic aberation are nearly eliminated by such combination.

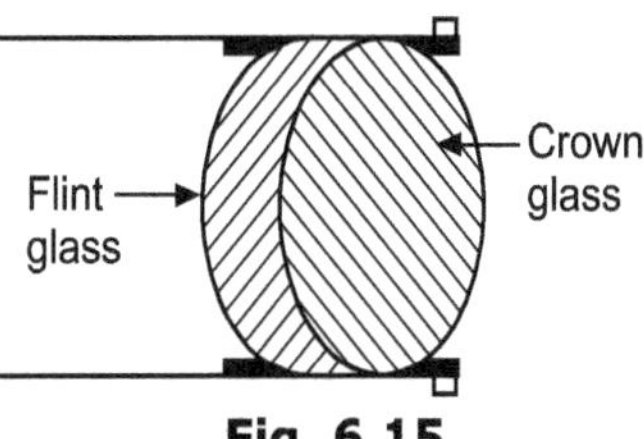

Fig. 6.15

2. Eye piece

- In most of the survey telescopes, Ramsden Eye piece is used.
- It is composed of two equal plano-convex lens of equal focal length.
- They are placed with their convex faces towards one another, at a distance of two-thirds of the focal length of either lens.

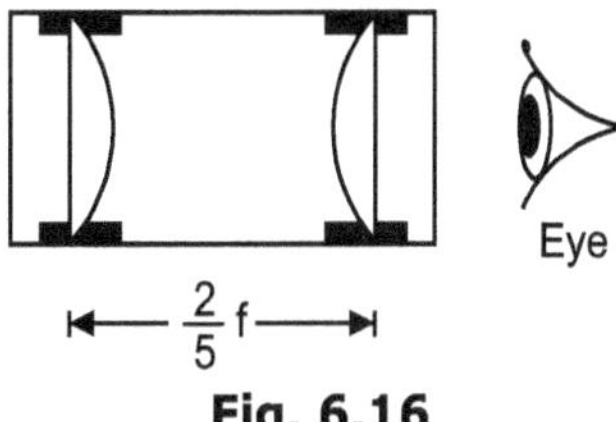

$$\frac{2}{5}f$$

Fig. 6.16

- It is placed at a distance of one-fourth the focal length of either lens from the diaphragm. The image formed by this eye piece is inverted but clear. The object of eye piece is to magnify both the image and the cross-hairs.

3. The diaphragm

- The diaphragm ring is of brass or gun metal inside the telescope tube, just infront of the eye piece.

- It is held in position by means of either two or four capstan headed screws which are capable of adjustment.

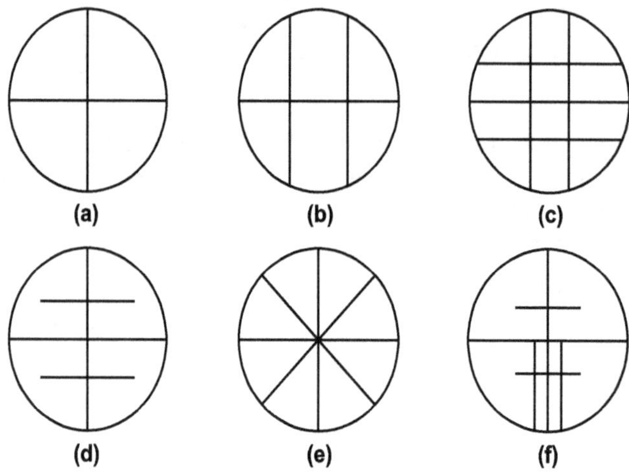

Fig. 6.17 : Diaphragms

- The ring carries the recticule of cross hairs formed by fine lines etched upon glass and is known as *diaphragm*.
- The staff readings are taken with respect to the central horizontal hair. The vertical hairs enable the observer to see the verticality of the staff.
- The diaphragm having three horizontal lines and one or two vertical or inclined lines is known as *stadia diaphragm* which is used in techeometric surveying.

6.15.3 Definitions of the Terms used During Levelling Operations

(1) **Back sight or back sight readings (B.S.)** **(W-06, 07, 08)** : It is a staff reading taken on a point of known elevation i.e. B.M. or change point. It is the first reading taken after the level is set up and levelled.

(2) **Fore sight or Fore sight readings (F.S.)** **(S-11)** : It is a staff reading taken on a point whose elevation is to be determined as on a change point. It is the last staff reading denoting the shifting of the instrument.

(3) **Intermediate sight (I.S.)** **(W-11)** : It is a staff reading taken on a point whose elevation is to be determined. All sights between B.S. and F.S. are intermediate sights.

Note :

(i) Back sight and fore sight denote staff readings.

(ii) For every set up of level, there will be one B.S. and one F.S. and any number of intersight inbetween.

(iii) Back sight is denoted as B.S., Fore sight as F.S., Intermediate sights as I.S., Reduced level by R.L. and Bench mark as B.M., Change point by, C.P., or S.P or T.P.

(4) Change point (C.P.) (W-07, 08, S-11, W-11, S-12) : It is a point on which fore and back sights are taken. When the instrument is to be shifted from one position to the other such points are taken in levelling operations and R.L. of these points are accurately determined. During the process of leveling sometime some stall readings are not possible. In such circumstances with respect to last stall position, the instrument is shifted to new position and levelling is continued. The change point is taken on any stable, well defined object such as boundary stone, rail, rock, kilometre stones, plinth etc. It is also called a *turning point* or *shifting point.*

(5) The height of instrument (H.L.) (W-11) : It is the elevation (R.L.) of the plane of collimation with respect to the datum when the instrument is correctly levelled. It does not mean the height of the centre of the telescope above the ground where the level stands.

(6) Focussing : Setting of eye piece and objective at the proper distance apart for the clear vision of the object sighted. The focus of the eye piece and that of the objective must coincide with the cross hair of the diaphragm; since the diaphragm is placed at the common focus.

(7) Parallax (S-05, 11, W-11) : It is the apparent movement of the image relatively to the cross hairs when the image formed by the objective does not fall in the plane of diaphragm. It is a source of error in levelling. It can be removed entirely by exact focussing. Parallax appears due to the poor focussing of the objective. It can be tested by moving the eye up and down.

- **Station:** It is the point where the leveling staff is held and not the point where the Level is set

- **Negetive Staff Reading:** The staff reading taken is said to be Negative if the Station is above the line of collimation and in such cases the staff is held inverted. Eg. Lying Chejja, ceiling of a building etc

- **Rise:** If the difference between two successive readings (BS-IS or IS-IS or IS-FS) is Positive, then it is Rise.

- **Fall:** Rise: If the difference between two successive readings (BS-IS or IS-IS or IS-FS) is Negative, then it is Fall

6.16 CLASSIFICATION OF LEVELLING

The levelling is classified as under :

(1) Fly levelling (S-09; W-06, 09, 10) : It is the levelling operation in which only BS and FS are taken and no intermediate sights are observed . Fly leveling is done for connecting the BM to the starting point of any project. It is used to establish bench mark. A series of levels are taken from one B.M. to the other. It is also known as *differential levelling or compound levelling.*

(2) Check levelling (W-07, 10; S-11) : In case of profile or longitudinal leveling, at the end of day's work the finishing point is connected to the starting point of that day's work by fly leveling, to check the accuracy of the work. This operation is called check leveling.

It is a process of running a series of levels to check the levels of T.B.M. with the B.M. at the end of each day's work, levels are taken, returning to the starting point on that day say B.M. with a view to check the day's work. If the levelling line closes on itself or on a benchmark of known elevation, it is called as a 'Good check'. In this, an error at an intermediate point cannot be carried forward even if it does not check any reading on a intermediate point.

(3) Reciprocal levelling (W-11) : It is adopted when it is required to find the difference in level between the two points accurately which are considerably apart. This process is also used when it is not possible to set up the level in between the two points due to river or pond etc. In this case level is setup on both the banks of the river or valley and two sets of staff readings are taken by holding the staff on both banks.

(4) Profile levelling (S-09; W-05, 09) : It is adopted to know the accurate outline of the surface of the ground along a given line. The levels are taken at some regular intervals, it is also called longitudinal levelling.

(5) Cross-sectioning : It is the operation of levelling to know the undulations of the ground surface run at right angles to a given line and on either side of it. It is used for plotting details of cross-section

(6) Trigonometrical levelling : In this method, elevations of points are computed from the observed vertical angles and the horizontal distances are measured in the field.

6.17 TYPES OF LEVELLING

6.17.1 Simple Levelling   (W-08)

It is the simplest levelling operation in which difference in elevation between two points is found out. The instrument may be set any where in between the two points, both visible from the instrument.

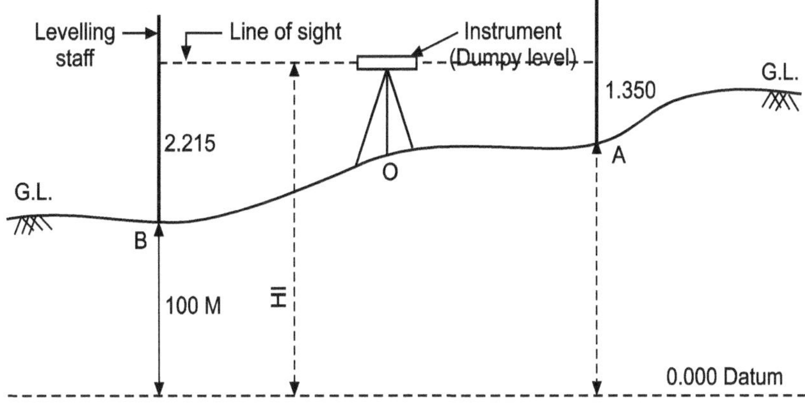

Fig. 6.18

Procedure : Suppose it is required to find out the difference in elevation (R.L.) between A and B.

(1) Set-up the level at O between A and B. The level may be set anywhere but to eliminate the errors in instrument, it is approximately set-up midway between two points.

(2)   Level the instrument carefully.

(3) Direct the telescope towards the staff held vertically at A and focuss it.

(4) The reading at which the horizontal hair appears to cut the staff.

(5) Hold the staff vertically at B.

(6) Direct the telescope on the staff B and focus it, and then take the staff reading. For example : Care should be taken that the bubble should be in centre while taking the reading.

   For example : Let the reading be 1.350 at A and 2.215 at B. The difference between these readings (2.215 – 1.350) gives the difference of level between A and B.

   If R.L. of A = 100.000 m

   H.I. at O = 100 + 1.350 = 101.350 m

   R.L. of B = 101.350 – 2.215 = 99.135 m

When the staff point is lower, the staff reading is greater and the R.L. is smaller and when the point is higher, the staff reading is smaller and the R.L. is more. To get the true difference between the two points the level must be set-up exactly midway between them.

6.17.2 Differential Levelling or Compound Levelling (W-08)

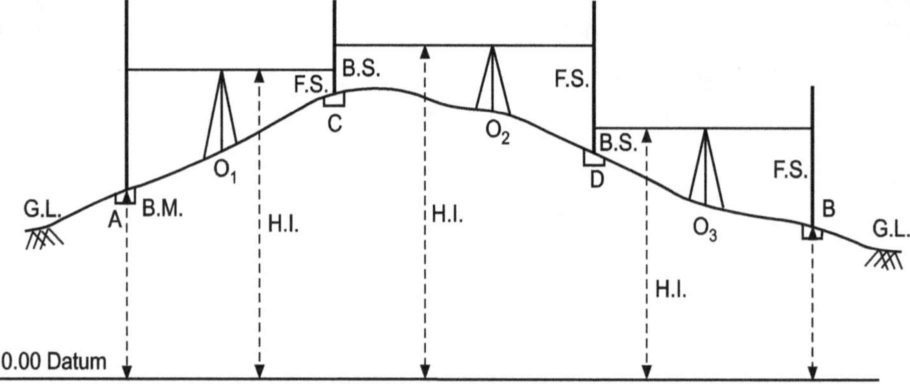

Fig. 6.19 : Differential Levelling

Differential levelling is used when it is required to find out the difference in elevation between the two points under the following circumstances.

(i) if the points are too far apart.

(ii) if the difference in elevation between the points is far great.

(iii) if there are some obstacles in levelling so that the points are not visible from one set-up of the instrument. Here, it is necessary to set-up the instrument at number of places and to work in a series of stages. Thus, the method of simple levelling is employed at each of the succesive stages. This is also known as compound or continuous levelling.

Illustration :

- Let A and B be the two points which are too far apart. It is required to find the difference of level between these two points. Set-up the level at O_1 and correctly level it.

- With the bubble central, take the reading on staff held at A. Select a firm point C so that the distance from O is approximately equal to that of A from O. (i.e. equalising B.S. and F.S. distances).

- Take the reading on the staff held at C. Now, shift the instrument to O_2 and set-up the level carefully and take the reading on staff held at C.

- Again choose a firm point D as before so that the instrument station O_2 is approximately midway between C and D.

- Take the reading on D.

- Care should be taken that the bubble should be exactly in the centre while taking reading. Repeat the process until the point B is reached.

Note :

(1) Each change point (C.P.) is read twice, once before shifting the instrument (F.S.) and second after shifting it (B.S.).

(2) The change point must be taken on firm object. The distance of C.P. should be within 100 m from the level.

(3) The level must remain stationary when the staff is being moved.

(4) The level must be set on firm ground and the bubble must be in centre while taking reading.

(5) To eleminate the instrumental errors due to imperfect adjustments, the fore sight and back sight distances should be approximately equal.

(6) Parallax, if any should be removed by correct focussing, each reading should be taken twice.

$$\text{The difference between A and B} = \text{Algebraic sum of these differences}$$
$$= \Sigma \text{ B.S.} - \Sigma \text{ F.S.}$$

If the difference is positive, it indicates that B is higher than point A and if negative, the point B is lower than the point A.

If R.L. of A is known, then,

$$\text{R.L. of B} = \text{R.L. of A} + \Sigma \text{ B.S} - \Sigma \text{ F.S.}$$

The R.L.s of the intermediate points are found out by,

$$\text{R.L of a point} = (\text{R.L. of B.M.} + \text{B.S.}) - \text{I.S.}$$
$$= \text{H.I.} - \text{I.S.}$$

6.18 PROFILE LEVELLING   (S-08; W-05, S-12)

- *Profile levelling* is the process of determining the elevations of points at measured intervals along a fixed line such as highway, canal, the centre line of railway etc.

- The object of profile levelling is to determine the undulations of the ground surface along a given line for the alignment of road, railway, canal or pipe line. The levelling is started from a bench mark.

- Fly levels may be run to carry the bench mark from a permanent bench mark, and B.M. is established on the side.

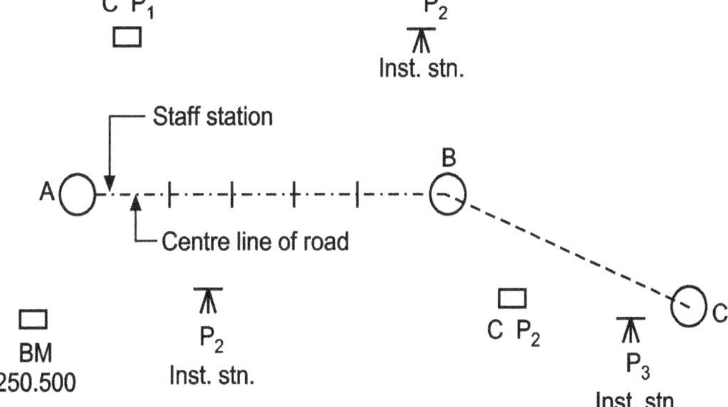

Fig. 6.20 : Profile Levelling Plan

Procedure :

- Let ABC be the given line of section. Points at 10 m intervals are marked on this line. Level is set-up on a firm ground at a suitable point say (P_1) in a commanding position.

- It is accurately levelled and B.S. is taken on the B.M. The R.L. of collimation is worked out by adding B.S. to the R.L. of B.M. The chain is stretched from A towards the point B.

- The fore bearings of the lines AB, BC etc. are taken with the compass and noted in the field book. The staff readings are taken starting from the point A at every 10 m distance, and recorded in field book against the respective distance. Besides these readings additional readings if necessary should be taken to represent the true surface of the ground.

- The instrument is then shifted when sights go long beyond 100 m or when further points are not visible due to high ground or valley or any other obstruction. C.P.1 is taken at suitable position, it need not be on the section line. The instrument is then moved forward and set-up at new position say (P_2) as before. Back sight is taken on C.P. and new H.I. is worked out.

- Chaining and readings are then continued as before until the reading is obtained on the last point B. The B.M. should be checked during the progress of work. In case of large descripancy the work should be repeated.

- The chaining and levelling operations are carried further from the point B to C and so on. Neat sketches of Bench marks and the features such as nalla, road crossing etc. should be drawn in the field book with full description.

6.18.1 Important Points to be Noted while Running a Profile Levelling (General Precautions During Levelling)

(i) The chainage of staff stations are continuous from the beginning to the end of the line.

(ii) The B.S. and F.S. distance should be equalised approximately to eliminate the instrumental errors.

(iii) Readings of B.S., F.S. should be taken very accurately with the bubble exactly in the centre of its run.

(iv) The features such as nalla, river, road, canal, cart track etc. crossed by the line should be fully located by taking bearing of their centre lines, their width etc.

6.19 THE WORKING PROFILE EXIBITS THE FOLLOWING INFORMATION

(i) The original ground levels.

(ii) The formation level.

(iii) The finished surface level.

(iv) The depths of cutting and heights of banking.

(v) The proposed gradient.

(vi) Any other information, which is likely to be useful during the execution of the work.

6.20 CROSS-SECTIONING (W-09, W-11)

- Cross-sections are run at right angle to the centre line on either side of it. These lines of cross-section are perpendicular to the lines in longitudinal section. The object of running the cross-sections is to determine the lateral outline of the ground surface.

- Cross-sections are taken at every 20 m or 30 m distance along the centre line. The length of cross-section may be run at closer intervals to outline the features of nala, road crossings etc.

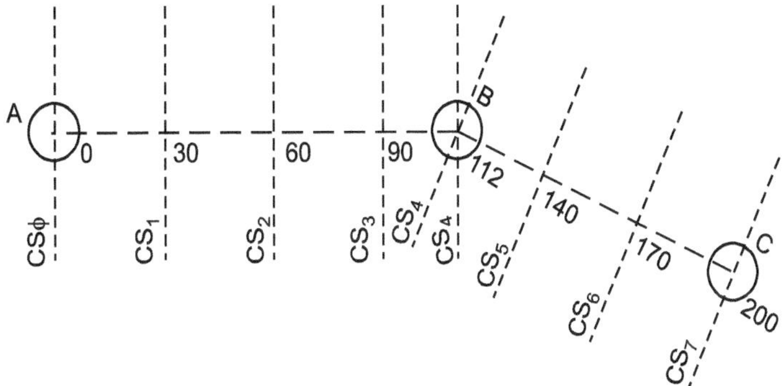

Fig. 6.21 : Cross-sectioning (Plan)

- Short cross-sections are generally set by an eye. Long cross-sections are set by an optical square or theodolite. The length of cross-section depend upon nature of work. The chainages are continuous from the starting point.

6.21 PLOTTING THE CROSS-SECTIONS

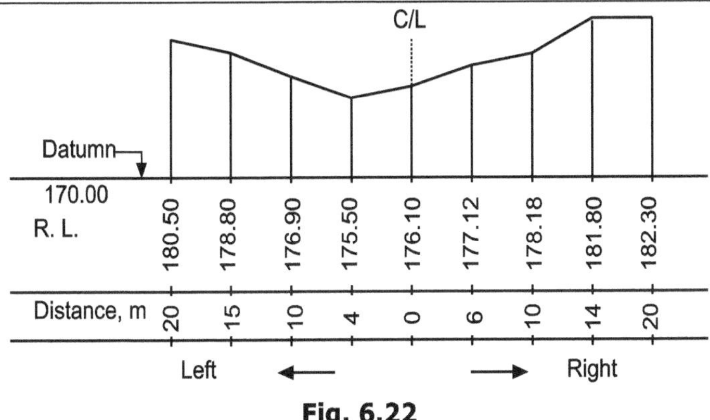

Fig. 6.22

- The cross-sections are plotted in the same manner as that of profiles, except that the scale used for plotting the horizontal and vertical distances are same.

- The scales commonly used are,

  1 in 100 and 1 in 200.

  The datum may be suitably assumed.

6.22 RECIPROCAL LEVELLING

This method is adopted to accurately determine the difference of level between two points which are far apart. It is also used when it is not possible to set-up the level midway between the two points due to deep valley or a river.

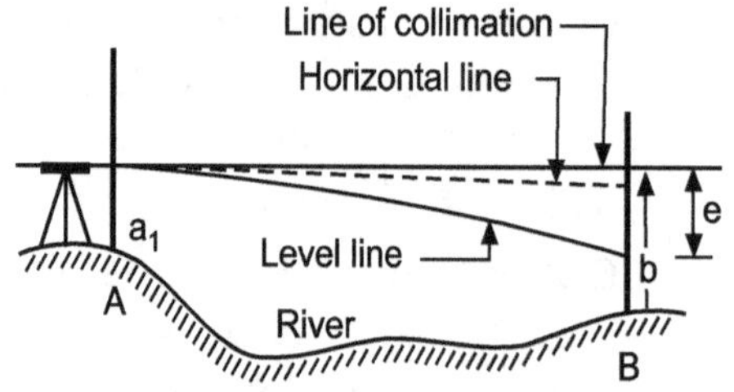

Fig. 6.23 (a)

The following errors are eliminated by this process :

(1) The error due to curvature and refraction.

(2) The collimation error (The line of collimation not being exactly parallel to the bubble axis).

(3) The error in instrument adjustment.

Procedure : (i) Let A and B be the two points on opposite banks of the river. (ii) It is required to find out the level difference between A and B. (iii) Set-up the level very near A and with bubble centered, take the reading on the staff held at A and B. (iv) The reading on A being very close should be taken through the object glass.

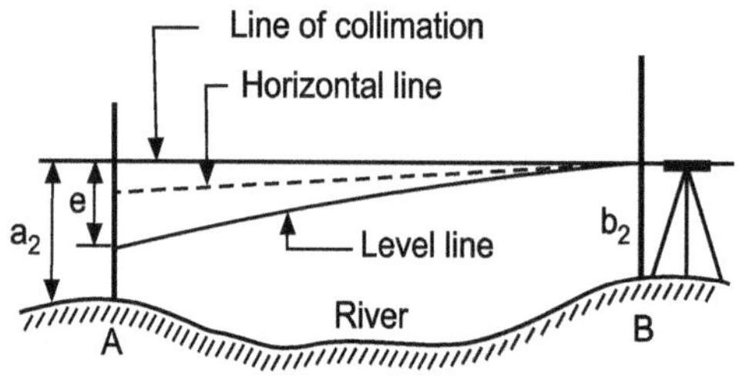

Fig. 6.23 (b)

(v) Let these readings be a_1 and b_1 respectively. [Fig. 6.23 (a)]

(vi) Shift the level and set up very near B.

(vii) Take the readings on A and B, with the bubble centered in the similar manner. Let readings be a_2 and b_2 respectively. [Fig. 6.23 (b)]

(viii) Let d = true difference of level between A and B and e = error due to curvature refraction and imperfect adjustment (total error).

Then correct reading on B in first case = b_1 – e.

In second case, correct reading on

$$A = a_2 - e.$$

From A, the true difference of level between A and B (true fall from A to B)

$$= (b_1 - e) - a_1$$

or $d = (b_1 - a_1) - e$ ... (1)

From B, the true differnce of level between A and B (true fall from A to B)

∴ $d = b_2 - (a_2 - e)$

$$= (b_2 - a_2) - e$$ ... (2)

Adding equation (1) and (2) the total error 'e' is eliminated.

$$\text{and} \qquad d = \left(\frac{(b_1 - a_1) + (b_2 - a_2)}{2}\right)$$

$$\text{or} \qquad e = \left(\frac{(b_1 - a_1) + (b_2 - a_2)}{2}\right)$$

Thus, the errors due to curvature, refraction, imperfect adjustment of level are eliminated.

6.23 ERRORS IN LEVELLING　　(S-08, 09; W-07, 08, 10, W-11, S-12)

The errors in levelling are due to the following principal sources.

1. Instrumental errors
2. Errors of manipulation.
3. Imperfect sighting.
4. Errors due to settlement of staff and level stand.
5. Errors due to natural sources.

(1) Instrumental Errors :

(i) Error due to imperfect adjustment : When the level is not in adjustment, line of sight will be inclined upwards or downwards and this will cause serious errors. The axis of the bubble not being at right angles to the vertical axis, and second, the line of collimation not being parallel to the bubble axis. It is, therefore, essential that the instrument should be tested and adjusted before use. The error due to the inclination of the line of collimation may be eliminated by equalising the backsight and foresight distance while taking change points.

(ii) Bubble being sluggish : If the bubble is sluggish it may apparently be in the centre though the bubble line is not horizontal. Sluggish bubble should be replaced by good one or the error can be partially avoided by observing the bubble after the target has been sighted.

(iii) Faulty focussing tube : Sometimes the focussing tube is faulty. Due to this, the objective does not move in horizontal plane but moves in inclined direction during focussing. This error is compensating and can be eliminated by balancing back sight and fore sight without changing focus and without moving slide.

(iv) The levelling staff : Erroneous divisions of the levelling staff will cause some errors which are negligible in ordinary works.

(2) Personal Errors :

(i) Errors of Manipulation :

(a) Careless levelling of the instrument (b) The bubble not being exactly in centre while sighting.(c) Resting the hand on tripod legs while taking staff readings. (d) The staff not being held exactly vertical.

(ii) Imperfect sighting : The error is caused due to poor focussing of eye piece and object glass. The readings are taken without removing the parallax.

(iii) Error due to settlement of staff and level : The level, staff or change point settles if proper precautions are not taken and cause cummulative errors and may be very serious. They can be avoided by planting the instrument on firm ground and proper selection of change point.

(3) Errors due to Natural Causes :

Errors are caused due to : (i) Curvature of earth (ii) Refraction and (iii) Effect of wind and sun on the level.

In ordinary levelling the errors due to curvature and refraction are not considered as they are too minor in quantity, even less than 0.003 m for a sight of 300 m length. The level should be sheltered from the sun or wind by survey umbrella. The object glass should be shaded by the rayshade or by hand so that the sun will not shine on the object glass. The levelling work should be suspended during wind or a heated atmosphere.

For more distances and for some precise work these errors are considerable.

In levelling operation the following common mistakes should be avoided :

(i)	Reading the staff in wrong direction when the staff is graduated erect and numbers on it should be read downwards and vice versa.

(ii)	At change point, the reading of fore sight and back sight are not taken exactly at the same point.

(iii)	Taking reading on top or bottom hair instead of central hair on stadia diaphragm.

(iv)	Mistakes in recording such as entering B.S. in F.S. and vice versa.

(v)	Mistakes in calculation of H.I. or Rise and Fall.

(vi)	Omitting some entries in field book.

(vii)	The levelling staff not being held in plumb or not being fully extended.

## 6.24 CLOSING ERROR IN LEVELLING	(W-10)

The levelling work is generally started from a point of known Reduced level (B.M.) and after carrying out the required levelling the work is finally closed on the starting point by taking fore sight on it.

The difference in reduced level of the starting point indicates the closing error in levelling.

6.25 DEGREE OF PRECISION

The degree of precision in levelling depends upon:

1. the quality of instrument.

2. skill of the level man.

3. character of area to be surveyed.

4. atmospheric condition.

5. purpose of levelling.

The precision also depends upon the number of set-ups and length of sights.

There is no hard and fast rule for it.

However, the magnitude of permissible closing error may be expressed as :

$$E = C \sqrt{K}$$

where, E = The permissible error in millimetre

C = The constant.

K = Distance in kilometres.

The value of constant 'C' depends upon :

(i)   the quality of instrument.

(ii)   skill of the level man.

(iii)   character of area.
(iv)   the atmospheric condition.

1.   For rough levelling, $E = \pm 96 \sqrt{K}$

2.   For ordinary levelling, $E = \pm 24 \sqrt{K}$

3.   For accurate levelling, $E = \pm 12 \sqrt{K}$

4.   For precise levelling, $E = \pm 6 \sqrt{K}$

5.   For very high precision, $E = \pm 1 \sqrt{K}$

6.25.1 Difficulties Faced in Levelling (W-08)

1.   If the length of sight is too long then you cannot read the reading properly.
2.   In soft ground the level is sink down in ground.
3.   In rainy and windy days to take the reading by dumpy level is very difficult.
4.   On uneven ground, the levelling to dumpy level is very difficult.
5.   The staff is not held exactly vertical therefore there is error in reading.

6.25.2 Precautions in Levelling to Eliminate Errors (S-12)

(i)   Do not take length of sight too large. Take about 100 m.

(ii)   Held the staff exactly vertical to get correct readings.

(iii)   Do the adjustments of the level properly and test them carefully.

(iv)   While taking B.S. and F.S. reading bubble must be in the centre.

(v)   Different surveyors must take levels on different days for checking.

(vi)   Atmospheric conditions like light, temperature etc. must be favourable during levelling.

(vii)   During rainy and windy day levelling must be avoided.

(viii) B.S. and F.S. distance must be approximately same to avoid instrumental errors.

6.26 BOOKING THE LEVEL FIELD BOOK   (W-11)

The following important points should be kept in mind while booking the staff readings in a level field book :

(1) The reading should be recorded in respective columns in order of their observations.

(2) The first entry on a page is always a back sight (B.S.) and last one is foresight (F.S.).

(3) The fore sight and back sight of the change point should be written on the same horizontal line.

(4) The R.L. of plane of collimation should be written opposite to the B.S. on the same horizontal line.

(5) In carrying forward the reading from one page to the next, if the last entry is an I.S., it is entered in both I.S. and F.S. columns, and in B.S. and I.S. columns as the first entry on the next page. The entries in the remaining columns against it should be repeated on the next page.

(6) Bench marks, change points, and other important points in levelling should be briefly but accurately described in the remark column. Sketches if necessary should be drawn on blank page on left side of the page.

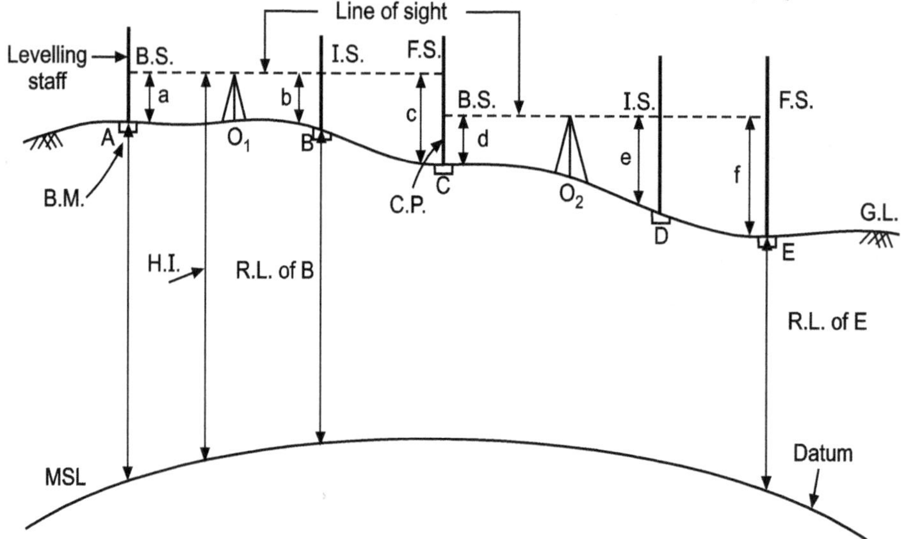

Fig. 6.24 : Levelling Operations

6.27 REDUCED LEVELS   (S-09; W-07, 09)

The system of working out the reduced levels of points from the staff reading taken in the field is termed as reducing levels. The reduced level (R.L.) of a point is the elevation of the point with reference to some datum.

There are two systems of finding reducing levels :

1. The plane of collimation system.

2. The rise and fall system.

6.27.1 The Plane of Collimation System

(Height of Instrument Method)

In this system, the R.L. of plane of collimation (H.I.) is found out for every set-up of the level and then the reduced levels of the points are worked out with the respective plane of collimation as described below :

Before starting work of levelling we must prepare the level page of the field book.

Table 6.1

Staff station	Reading			H.I. (Collimation plane level)	Reduced level	Remarks
	B.S.	I.S.	F.S.			
B.M.						B.M.
1						:
2						:
3						CP_1
:						:
:						:
:						CP_2
:						:
:						:

(1) Determine the R.L. of plane of collimation for the first set-up of the level by adding B.S. to the R.L. of B.M. i.e. (R.L. of plane of collimation = R.L. of B.M. + B.S.)

(2) Obtain the R.L.s of the intermediate points and the first change point (C.P.) by subtracting the staff readings (I.S. and F.S. from the R.L. of plane of collimation (H.I.). (R.L. of a point = R.L. of plane of collimation (H.I.) – I.S. or F.S.)

(3) When the instrument is shifted and set up at new position take a back sight reading on change point. A new plane of collimation is determined by addition of B.S. to the R.L. of change point.

Thus, the levels from two set-ups of the instruments can be corelated by means of B.S. and F.S. taken on C.P.

∴ R.L. of new collimation point = R.L. of change point + B.S. reading

(4) Find out the R.L.s of the successive points and the second C.P. by subtracting their staff readings from this plane of collimation R.L.

(5) Repeat the procedure until all the R.L.s are worked out.

Arithmetical check : The difference between the sum of the back sights and the sum of the fore sights should be equal to the difference between the last and first reduced levels.

i.e. Σ B.S. $-$ Σ F.S. $=$ Last R.L. $-$ First R.L.

The calculations of reduced levels of the plane of collimation and of the change points only are checked. There is no check on the reduction of intermediate reduced levels.

6.27.2 Rise and Fall System   (W-05, S-11)

In this system, there is no need to determine R.L. of plane of collimation. The difference of level between consecutive points is obtained as described below :

Before starting work of levelling, we must prepare the level page of the field book.

Table 6.2

Staff station	Readings			Rise (+)	Fall (−)	Reduced level	Remarks
	B.S.	I.S.	F.S.				
B.M.							B.M.
A							:
B							CP$_1$
C							:
D							:
:							CP$_2$
:							:

(1) Determine the difference in staff readings between the consecutive point comparing each point after the first with that immediately preceeding it.

(2) Obtain the rise or fall from the difference of their staff readings accordingly to the staff reading at the point is smaller or greater than that of preceeding point.

i.e.   Rise or Fall $=$ Previous reading $-$ Current reading

If difference is +ve $\rightarrow$ Rise

If difference is −ve $\rightarrow$ Fall

(3) Find out the reduced level of each point by adding rise to or subtracting fall from the R.L. of a preceeding point.

i.e. Reduced level of any point $=$ Reduced level of preceding point $\pm$ Rise or Fall

$+ \rightarrow$ When rise

$\rightarrow$ When fall

Arithmetical Check :

The difference between the sum of back sight and the sum of fore sights

= the difference between the sum of Rise and the sum of Fall

= the difference between the last R.L. and the First R.L.

$\therefore \qquad \Sigma \text{ B.S.} - \Sigma \text{ F.S.} = \Sigma \text{ Rise} - \Sigma \text{ Fall} = \text{Last R.L.} - \text{First R.L.}$

Thus, there is check on calculation of all readings.

It may be noted that there is no check on the reading taken in the field. The above checks are only for the accuracy of recording and reducing the levels.

6.28 COMPARISON BETWEEN PLANE OF COLLIMATION SYSTEM

(H.I) AND RISE AND FALL SYSTEM   (S-08; W-06, 09, W-11, S-12)

Plane of Collimation System	Rise and Fall System
(1) The method is more rapid, less tedious and simple as it involves less calculations.	(1) This method is more labrious as it involves more calculations.
(2) There is no check on calculation of R.L.s of intermediate sights. Hence, mistake made remains unchecked.	(2) There is complete check on all calculation work.
(3) The error in calculating the R.L. of any point is not carried forward as the R.L.s are calculated from the respective plane of collimation.	(3) The mistake made in calculating the R.L. of any point will be carried forward.
(4) It is used for calculating R.L.s of profile levelling operations, giving levels in constructional works such as canal, roads etc.	(4) It is used for calculating R.L.s of precise levelling works, check levelling etc.

SOLVED EXAMPLES

TYPE I : PROBLEMS ON H.I. METHOD

Example 6.1 : *The level page of field book is given below. The R.L. of first point is 275 m. Calculate the R.L. of remaining points by H.I. method.*

Level Page of the Field Book

Station	Reading			H.I.	Reduced Level	Remarks
	B.S.	I.S.	F.S.			
A	0.475				275.00	B.M.
B	1.060		1.975			CP$_1$
C		1.550				
D		2.120				
E	2.380		1.785			CP$_2$
F	1.375		0.895			CP$_3$
G			1.750			

Solution :

The R.L. of plane of collimation = R.L. of B.M. + B.S.

= 275.000 + 0.475

= 275.475

Similarly, at change point No. 1

R.L. of B = H.I. – F.S.

= 275.475 – 1.975

= 273.500

New R.L. of plane of collimation (H.I.) = R.L. of C.P. 1 + B.S.

= 273.500 + 1.06

= 274.560

The same method is adopted for calculating new H.I. at C.P.2, C.P.3 and corresponding reduced levels are worked out.

For calculating R.Ls. use new height of collimation. The last reading is always entered in F.S. column.

Hence, 1.750 is entered in F. S.

Station	Reading				Reduced Level	Remarks
	B.S.	I.S.	F.S.	H.I.		
A	0.475			275.475	275.000	B.M. on the plinth of building
B	1.060		1.975	274.560	273.500	C.P.1
C		1.550			273.010	
D		2.120			272.440	
E	2.380		1.785	275.155	272.775	C.P.2
F	1.325		0.895	275.585	274.260	C.P.3
G			1.750		273.835	T.B.M. on Boundary stone
Arithmetical Check :	Σ B.S. – Σ F.S. = 5.240 – 6.405 = –1.165			Last R.L. – First R.L. = 273.835 – 275.000 = – 1.165		

Example 6.2 : *The following consecutive readings were taken with a level and a 4 metre levelling staff on continuosly sloping ground from A to B at every 30 metre interval.*

0.355 on A 0.730,　1.055,　2.690,　3.950,　0.485,
1.020　　1.895,　2.535,　3.855,　0.675,　1.715,
2.985,　　3.600 on B.

The R.L. of A was 560.250 m. Enter the readings in a level field book and check your calculations by usual method. Determine the Gradient of the line AB. Use plane of collimation method.

Solution : Since the readings were taken on continuosly sloping ground and the largest reading that can be taken on this staff is 4 m, the level was shifted after the reading 3.950 and 3.885. Therefore, these readings are entered in F.S. column and the reading 0.485 and 0.675 are B.S. readings which should be entered in B.S. column.

The last reading is always a fore sight reading.

The remaining readings are entered in I.S. column. The reduced levels of the points are calculated by the collimation method and results are tabulated as under :

Here, first we calculate H.I.

$$\therefore \quad H.I. = B.S. \text{ reading of A} + R.L. \text{ of B.M.}$$
$$= 0.355 + 560.250$$
$$= 560.605$$

Now, calculate R.Ls. of next points

$$R.L. \text{ of point} = H.I. - I.S. \text{ of that point}$$
$$\therefore \quad \text{For point 1} = 560.605 - 0.730$$
$$= 559.875$$
$$\text{For point 2} = 560.605 - 1.055$$
$$= 559.550$$
$$\text{For point 3} = 560.605 - 2.690$$
$$= 557.915$$
$$\text{For point 4} = H.I. - F.S. \text{ of that point}$$
$$= 560.605 - 0.485$$
$$= 556.655$$

Next, $\qquad$ New H.I. $= B.S.$ reading of C.P.1 $+ R.L.$ of C.P.1
$$= 0.485 + 556.655$$
$$= 557.140$$

Now, we find next R.L.s

$$R.L. \text{ of point 5} = 557.140 - 1.020$$
$$= 556.120$$
$$R.L. \text{ of point 6} = 557.140 - 1.895$$
$$= 555.245$$
$$R.L. \text{ of point 7} = 557.140 - 2.535$$
$$= 554.605$$
$$R.L. \text{ of point 8} = 557.14 - 3.855 = 553.255$$
$$\text{Next new H.I.} = B.S. \text{ of C.P. 2} + R.L. \text{ of C.P. 2}$$
$$= 0.675 + 553.255$$
$$= 553.930$$

Next R.L.s : $\quad$ R.L. of point 9 $= 553.930 - 1.715$
$$= 552.215$$

$$\text{R.L. of point 10} = 553.930 - 2.985$$
$$= 550.945$$
$$\text{R.L. of point 11} = \text{H.I.} - \text{F.S.} = 553.930 - 3.600$$
$$= 550.33$$

Level Page of the Field Book

Station	Distance (m)	Readings			H.I.	R.L.	Remarks
		B.S.	I.S.	F.S.			
A	0	0.355			560.605	560.250	B.M.
1	30		0.730			559.875	
2	60		1.055			559.550	
3	90		2.690			557.915	
4	120	0.485		3.950	557.140	556.655	C.P.1
5	150		1.020			556.120	
6	180		1.895			555.245	
7	210		2.535			554.605	
8	240	0.675		3.885	553.930	553.255	C.P.2
9	270		1.715			552.215	
10	300		2.985			550.945	
B	330			3.600		550.330	last point
		Σ B.S = 1.515		Σ F.S. = 11.435			

Arithmetical check : Σ B.S. $- \Sigma$ F.S. $= 1.514 - 11.435 = -9.92$

and Last R.L. $-$ First R.L. $= 550.330 - 560.250 = -9.92$

$$\text{Difference} = 9.920$$

Then it is fall of 9.92 m from A to B

$$\text{The distance AB} = 330 \text{ m}$$

$$\therefore \quad \text{Gradient of the line AB} = \frac{9.92}{330} \qquad \text{Gradient of line} = \frac{V}{H}$$

$$= \frac{1}{33.26}$$

i.e.　　1 in 33.26 (Falling)

Example 6.3 : *The following consecutive readings were taken with a tilting level :*

3.865,　　3.345,　　2.930,　　1.950,　　　0.855,　　3.795,

2.640,　　1.540,　　1.935,　　0.865, &　　0.665

The level was shifted after the 5th and the 8th reading. The first reading was taken on a B.M. of R.L. 150.250. Calculate the R.Ls of change points and difference of level between the first and the last point. Apply, usual checks.　　**(S-11)**

Solution : The level was shifted after the 5th reading. Hence, the fifth reading 0.855 should be recorded in F.S. column and next reading i.e. 6th reading 3.795 should be recorded in B.S. column on the same horizontal line. Similarly, the 8th reading i.e. 1.540 should be recorded in F.S. and 9th reading i.e. 1.935 should be recorded against the F.S. in B.S column on the same horizontal line. The remaining readings are calculated below.

We know that

$$\text{H.I.} = \text{B.S. reading} + \text{R.L.}$$
$$= 3.865 + 150.250 = 154.115$$

Now,

$$\text{R.L. of C.P.1} = \text{H.I.} - \text{F.S.}$$
$$= 154.115 - 0.855 = 153.260$$
$$\text{New H.I.} = \text{B.S. of C.P.1} + \text{R.L. of C.P.1}$$
$$= 3.795 + 153.260$$
$$= 157.055$$
$$\text{R.L. of C.P.2} = \text{New H.I.} - \text{F.S.}$$
$$= 157.055 - 1.540$$
$$= 155.515$$
$$\text{New H.I.} = \text{B.S. of C.P.2} + \text{R.L. of C.P.2}$$
$$= 1.935 + 155.515 = 157.450$$
$$\text{R.L. of last point} = \text{New H.I.} - \text{F.S.}$$
$$= 157.450 - 0.665 = 156.785$$

Level Page of the Field Book

Stations	Readings			R.L. of Plane of Collimation	Reduced Level	Remarks
	B.S.	I.S.	F.S.	(H·I)		
1	3.865			154.115	150.250	B.M. of R.L. 150.250
2		3.345				
3		2.930				
4		1.950				
5	3.795		0.855	157.055	153.260	C.P.1
6		2.640				
7	1.935		1.540	157.450	155.515	C.P.2
8		0.865				
9			0.665		156.785	Last point
	Σ B.S. = 9.595		Σ F.S. = 3.060			

Arithmetic check : Σ B.S. – Σ F.S   Last R.L. – First R.L.

   = 9.595 – 3.060 = 6.535 = 156.785 – 150.250 = 6.535

Difference in level between the first and the last point

R.L. of last point	=	156.785
R.L. of 1st point	=	150.250
Difference	=	6.535

There is a rise from point 1 to last point.

Example 6.4 : *Determine the gradient of line 'AB' if the following readings were taken from point A to B i.e. 0.620 m, 1.680, 2.350, 0.400, 1.100, 2.680, 0.300, 0.900, 1.500, 2.000, 1.000.*

The staff used for the work was 3 m staff, R.L. of first point = 150.000 m. Give the position of change points on line AB. The horizontal distance AB is 300 m. **(W-05)**

Solution :

Level Page of the Field Book

Staff station	B.S.	I.S.	F.S.	H.I.	R.L.	Remark
A	0.620			150.620	150.000	B.M.
1		1.680			148.94	
2	0.400		2.350	148.67	148.27	C.P.1
3		1.100			147.57	
4	0.300		2.680	146.29	145.99	C.P.2
5		0.900			145.39	
6		1.500			144.79	
7		2.000			144.29	
B			1.000		145.29	
	ΣB.S. = 1.320		ΣF.S. = 6.03			

$$H.I. = R.L. \text{ of } B.M. + B.S. \text{ at station } A$$
$$= 150 + 0.620 = 150.620$$
$$R.L. \text{ of station } 1 = H.I. - I.S. \text{ of station } 1$$
$$R.L. \text{ of station } 1 = 150.620 - 1.680 = 148.94$$
$$R.L. \text{ of station } 2 = H.I. - F.S. \text{ of station } 2$$
$$R.L. \text{ of station } 2 = 150.620 - 2.350 = 148.27$$

For Change Point 1 : Now,

$$New H.I. = R.L. \text{ of } 2 + B.S. \text{ of station } 2$$
$$= 148.27 + 0.400 = 148.67$$
$$R.L. \text{ of station } 3 = H.I. - I.S. \text{ of station } 3$$
$$= 148.67 - 1.100 = 147.57$$

$$\text{R.L. of station 4} = \text{H.I.} - \text{F.S. of station 4}$$
$$= 148.67 - 2.680 = 145.99$$

For change Point 2 :

$$\text{New H.I.} = \text{R.L. of station 4} + \text{B.S. of station 4}$$
$$= 145.99 + 0.300$$
$$\text{H.I.} = 146.29$$
$$\text{R.L. of station 5} = \text{H.I.} - \text{I.S. of station 5}$$
$$= 146.29 - 0.900 = 145.39$$
$$\text{R.L. of station 6} = \text{H.I.} - \text{I.S. of station 6}$$
$$= 146.29 - 1.500 = 144.79$$
$$\text{R.L. of station 7} = \text{H.I.} - \text{I.S. of station 7}$$
$$= 146.29 - 2.000 = 144.29$$
$$\text{R.L. of station B} = \text{H.I.} - \text{F.S. of station 8}$$
$$= 146.29 - 1.00 = 145.99$$

Arithmetic Check :

$$\Sigma\, \text{B.S.} - \Sigma\, \text{F.S.} = \text{Last R.L.} - \text{First R.L.}$$
$$\therefore \quad 1.320 - 6.03 = 145.29 - 150.000$$
$$\therefore \quad -4.71 = -4.71$$

$$\text{Gradient of line AB} = \frac{\text{First R.L.} - \text{Last R.L.}}{\text{Distance between point A and point B}}$$
$$= \frac{150.000 - 145.29}{300} = \frac{4.71}{300} = \frac{1}{63.69}$$

$$\text{Gradient of line AB} = 1 \text{ in } 63.69 \text{ (falling gradient)}$$

Example 6.5 : *The following readings were taken with a level and 4 m staff. Draw up a level book page and calculate reduced levels by height of instrument method.*

0.578, 0.933, 1.768, 2.450, 3.005, 0.567, 1.181, 1.888, 3.679, 0.612, 0.705 and 1.810.

The instrument was shifted after 5th and 9th reading. The R.L. of first station is 58.250 m. **(W-06)**

Solution : The level was shifted after 5th reading. Hence, the fifth reading 3.005 should be recorded in F.S. column and next reading i.e. 6th reading 0.567 should be recorded in B.S. column on the same horizontal line. Similarly, the 9th reading i.e. 3.679 should be recorded in F.S. and 10th reading i.e. 0.612 should be recorded against the F.S. in B.S. column on the same horizontal line.

The reaming readings should be calculated and recorded as usual.

Level Page of the Field Book

Staff station	B.S.	I.S.	F.S.	H.I.	R.L.	Remark
BM	0.578			58.828	58.250	B.M.
1		0.933			57.895	
2		1.768			57.060	
3		2.450			56.378	
4	0.567		3.005	56.390	55.823	C.P.1
5		1.181			55.209	
6		1.888			54.502	
7	0.612		3.679	53.323	57.711	C.P.2
8		0.705			52.618	
9			1.810		51.513	
	Σ B.S. = 1.757		Σ F.S. = 8.494			

$$
\begin{aligned}
\text{H.I.} &= \text{R.L. of B.M.} + \text{B.S. reading at station A} \\
\text{H.I.} &= 58.250 + 0.578 \\
\text{H.I.} &= 58.828 \\
\text{R.L. of station 1} &= \text{H.I.} - \text{I.S. of station 1} \\
&= 58.828 - 0.933 \\
&= 57.895 \\
\text{R.L. of station 2} &= \text{H.I.} - \text{I.S. of station 2} \\
&= 58.828 - 1.768 \\
&= 57.06 \\
\text{R.L. of station 3} &= \text{H.I.} - \text{I.S. of station 3} \\
&= 58.828 - 2.450 \\
&= 56.378 \\
\text{R.L. of station 4} &= \text{H.I.} - \text{F.S. of station 4} \\
&= 58.828 - 3.005 \\
&= 55.823
\end{aligned}
$$

For change point 1 :

$$
\begin{aligned}
\text{New H.I.} &= \text{R.L. of station} - \text{B.S. of station 4} \\
&= 55.823 - 0.567 \\
&= 56.390 \\
\text{R.L. of station 5} &= \text{New H.I.} - \text{I.S. of station 5} \\
&= 56.390 - 1.181 \\
&= 55.209 \\
\text{R.L. of station 6} &= \text{New H.I.} - \text{I.S. of station 6} \\
&= 56.390 - 1.888 = 54.502
\end{aligned}
$$

$$\text{R.L. of station 7} = \text{New H.I.} - \text{F.S. of station 7}$$
$$= 56.390 - 3.679$$
$$= 52.711$$

For Change Point 2 :

$$\text{New H.I.} = \text{R.L of station 7} + \text{B.S. of station 7}$$
$$= 52.711 + 0.612 = 53.323$$
$$\text{R.L. of station 8} = \text{New H.I.} - \text{I.S. of station 8}$$
$$= 53.323 - 0.705$$
$$= 52.618$$
$$\text{R.L. of station 9} = \text{New H.I.} - \text{F.S. of station 9}$$
$$= 53.323 - 1.810 = 51.513$$

Arithmetic Check :

$$\Sigma \text{ B.S.} - \Sigma \text{ F.S.} = \text{Last R.L.} - \text{First R.L.}$$
$$\therefore \quad 1.757 - 8.494 = 51.513 - 58.250$$
$$\therefore \quad -6.737 = -6.737$$

Hence the check was fulfilled.

Example 6.6 : *The following consecutive readings were taken with a level and 4 m levelling staff on continuously sloping ground at common interval of 30 m. 0.585 on A, 0.935, 1.950, 2.845, 3.640, 3.930, 0.965, 1.035, 1.690, 2.540, 3.845, 0.955, 1.575, 3.015 on B. Elevation of A was 520.450. Make up a level book. Calculate R.L's. of all points and apply the usual checks.* **(W-07)**

Solution :

Level Page of the Field Book

Station	B.S.	I.S.	F.S.	H.I.	R.L.
0	0.585		–	521.035	520.450
30		0.935	–	–	520.100
60		1.950	–	–	519.085
90		2.845	–	–	518.190
120		3.640			517.395
150	0.965		3.930	518.07	517.105
180		1.035		–	517.035
210		1.690		–	516.380
240		2.540			516.530
270	0.955		3.845	515.18	514.225
300		1.575			513.605
330			3.015		512.165
	Σ B.S. = 2.505		Σ F.S. = 10.79		

Arithmetic Check :

$$\Sigma \text{ B.S.} - \Sigma \text{ F.S.} = \text{R.L. of last point} - \text{R.L. of first point}$$

$$\therefore \quad 2.505 - 10.790 = 512.165 - 520.450$$

$$\therefore \quad -8.285 = -8.285$$

Hence check is fulfilled.

Example 6.7 : *Following consecutive readings were taken with a dumpy level and 4 m levelling staff on a continuous sloping ground at 30 m interval 0.68, 1.455, 1.855, 2.33, 2.885, 3.380, 1.055, 1.86, 2.265, 3.540, 0.835, 0.945, 1.53, 2.250, R.L. of first point was 80.75. Rule out page of level book and enter above readings. Carry out reduction of levels by H.I. method and apply arithmetic check.* **(S-08)**

Solution :   **Level Page of the Field Book**

Station	B.S.	I.S.	F.S.	H.I.	R.L.	Remark
A	0.68			81.43	80.75	B.M.
B		1.455			79.975	
C		1.855			79.575	
D		2.330			79.100	
E		2.885			78.545	
F	1.055		3.380	79.105	78.05	C.P.1
G		1.86			77.245	
H		2.265			76.84	
I	0.835		3.540	76.4	75.565	C.P.2
J		0.945			75.455	
K		1.53			74.87	
L			2.250		74.15	
	Σ B.S. = 2.57		Σ F.S. = 9.17			

Arithmetic Check :

Σ B.S. $-\Sigma$ F.S. = 2.57 $-$ 9.17 = $-$ 6.6   Last R.L. $-$ First R.L. = 74.15 $-$ 80.75 = $-$ 6.6

Hence the check is complete.

Example 6.8 : *The following readings were taken with a dump level :*

0.895, 1.645, 3.015, 0.955, 0.695, 0.250, 1.535, 2.135.

The instrument was shifted after the third and sixth readings. The first reading was taken on a staff held on the Bench mark of R.L. 820.765. Calculate the reduced levels of all points by H.I. method. Enter the readings in a page of level field book. Apply usual checks. **(S-09)**

Solution :

Station	B.S.	I.S.	F.S.	H.I.	R.L.	Remark
1	0.895			821.66	820.765	B.M.
2		1.645			820.015	
3	0.955		3.015	819.6	818.645	C.P.1
4		0.695			818.905	
5	1.535		0.250	820.885	819.35	C.P.
			2.135		818.75	
	Σ B.S. = 3.385		Σ F.S. = 5.4			

Arithmetical Check :

Σ B.S. – Σ F.S. = 3.385 – 5.4 = – 2.015

And Last R.L. – First R.L. = 818.75 – 820.765 = – 2.015

Hence the check is fulfilled.

Example 6.9 : *The consecutive readings were taken with a dumpy level :*

3.875, 3.630, 2.865, 1.945, 0.920, 3.165, 2.860, 1.895, 2.125, 0.965 and 0.785. The level was shifted after fifth and eighth readings. The first reading was taken on benchmark of R.L. 260.865. Use collimation plane method to calculate reduced levels of all points with usual checks. **(W-09)**

Solution :　　　　　　**Level Page of the Field Book**

Station	B.S.	I.S.	F.S.	H.I.	R.L.	Remark
1	3.875			264.74	260.865	B.M.
2		3.630			261.11	
3		2.865			261.875	
4		1.945			262.795	
5	3.165		0.920	266.985	263.82	C.P.1
6		2.86			264.125	
7	2.125		1.895	267.215	265.09	C.P.2
8		0.965			266.25	
9			0.785		266.43	
	Σ B.S. = 9.165		Σ F.S. = 3.6			

Arithmetical Check :

Σ B.S. $-$ Σ F.S. = 9.165 $-$ 3.6 = 5.565 And Last R.L. $-$ First R.L. = 266.43 $-$ 260.865 = 5.565

Hence, the check is fulfilled.

TYPE II : PROBLEMS ON RISE AND FALL METHOD

Example 6.10 : *The level page of field book is given below. The R.L. of first point is 275.00 m. Calculate the R.L. of other points by rise and fall method.*

Station	Reading			Rise	Fall	Reduced	Remark
	B.S.	I.S.	F.S.	(+)	(−)	Level	
A	0.475					275.00	B.M.
B	1.060						
C		1.55					
D		2.12					
E	2.380		1.785				
F	1.325		0.895				
G			1.750				

Solution : Here the R.L. of plane of collimation (H.I.) is not at all worked out.

The difference of level between the two consecutive readings is found by comparing the staff readings i.e. 1.975 and 0.475.

The second point is lower than first by 1.975 − 0.475 = 1.500. It indicates fall which is to be deducted from previous R.L. i.e. 275.000.

Hence,   R.L. of B = R.L. of A − Fall = 275.000 − 1.5

                                                    = 273.50

Similarly, difference between B and C = 1.550 − 1.060

                                                    = 0.49

Hence,   R.L. of C = R.L. of B − Fall

                                                    = 273.50 − 0.49

                                                    = 273.01

Similarly, by deducting fall from and adding rise to the preceeding R.L. the R.L.s of points D, E, F and G are worked out as shown in the table.

Level Page of the Field Book

Station	Readings			Rise (+)	Fall (−)	Reduced Level	Remarks
	B.S.	I.S.	F.S.				
A	0.475					275.000	B.M. on plinth of the building
B	1.060	...	1.975	...	1.500	273.500	C.P.1
C	...	1.550	...	...	0.49	273.010	
D	...	2.120	...	...	0.570	272.440	
E	2.380	...	1.785	0.335	...	272.775	C.P.2
F	1.325	...	0.895	1.485	...	274.260	C.P.3
G	...	...	1.750	...	0.425	273.835	T.B.M. on boundary stone.
	∑ B.S. = 5.240		∑ F.S. = 6.405	∑ Rise = 1.820	∑ Fall = 2.985		

Arithmetical check : ∑ B.S. − F.S. = ∑ Rise − ∑ Fall = Last R.L. − First R.L.

∴　　　　5.240 − 6.405 = 1.820 − 2.985 = 273.835 − 275.000

∴　　　　　　　− 1.165 = − 1.165 = − 1.165

Example 6.11 : *The following are the consecutive readings on a 4 m levelling staff on a continuously sloping ground at a interval of 30 m.*

0.880, 1.600, 1.970, 2.550, 2.990, 3.485, 1.250, 1.980, 2.465, 3.740, 0.920, 1.145, 1.850, 2.740.

The R.L. of first point is 200.00 m. Rule out a page of level field book and enter the above readings. Calculate the reduced levels of all the points by rise and fall method. Also find the gradient of the line joining the first and the last point. **(S-06)**

Solution : The level was shifted after the 6th reading. Hence, the sixth reading 3.485 should be recorded in F.S. column and next reading i.e. 1.250 should be recorded in B.S. column on the same horizontal line.

Similarly, 10th reading i.e. 3.740 should be recorded in F.S. and 11th reading i.e. 0.920 should be recorded against the F.S. in B.S. column on the same horizontal line.

Now, 14th i.e. last reading 2.740 should be recorded in F.S. column.

Level Page of the Field Book

Staff station	B.S.	I.S.	F.S.	Rise (+)	Fall (−)	R.L.	Remark
(A) 0	0.880			−		200.00	B.M.
30		1.600		−	0.720	199.280	
60		1.970		−	0.370	198.910	
90		2.550		−	0.580	198.330	
120		2.990		−	0.440	197.890	
150	1.250		3.485	−	0.495	197.395	C.P.1
180		1.980		−	0.730	196.665	
210		2.465		−	0.485	196.180	
240	0.920		3.740	−	1.275	194.905	C.P.2
270		1.145		−	0.225	194.680	
300		1.850		−	0.705	193.975	
(B) 330			2.740	−	0.89	193.085	
	Σ B.S. = 3.05		Σ F.S. = 9.965		Σ Fall = 6.915		

Arithmetic Check :

$$\Sigma \text{ B.S.} - \Sigma \text{ F.S.} = \Sigma \text{ Rise} - \Sigma \text{ Fall} = \text{Last R.L.} - \text{First R.L.}$$
$$3.05 - 9.965 = 0 - 6.915 = 193.085 - 200$$
$$- 6.915 = - 6.915 = - 6.915$$

Hence the check was fulfilled.

Gradient of line joining the first and the last point

$$\text{i.e. line AB} = \frac{\text{First R.L.} - \text{Last R.L. (V)}}{\text{Distance between point A and point B (H)}}$$

$$= \frac{200.00 - 193.085}{330} = \frac{6.915}{330} = \frac{1}{47.72}$$

∴ Gradient 1 in 47.72 is falling gradient.

Example 6.12 : *The following consecutive readings were taken with a dumpy level, 3.875, 3.630, 2.865, 1.945, 0.920, 3.165, 1.895, 2.125, 0.965 and 0.785.*

The level was shifted after the fifth and eight readings. The first reading was taken on the bench mark of R.L. 260.865. Use rise and fall method to calculate the reduced levels of all points and apply usual checks.

Solution : The level was shifted after the 5th reading. Hence, the fifth reading 0.920 should be recorded in F.S. column and next reading i.e. 6th reading 3.165 should be recorded in B.S. column on the same horizontal line.

Similarly, the 8th reading i.e. 1.895 should be recorded in F.S. and 9th reading i.e. 2.125 should be recorded against the F.S. in B.S. column on the same horizontal line. The remaining readings were calculated and recorded as usual.

Level Page of the Field Book

Staff station	B.S.	I.S.	F.S.	Rise (+)	Fall (−)	R.L.	Remarks
1	3.875					260.865	
2		3.630		0.245	−	261.111	
3		2.865		0.765	−	261.875	
4		1.945		0.920	−	262.795	
5	3.165		0.920	1.025	−	263.820	C.P.1
6		2.860		0.305	−	264.125	
7	2.125		1.895	0.965	−	265.090	C.P.2
8		0.965		1.160	−	266.250	
9			0.785	0.180	−	266.430	
	Σ B.S. = 9.165		Σ F.S. = 3.6	Σ Rise = 5.565			

Arithmetic check :

$$\Sigma \text{ B.S.} - \text{F.S.} = \Sigma \text{ Rise} - \Sigma \text{ Fall} = \text{Last R.L.} - \text{First R.L.}$$
$$= 9.165 - 3.60 = \Sigma\, 5.565 - 0 = 266.430 - 260.865$$
$$= 5.565 \qquad = 5.565 \qquad = 5.565$$

Hence all the checks are fulfilled.

TYPE III : PROBLEMS ON MISSING READING

Sometimes the entries of few readings are missing due to the field book being spoiled or getting wet etc. or omitted due to some difficulties. However, such missing readings can be computed from the available entries of B.M., H.I. and other staff readings. The following rules of reduction should be kept in mind while attempting such problems.

(1) Collimation System :

(a) Collimation R.L. (H.I.) = B.M. + B.S.

　　At change points, the new H.I. is calculated.

　　New H.I. = R.L. of C.P. + Backsight Reading on C.P.

(b) Reduced level = H.I. − Staff reading (I.S. or F.S.)

　　R.L. of a point is calculated from the H.I. with reference to which the reading on the point is taken .

(c) Readings calculated are correct if check, 'Σ B.S. − Σ F.S. = Last R.L. − First R.L.' is true.

(2) Rise and Fall Method :

(a) Rise or fall is found by comparing the staff reading with the immediately preceeding reading.

(b) Rise is added or fall is subtracted from the preceeding R.L. to get the R.L. of the point.

(c) Readings calculated are correct if check, 'Σ B.S. $-$ Σ F.S. $=$ Σ Rise $-$ Σ Fall = Last R.L. $-$ First R.L.' is ture.

Problems on Missing Reading by H.I. Method :

Example 6.13 : *The following is the page of a field book. Fill in the missing readings. Calculate the reduced levels of all the points. Check the accuracy of the calculation.*

Level Page of the Field Book

Sr. No.	Reading			Rise	Fall	Reduced level	Remarks
	B.S.	I.S.	F.S.				
1.	2.150					450.000	B.M.No.1
2.	1.645		×	0.500			
3.		2.345			×		
4.	×	1.965		×			
5.	2.050	1.825			0.400		
6.		×		×		451.500	B.M.No.2
7.	1.690		×	0.120			
8.	2.865		2.100		×		
9.			×	×		452.260	B.M.No.3

Solution : The foresight of station No. 2 is missing. But it can be calculated from the given difference of station 1 and station 2.

Station 2 is higher than station 1 by 0.500.

Hence, missing reading at Station 2 = 2.150 – 0.500 = 1.650.

The fall of station 3 is missing. It is the difference of staff reading on station 2 and station 3 = 2.345 – 1.645 = 0.700.

The rise of station 4 = 2.345 – 1.965 = 0.380

Similarly, the B.S. reading of Station 4 is found from the fall of Station 5

$$= 1.825 - 0.400 = 1.425.$$

The R.Ls. of station 1 to station 5 can now be worked out as all the readings upto station 5 are available. From the difference in R.L. of station 5 and station 6 the missing rise of station 6 is calculated i.e.

$$451.500 - 449.780 \qquad = 1.720$$

Hence, the missing I.S. of station 6 $\qquad = 2.05 - 1.72$

$$= 0.33$$

F.S. of station No. 7 = 0.330 – 0.120 $\qquad = 0.210$

Fall of station No. 8 = 2.100 – 1.690 $\qquad = 0.410$

The R.Ls of station 6 to station 8 can now be worked out. The R.L. of station 8 is 451.200.

The difference in R.Ls. of station 9 and 8 gives the missing Rise.

i.e. 452.260 – 451.210 = 1.050

Hence, missing F.S. of station No. 9 = 2.865 – 1.050 = 1.815

Thus, all the missing readings are worked out and R.Ls. are calculated. The results are entered in the following table –

The readings which were missing are bold :

Arithmetic check : Σ B.S. – Σ F.S. = Σ Rise – Σ Fall = Last R.L. – First R.L.

$\therefore$ 11.825 – 9.565 = 3.77 – 1.51 = 452.26 – 450.00 = 2.26

Level Page of the Field Book

Sr. No.	Reading			Rise	Fall	Reduced level	Remarks
	B.S.	I.S.	F.S.				
1.	2.150					450.000	B.M.No.1
2.	1.645		**1.650**	0.500		**450.500**	C.P.
3.		2.345			**0.700**	**449.800**	
4.	**1.425**		1.965	**0.380**		**450.180**	C.P.
5.	2.050		1.825		0.400	**449.780**	C.P.
6.		**0.330**		**1.720**		451.500	B.M.No.2
7.	1.690		**0.21**	0.120		**451.620**	C.P.
8.	2.865		2.100		**0.410**	**451.210**	C.P.
9.			**1.815**	**1.050**		452.260	B.M.No.3
	Σ B.S. = 11.825		Σ F.S. = 9.565	Σ Rise = 3.77	Σ Fall = 1.51		

Arithmetical Check :

$$\Sigma \text{ B.S.} - \Sigma \text{ F.S.} = \Sigma \text{ Rise} - \Sigma \text{ Fall} = \text{Last R.L.} - \text{First R.L.}$$

$\therefore$ 11.825 – 9.565 = 3.77 – 1.51 = 452.260 – 450.000

$\therefore$ 2.26 = 2.26 = 2.26

Hence the check is fulfilled.

Example 6.14 : *The following is the page of a level field book. Fill up the missing reading and complete the page. Apply usual checks.* **(W-11)**

Level Page of the Field Book

Sr. No.	Reading			Collimation R.L.	Reduced level	Remarks
	B.S.	I.S.	F.S.			
1.	2.650			X	100.000	B.M.
2.		3.740			98.910	
3.		X			98.820	
4.	4.640		X	X	98.380	C.P. 1
5.		0.380			X	
6.	1.640		X	103.700	102.060	C.P.2
7.		2.840			100.860	
8.	X		3.480	104.900	100.220	C.P.3
9.			X		102.700	Last point

The R.L. of collimation in the beginning = R.L. of B.M. + B.S.

$$= 100.000 + 2.65 = 102.650$$

The missing I.S. at station 3 = R.L. of collimation – R.L. of station 3

$$= 102.650 - 98.820 = 3.830$$

The missing F.S. at station 4 = 102.650 – 98.380 = 4.270

The new R.L. of collimation C. P. 1 = R.L. + B.S.

$$= 98.380 + 4.640 = 103.020$$

and F.S. at station 6 = 103.02 – 102.060 = 0.960

and F.S. at station 9 = 104.900 – 102.700 = 2.200

The missing readings are thus worked out and entered in the table below :

Level Page of the Field Book

Sr. No.	Reading			Collimation R.L.	Reduced level	Remarks
	B.S.	I.S.	F.S.			
1.	2.650			**102.650**	100.000	B.M.
2.		3.740			98.910	
3.		**3.830**			98.820	
4.	4.640		**4.270**	**103.020**	98.380	C.P. 1
5.		0.380			**102.640**	
6.	1.640		**0.960**	103.700	102.060	C.P.2
7.		2.840			100.860	
8.	**4.680**		3.480	104.900	100.220	C.P.3
9.			**2.200**		102.700	Last point
	Σ B.S. = 13.610		Σ F.S. = 10.910			

Arithmetical Check :

$$\Sigma\ B.S. - \Sigma\ F.S.\ = \text{Last R.L.} - \text{First R.L.}$$

$$\therefore\quad 13.610 - 10.910\ = 102.700 - 100.000$$

$$\therefore\quad 2.700\ = 2.700$$

Hence, the check is fulfilled.

Problems on Missing Reading by Rise and Fall Method :

Example 6.15 : *The following is defaced page of a level field book. Insert missing entries (X). Fill the missing readings. Calculate R.L.s of all stations. Apply usual arithmetical checks.*

Level Page of the Field Book

Station	B.S.	I.S.	F.S.	Rise	Fall	R.L.	Remark
1	2.345					129.250	BM I
2	1.650		X	0.035			
3		2.210			X		
4	X		1.850	X			
5	1.850		1.925		0.455		
6			X	0.37		129.000	BM II

(W-07)

Solution : We start from station 2.

For Station 2 :

$$\text{Rise at station 2} = \text{B.S. of station 1} - \text{F.S. of station 2}$$

$\therefore \quad 0.035 = 2.345 - X$

$\therefore \quad X = 2.345 - 0.035$

$\therefore \quad \text{F.S. of station 2} = 2.310 \text{ m}$

For Station 3 :

$$\text{Rise at station 3} = \text{B.S. of station 2} - \text{I.S. of station 3}$$

$\therefore \quad X = 1.650 - 2.210$

$\therefore \quad X = -0.560 \text{ m}$

Because of minus sign it is fall at station 3.

For Station 4 :

$$\text{Rise at station 4} = \text{I.S. of station 3} - \text{F.S. of station 4}$$

$\therefore \quad X = 2.210 - 1.850$

$\therefore \quad \text{Rise of station 4} = 0.360 \text{ m}$

For Station 5 :

$$\text{Fall of station 5} = \text{B.S. at station 4} - \text{F.S. at station 5}$$

$\quad -0.455 = X - 1.925$

$\therefore \quad X = -0.455 + 1.925$

$\therefore \quad X = 1.47$

$\therefore \quad \text{B.S. at station 4} = 1.47$

For Station 6 :

Rise at station 6 = B.S. of station 5 – F.S. at station 6

∴   0.37 = 1.850 – X

∴   X = 1.850 – 0.37

∴   F.S. at station 6 = 1.480 m

The missing readings worked out are entered the table below :

Level Page of Field Book

B.S.	I.S.	F.S.	Rise	Fall	R.L.
2.345					129.25
1.65		**2.310**	0.036		129.285
	2.210			**0.560**	128.726
1.470		1.850	**0.360**		129.085
	1.85	1.925		0.496	128.63
1.860		**1.480**	**0.370**		129.00

Arithmetical Check :

ΣB.S. – ΣF.S. = ΣRise – ΣFall = Last R.L. – First R.L.

∴   7.315 – 7.565 = 0.765 – 1.015 = 129.000 – 129.250

∴   – 0.25 = – 0.25   = – 0.25

Hence, check was fulfilled.

Example 6.16 : *Below is the page of a level book in which some of the readings are missing and are marked as 'X'. Find the values of the missing readings. Calculate R.Ls. of all points. Apply usual checks.*

Level Page of the Field Book

Stn.	B.S.	I.S.	F.S.	Rise	Fall	R.L.	Remarks
A	X					275.000	B.M.
B	1.060		1.975		1.500	X	C.P.1
C		1.550					
D		X				272.440	
E	2.380		1.785				C.P.2
F	1.325		0.895			X	C.P.3
G			X			X	Last point

Solution : We calculate here the missing readings.

For Station A :

$$\text{B.S. of A} - \text{F.S. of B} = \text{Fall at B}$$

$$\therefore \quad X - 1.975 = -1.500$$

$$\therefore \quad X = -1.500 + 1.975$$

$$\therefore \quad X = 0.475$$

$$\therefore \quad \text{B.S. of A} = 0.475 \text{ m}$$

For Station B :

$$\text{R.L. of B} = \text{R.L. of A} - \text{Fall at B}$$

$$\therefore \quad X = 275.000 - 1.500$$

$$\therefore \quad X = 273.5$$

$$\therefore \quad \text{R.L. of B} = 273.5 \text{ m}$$

For Station C :

$$\text{Fall at C} = \text{B.S. of B} - \text{I.S. of C}$$

$$= 1.060 - 1.550$$

$$= -0.49 \text{ m}$$

Now, $\quad \text{R.L. at C} = \text{R.L. at B} - \text{Fall at C}$

$$= 273.5 - 0.49$$

$$= 273.01 \text{ m}$$

For Station D :

$$\text{Fall at D} = \text{R.L. at C} - \text{R.L. at D}$$

$$= 273.01 - 272.440$$

$$= -0.57 \text{ m}$$

Now, $\quad \text{I.S. of C} - \text{I.S. of D} = -0.57$

$$\therefore \quad 1.550 - \text{I.S. of D} = -0.57$$

$$\therefore \quad \text{I.S. of D} = +0.57 + 1.550$$

$$= 2.12$$

For Station E :

$$\text{Rise at E} = \text{I.S. of D} - \text{F.S. of E}$$

$$= 2.12 - 1.785$$

$$= 0.335$$

Now, $\quad \text{R.L. at E} = \text{R.L. at D} + \text{Rise at E}$

$$= 272.440 + 0.335$$

$$= 272.775$$

For Station F :

$$\text{Rise at F} = \text{B.S. of E} - \text{F.S. of F}$$
$$= 2.380 - 0.895$$
$$= 1.485$$

$\therefore$
$$\text{R.L. at F} = \text{R.L. at E} + \text{Rise at F}$$
$$= 272.775 + 1.485$$
$$= 274.26$$

For Station G :

$$\text{Rise at G} = \text{R.L. at G} - \text{R.L. at F}$$
$$= 275 - 274.26$$
$$= 0.74$$

Now,
$$\text{Rise at G} = \text{B.S. of F} - \text{F.S. of G}$$

$\therefore$
$$0.74 = 1.325 - \text{F.S. of G}$$

$\therefore$
$$\text{F.S. of G} = 1.325 - 0.74$$
$$= 0.585$$

The calculated missing readings are tabulated in the table below :

Level Page of the Field Book

Stn.	B.S.	I.S.	F.S.	Rise	Fall	R.L.	Remarks
A	**0.475**					275.000	B.M.
B	1.060		1.975		1.500	**273.5**	C.P.1
C		1.550			0.490	273.01	
D		**2.12**			0.570	272.44	
E	2.380		1.785	0.335		272.775	C.P.2
F	1.325		0.895	1.485		**274.26**	C.P.3
G			**0.585**	0.74		**275.00**	Last point
	Σ B.S. = 5.24		Σ F.S. = 5.24	Σ Rise = 2.56	Σ Fall = 2.56		

Arithmetical Check :

$$\Sigma \text{ B.S.} - \Sigma \text{ F.S.} = \Sigma \text{ Rise} - \Sigma \text{ Fall} = \text{Last R.L.} - \text{First R.L.}$$

$\therefore$
$$5.24 - 5.24 = 2.56 - 2.56 = 275.00 - 275.00$$

$\therefore$
$$0 = 0 = 0$$

Hence, the check is fulfilled.

Example 6.17 : *The following is the extract of a level field book. Find out the missing reading marked (X) and complete the page. Check your calculations.*

B.S.	I.S.	F.S.	H.I.	R.L.	Ramarks
2.410			(X)	(X)	Station A
3.260		0.480	(X)	(X)	Station B
	(X)			184.430	
	2.390			(X)	
	1.320			186.610	
(X)		2.150	188.500	(X)	Station C
2.020		(X)	(X)	188.120	Station D
	1.740			(X)	
		1.220		(X)	Station E
∑ B.S. = 10.410		∑ F.S. = 4.230			

Ans.

B.S.	I.S.	F.S.	H.I.	R.L.	Ramarks
2.410			**185.150**	**182.740**	Station A
3.260		0.480	**187.930**	**184.670**	Station B
	3.500			184.430	
	2.390			**184.540**	
	1.320			186.610	
2.710		2.150	188.500	**185.780**	Station C
2.020		**0.380**	**190.140**	188.120	Station D
	1.740			**188.400**	
		1.220		**188.920**	Station E
∑ B.S. = 10.410		∑ F.S. = 4.230			

Arithmetical Check :

$$\Sigma \text{ B.S.} - \Sigma \text{ F.S} = \text{Last R.L.} - \text{First R.L.}$$

$$\therefore \quad 10.410 - 4.230 = 188.920 - 182.740$$

$$6.180 = 6.180$$

TYPE IV : MISCELLANEOUS PROBLEMS

Example 6.18 : In levelling between two points A and B on opposite banks of the river, the following observations were nade :

Instrument at	Staff readings on	
	A	B
A	2.245	3.390
B	1.790	3.010

Find the true difference of level between A and B.

Solution : Case I : Apparent differene of level between A and B

$$= 3.390 - 2.245 = 1.145$$

Case II : Apparent difference between A and B

$$= 3.040 - 1.790 = 1.250$$

The true difference of level between A and B

$$= \frac{\text{Sum of the two apparent differences of level}}{2}$$

$$= \frac{1.145 + 1.250}{2} = \frac{2.395}{2} = 1.197 \text{ m}$$

(True fall from A to B) i.e. 1 in 33.26 (Falling)

Example 6.19 : *A line of levels was run from a bench mark No. 1 of R.L. 584.570 to a bench mark No.2 of R.L. 586.675. The sum of back sight was 6.515 and that of foresight was 4.495. Find out the closing error of the levelling work.*

Solution : R.L. of B.M. No.2

$$= \text{R.L. of B.M. No. 1} + \Sigma \text{ B.S.} - \Sigma \text{ F.S.}$$
$$= 584.570 + 6.515 - 4.495$$
$$= 586.590$$

But the R.L. of B.M. No. 2 is 586.675.

Hence,   the closing error $= 586.675 - 586.590$
$$= 0.085 \text{ m} = (-) \ 0.085 \text{ m.}$$

Examples on Permanent Adjustment of Level :

Example 6.20 : *In a two peg test of a dumpy level, the following readings were taken.*

Instrument at	Reading on		Remarks
	A	*B*	
O (Midway between A and B)	*1.735*	*1.450*	*Distance between A and B = 100 m*
A	*1.530*	*1.215*	

Find the staff reading on B in order that line of collimation should be horizontal when the instrument was at A.   **(S-11)**

Solution : Level at O, staff reading on A   = 1.735

Level at O, staff reading on B   = 1.450

True difference of level   = 0.285
(True rise from A to B)

Level at A, staff reading on A   = 1.530

Deduct true rise   = 0.285

True staff reading on B   = 1.245

But observed staff reading on B   = 1.215 which is less than required.

∴   The line of collimation is inclined downwards, and the error is

$$1.245 - 1.215 = -0.030 \text{ in } 100 \text{ m}$$

∴   Staff reading on B to make the line of collimation horizontal = 1.245.   **... Ans.**

Example 6.21 : A dumpy level was tested by the two peg method and the following observations were made.

1. Instrument mid-way at O between A and B.

    Staff reading on A = 1.355

    Staff reading on B = 1.695.

2. Instrument at O_1 in the line BA, 20 m behind A

    Staff reading on A = 1.520

    Staff reading on B = 1.715

Distance between A and B = 100 m.

Find the staff readings on A and B to give the line of sight horizontal when the instrument is at O_1.

Solution :

(i) Instrument midway i.e. at O :

   True difference of level   = Staff reading on A – Staff reading on B

   $\qquad\qquad\qquad\qquad\qquad$ = 1.695 – 1.355

   $\qquad\qquad\qquad\qquad\qquad$ = 0.340

   (True fall from A to B)

(ii) Instrument at O_1 :

   Apparent difference of level = Staff reading on B – Staff reading on A

   $\qquad\qquad\qquad\qquad\qquad$ = 1.715 – 1.520

   $\qquad\qquad\qquad\qquad\qquad$ = 0.195

Since the two difference do not agree, the line of collimation is not in adjustment.

Now, instrument at O_1 :

Observed reading on A $\qquad\qquad$ =   1.520

+ True fall $\qquad\qquad\qquad\qquad$ = + 0.340

Corresponding reading on A (e_1)   1.860

Since the observed reading 1.715 on B is less than (e_1) i.e. 1.860, the line of collimation is *inclined* downwards.

The collimation error in 100 m = Corresponding reading A (e_1)

   $\qquad\qquad\qquad\qquad\qquad$ – Staff reading on B

   $\qquad\qquad\qquad\qquad\qquad$ = 1.860 – 1.715

   $\qquad\qquad\qquad\qquad\qquad$ = 0.145 = – 0.145

The correction therefore is additive.

Correct staff reading on B

$$= 1.715 + \frac{D + d}{D} (b_1 \sim e_1) = 1.715 + \frac{100 + 20}{100} (0.145)$$

$$= 1.715 + \frac{120}{100} \times 0.145$$

$$= 1.889 \qquad \text{... Ans.}$$

Correct staff reading on A $= 1.520 + \dfrac{20}{100} \times 0.145$

$$= 1.549 \qquad \text{... Ans.}$$

Important Points

- **Levelling** is "an art of determining relative heights or elevations of different points on the earth's surface so that the same may be represented on a plan or map". It is essentially a process dealing with the measurements in vertical plane.

- **Datum surface or line :** It is an arbitrary level surface (line) from which elevations of points may be referred. In India, mean sea level at Karachi is considered as datum of elevation zero.

- **Back sight (B.S.) :** It is a staff reading taken on a point of known elevation i.e. B.M. or change point. It is the first reading taken after the level is set up and levelled.

- **Fore Sight (F.S.):** It is a staff reading taken on a point whose elevation is to be determined as on a change point. It is the last staff reading denoting the shifting of the instrument.

- **Intermediate sight (I.S.) :** It is a staff reading taken on a point whose elevation is to be determined. All sights between B.S. and F.S. are intermediate sights.

- **Change point (C. P.) :** It is a point on which both fore sight and back sights are taken.

- **Line of collimation:** It is a line joining the intersection of the cross hairs of diaphragm to the optical centre of the object glass and its continuation. It is also known as *line of sight.*

- **The height of instrument (H.L.) :** It is the elevation (R.L.) of the plane of collimation with respect to the datum when the instrument is correctly levelled.

- **Parallax :** It is the apparent movement of the image relatively to the cross hairs when the image formed by the objective does not fall in the plane of diaphragm.

- **Bench mark** is a reference point of known elevation. There are four kinds of bench marks.
    - (a) (Great Trigonometrical Survey (G. T. S.) bench mark
    - (b) Permanent bench mark.
    - (c) Arbitrary bench mark.
    - (d) Temporary bench mark.

- **Temporary Adjustments of Dumpy Level**
  These adjustments are to be performed at each set-up of the level before taking any observation.
  (a) Setting up of the level.
  (b) Levelling of the level.
  (c) Focussing the eye piece.
  (d) Focusing the object glass to remove the parallax.
- During temporary adjustments the bubble will move in the direction of movement of the left thumb.
- Always remember that centering is not carried out in levelling as no horizontal measurements are taken.
- Automatic levels have two principal adjustments (1) Circular bubble (2) Line of sight. It should be checked that the compensator is functioning properly
- **Station :** It is the point where the levelling staff is held and not the point where the Level is set
- **Negative Staff Reading :** The staff reading taken is said to be Negative if the Station is above the line of collimation and in such cases the staff is held inverted. For example : Chejja, ceiling of a building etc
- **Rise :** If the difference between two successive readings (BS-IS or IS-IS or IS-FS) is Positive, then it is Rise.
- **Fall :** If the difference between two successive readings (BS-IS or IS-IS or IS-FS) is Negative, then it is Fall
- **Fly levelling :** It is the levelling operation in which only BS and FS are taken and no intermediate sights are observed. Fly levelling is done for connecting the BM to the starting point of any project.
- **Check levelling:** In case of profile or longitudinal leveling, at the end of day's work the finishing point is connected to the starting point of that day's work by fly levelling, to check the accuracy of the work. This operation is called check levelling.
- **Reciprocal levelling:** This process is used when it is not possible to set up the level in between the two points due to river or pond etc. In this case level is setup on both the banks of the river or valley and two sets of staff readings are taken by holding the staff on both banks.
- **Profile levelling :** It is adopted to know the accurate outline of the surface of the ground along a given line. The levels are taken at some regular intervals, it is also called longitudinal levelling.
- **Cross-sectioning :** It is the operation of levelling to know the undulations of the ground surface run at right angles to a given line and on either side of it.
- The errors in levelling are due to the following principal sources.
  1. Instrumental errors
  2. Errors of manipulation.
  3. Imperfect sighting.
  4. Errors due to settlement of staff and level stand.
  5. Errors due to natural sources.

- **CLOSING ERROR IN LEVELLING**

  The levelling work is generally started from a point of known Reduced level (B.M.) and after carrying out the required levelling the work is finally closed on the starting point by taking fore sight on it. The difference in reduced level of the starting point indicates the closing error in levelling.

- The magnitude of permissible closing error may be expressed as :

$$E = C \sqrt{K}$$

  where, E = The permissible error in millimetre

      C = The constant.

      K = Distance in kilometres.

- **Arithmetical check :**

$$\Sigma \text{ B.S.} - \Sigma \text{ F.S.} = \Sigma \text{ Rise.} - \Sigma \text{ Fall} = \text{Last R.L.} - \text{First R.L.}$$

Practice Questions

1. Draw a neat sketch of dumpy level and name all the important parts.

2. Explain the essential difference between the dumpy level and tilting level. State under what circumstances each is used.

3. Describe the level field book, and explain how the staff reading and other relevant entries are booked in it.

4. State the methods of reducing levels ? Discuss their merits and demerits.

5. What are the various types of levelling staffs ? Draw a neat sketch of levelling staff 4 m showing the details of graduations.

6. Write short notes on :

    (1) Simple levelling. (2) Differential levelling. (3) Precise levelling.

7. Explain the procedure for profile levelling and cross-sectioning.

8. Explain what is meant by Reciprocal levelling ? Under what circumstances it is used ? What are the errors eliminated by using Reciprocal levelling ?

9. Describe any four personal errors in levelling.

10. Describe any four natural errors in levelling.

11. Explain instrumental error in level and state four sources of instrumental error.

12. Why permanent adjustments are necessary in case of levels ?

13. Explain the temporary adjustment of tilting level. How does it differs from dumpy level ?

14. Explain in brief, in case of dumpy level :

    (i) Adjustment of bubble axis.

    (ii) Adjustment of line of collimation by two peg method.

15. Describe the various types of Bench marks.

16. What is meant by fly levelling ? When is it carried out ?

17. What do you understand by closing error in levelling ? State the limits of precision in carrying out levelling work for important project site.

18. Describe H.I. method of booking and finding R.L. with a specimen page of level book.

19. Flying levels were run from a bench mark of R.L. 250.550 to bench mark of R.L. 263.915. The sum of back sights was 29.565 and that of foresights was 16.225. Find the closing error of the levelling work.

    [**Ans.** – 0.025 m.]

20. The following consecutive readings were taken with a dumpy level :

    0.895, 1.645, 2.895, 3.015, 0.955, 0.695, 0.585, 0.250, 1.535, 0.995, 2.135 .

    The instrument was shifted after the fourth and eight reading. The first reading was taken on a staff held on the Bench mark of R.L. 820.765. Rule out a page of level field books and enter the above readings. Calculate the reduced levels of change points by Height of collimation method and apply usual checks. What is the difference of levels between the first and the last point.

    [**Ans.** –2.015 m.]

21. The following consecutive readings were taken with a level and 4 m staff on continuously sloping ground at a common interval of 30 m.

    0.760, 1.510,   1.935,   2.400,   2.985,   3.650,   1.015,

    1.855, 2.490,   3.570,   0.875,   1.025,   1.690,   2.335.

    The Reduced level of the first point was 150.250.

    Rule out a page of a level field book and enter the above readings.

    Calculate the reduced level of the points by the Rise and Fall method and also the gradient of the line joining the first and last point.

    [**Ans.** Gradient 1 in 47.82]

22. Find the height of chhajja above the floor from the following data :

    R.L. of floor level = 50.000

    Staff reading on the floor = 1.525

    Reading on the staff held inverted, the bottom touching the underside of chhajja = 3.515.

    [**Ans.** 5.04 m.]

MSBTE Questions & Answers

Summer 2011

1. Define line of collimation.

Ans. Refer Section 6.6.1 (ii).

2. What is the parallax ?

Ans. Refer Section 6.15.3 (7).

3. What is check levelling ?

Ans. Refer Section 6.16 (2).

4. How to over come difficulty in levelling due to obstruction of wall ?

Ans. Refer Section 6.15.3 (4). **Hint :** By choosing suitable change point)

5. Fill the missing readings and apply usual check in the reading taken in the page of field book.

Station	Readings			Height of	R.L.	Remarks
	B.S.	I.S.	F.S.	instrument		
A	x			300.785	300	B.M.
	1.232				x	
	x				298.375	
	2.645				x	
	x				296.236	
			x		294.765	Last point

Ans.

Station	B.S.	I.S.	F.S.	H.I.	R.L.	Remark
1	**0.785**			300.785	300.00	B.M.
2		1.232			**299.553**	
3		**2.41**			298.375	
4		2.645			**298.14**	
5		**4.549**			296.236	
6			6.02		294.765	L.P.
Σ B.S. = 0.785		Σ F.S. = 6.02				

Arithmetic check :

$$\Sigma \text{B.S.} - \Sigma \text{F.S.} = \text{Last R.L.} - \text{First R.L.}$$

$$0.785 - 6.02 = 294.765 - 300$$

$$-5.235 = -5.235 \Rightarrow \text{Checked}$$

6. The following consecutive readings were taken with a dumpy level and 4 m levelling staff on continuously sloping ground A to B at every 30 m interval.

0.355 m on A, 0.730, 1.055, 2.690, 3.950, 0.485, 1.020, 1.895, 2.535. The R.L. of A was 560.250 m. Prepare a page of level book and check your calculations by usual method.

Determine the gradient of the line AB.

Ans. As it is a continuously sloping ground readings should increase continuously, otherwise there will be change points as shown in the table.

Station	B.S.	I.S.	F.S.	H.I.	R.L.	Remark
1	0.355			560.605	560.25	B.M.
2		0.73			559.875	
3		1.055			559.55	
4		2.69			557.915	
5	0.485		3.95	557.14	556..655	C.P.$_1$
6		1.02			556.12	
7		1.895			555.245	
8			2.535		554.605	
	0.84		6.485			

Arithmetic check :

$$\Sigma \text{ B.S.} - \Sigma \text{ F.S.} = \text{Last R.L.} - \text{First R.L.}$$
$$0.84 - 6.485 = 554.605 - 560.25$$
$$-5.645 = -5.645 \Rightarrow \text{Checked}$$
$$\text{Gradient} = \frac{\text{Elevation Diff.}}{\text{Horizontal distance}} = \frac{5.645}{210} = \frac{1}{37.201}$$

(Horizontal distance is 210 m because 8 station points means $7 \times 30 = 210$ m)

$$\text{i.e. Gradient} = \frac{1}{37.201} \text{ i.e. 1 m in 37.201 m}$$

7. The following consecutive readings were taken with level 3.865, 3.345, 2.930, 1.950, 0.855, 3.795, 2.640, 1.540. The level was shifted after 5th readings. The first reading was taken on B.M. of R.L. 150.250. Calculate the reduced levels of change points and difference of level between the first and last points. Apply usual checks.

Ans.

Station	B.S.	I.S.	F.S.	H.I.	R.L.	Remark
	3.865			154.115	150.25	
		3.345			150.77	
		2.93			151.185	
		1.95			152.165	
	3.795		0.855	157.055	153.26	
		2.64			154.415	
			1.54		155.515	
	Σ B.S. = 7.66		Σ F.S. = 2.395			

Check ;

$$\Sigma \text{ B.S.} - \Sigma \text{ F.S.} = \text{Last R.L.} - \text{First R.L.}$$
$$7.66 - 2.395 = 155.515 - 150.25$$
$$5.265 = 5.265 \Rightarrow \text{Checked}$$

Winter 2011

1. What is the reciprocal levelling ?

Ans. Refer Section 6.16 (3).

2. Define change point.

Ans. Refer Section 6.15.3 (4).

3. Define Benchmark and state its types.

Ans. Refer Section 6.3.

4. Write the different points considered while booking the staff readings in level field book.

Ans. Refer Section 6.26.

5. Write the sources of errors in levelling.

Ans. Refer Section 6.23.

6. The following is page of level field book. Fill up the missing readings and complete page Apply usual checks.

Sr. No.	Readings			Collimation	Reduced	Remarks
	B.S.	I.S.	F.S.	R.L.	level	
1.	2.650			X	100.000	B.M.
2.		3.740			98.910	
3.		X			98.820	
4.	4.640		X	X	98.380	C.P.1
5.		0.380			X	
6.	1.640		X	103.700	102.060	C.P.2
7.		2.840			100.860	
8.	X		3.480	104.900	100.220	C.P.3
9.			×		102.700	Last point

Ans.

Station	B.S.	I.S.	F.S.	H.I.	R.L.	Remark
1	2.65			**102.65**	**100.00**	
2		3.74			98.91	
3		**3.83**			98.82	
4	4.64		**4.33**	102.96	98.32	
5		3.8			**99.16**	
6	1.64		**0.9**	103.7	102.06	
7		2.84			100.86	
8	**4.68**		3.48	104.90	100.22	
9.			2.2		102.70	
Σ B.S. = 13.61		Σ F.S. = 10.91				

Arithmetic check :

$$\Sigma \text{B.S.} - \Sigma \text{F.S.} = \text{Last R.L.} - \text{First R.L.}$$
$$13.61 - 10.91 = 102.7 - 100$$
$$2.7 = 2.7 \Rightarrow \text{Checked}$$

Always remember :　　R.L. + B.S. = H.I.

　　　　　　　and　H.I. – I.S./F.S. = R.L.

7. Following consecutive readings were taken with dumpy level. The first readings was taken at B.M. of R.L. 212.00 with the 4 m staff. The instrument was shifted after 5th readings.

   2.700, 3.203, 2.909, 3.455, 3.890, 0.739, 1.372, 2.606.

   Prepare a page of level field book enter above readings and find reduced levels of all points apply arithmetic check.

Ans.

Station	B.S.	I.S.	F.S.	H.I.	R.L.	Remark
1	2.7			214.7	212.00	
2		3.203			211.497	
3		2.909			211.791	
4		3.455			211.245	
5	0.739		3.89	211.549	210.81	
6		1.372			210.177	
7			2.606		208.943	
Σ B.S. = 3.439		Σ F.S. = 6.496				

Arithmetic check :

$$\Sigma \text{B.S.} - \text{F.S.} = \text{Last R.L.} - \text{First R.L.}$$
$$3.439 - 6.496 = 208.943 - 212.00$$
$$-3.057 = -3.057 \Rightarrow \text{Checked}$$

8. A line of level was run from a benchmark No. 1 of R.L. 807.854 to a benchmark No. 2 of R.L. 809.652 the sum of the back sight was 2.194 and that of the foresight was 0.408. What was the closing error of the level work.

Ans. For Accurate work :

$$\Sigma \text{B.S.} - \Sigma \text{F.S.} = \text{Last R.L.} - \text{First R.L.}$$

Here　　　$2.194 - 0.408 = 809.652 - 807.854$

　　　　　　　$1.786 \neq 1.798$

Hence closing error is **0.012 m.**

9. What is cross-sectioning method of levelling write the use of it.

Ans. Refer Section 6.20.

10. Write any four errors in manipulation in levelling work.

Ans. Refer Section 6.23.

11. What are the temporary adjustments of dumpy level.

Ans. Refer Section 6.7.1.

12. Define the following :

(i) Height of instrument

Ans. Refer Section 6.6.1 (ii).

(ii) Parallax

Ans. Refer Section 6.15.3 (7).

(iii) Intermediate sight

Ans. Refer Section 6.15.3 (3).

(iv) Change point.

Ans. Refer Section 6.15.3 (4).

13. Compare between plane and height of instrument method and rise and all method of reducing level.

Ans. Refer Section 6.28.

Summer 2012

1. Define : (i) Level line, (ii) Horizontal line.

Ans. Refer Section 6.2 (2) and (4).

2. Differentiate between G.T.S. bench mark and permanent bench mark.

Ans. Refer Section 6.3 (i) and (ii).

3. State advantages of auto level over dumpy level.

Ans. Refer Section 6.11.

4. Following consecutive readings were taken with a dumpy level during a levelling work : 0.625, 0.910, 0.450, 1.240, 1.395, 0.855, 0.925, 1.110, 1.050, 0.885, 1.125, 0.555. First reading was taken on a Bench Mark of R.L. 100.250 and level was shifted twice after 5th and 9th reading during levelling work. Enter all readings in a page of level book and reduce levels of all station by collimation method.

Ans.

Station	B.S.	I.S.	F.S.	H.I.	R.L.s	Remarks
	0.625			100.875	100.25	B.M.
		0.91			99.965	
		0.45			100.425	
		1.24			99.635	
	0.855		1.395	100.335	99.48	CP_1
		0.925			99.41	
		1.11			99.225	
	0.885		1.05	100.17	99.285	CP_2
		1.125			99.045	
			0.055		100.115	LP
Σ B.S.	2.365		Σ F.S. = 2.5			

Arithmetic Check :

$$\Sigma \text{ B.S.} - \Sigma \text{ F.S.} = \text{Last R.L.} - \text{First R.L.}$$

$$2.365 - 2.5 = 100.115 - 100.25$$

$$-0.135 = -0.135$$

5. State the source of errors in levelling.

Ans. Refer Section 6.23.

6. What precautions would you take while levelling with a dumpy level ?

Ans. Refer Section 6.6.2 and 6.1.8.

7. Differentiate between height of instrument and rise and fall method of reduction of levels.

Ans. Refer Section 6.28.

8. Explain the procedure of profile levelling for construction of a road.

Ans. Refer Section 6.18.

9. Explain importance of change point and bench mark in levelling.

Ans. Refer Section 6.15.3 (4) and 6.2 (8).

10. State the fundamental axes of dumpy level. State relationship between the axes when dumpy level is in perfect adjustment.

Ans. Refer Section 6.6.1 and 6.6.2.

11. Following is the page of level field book were some reading are missing. Bind the missing reading and apply arithmetic check.

Station	BS	IS	FS	HI	RL	Remark
A	X			500.585	500.000	BM
		0.935			X	
		X			499.355	
		2.845			X	
		X			498.650	
B			X		497.225	Last point

Ans.

Station	B.S.	I.S.	F.S.	H.I.	R.L.	Remark
A	**0.585**			500.585	500.00	
		0.935			**499.65**	
		1.23			499.355	
		2.845			**497.74**	
		1.935			498.65	
			3.36		497.225	L.P.

Remember :   R.L. + B.S. = H.I.

         and H.I. – I.S./F.S. = R.L.s

Check : Σ B.S. – Σ F.S. = Last R.L. – First R.L.

         0.585 – 3.36 = 497.225 – 500

         – 2.775 = – 2.775 $\Rightarrow$ Checked

Winter 2012

1. Define :

    (i)   Bench mark

Ans. Refer Section 6.2 (8).

    (ii)   Reduced level

Ans. Refer Section 6.2 (8).

    (iii)   Line of collimation

Ans. Refer Section 6.16 (ii).

    (iv)   Axis of bubble tube.

Ans. Refer Section 6.6.1 (iii)

2. Following readings were taken with dumpy level and 4 m staff. The instrument was shifted after 5th and 8th readings, 2.865, 3.345, 2.935, 1.950, 0.855, 2.790, 2.640, 1.540, 0.935, 0.850 and 0.190 R.L. of starting station is 200 m. Calculate the R.L. of various points by plane of collimation (H.I.) method. Apply usual checks.

Ans. As the instrument was shifted after 5th and 8th readings, 5th and 8th readings will be FS and 6th and 9th will be B.S. ofcourse first reading is B.S. and last reading F.S. and remaining will be I.S.

Stn.	Readings			H.I.	RLs	Remarks
	B.S.	I.S.	F.S.			
1.	2.865			202.865	200.000	Start point (B.M.)
2.		3.345			199.520	
3		2.935			199.930	
4		1.95			200.915	
5	2.79		0.855	204.80	202.01	CP_1
6		2.64			202.16	
7	0.935		1.54	204.195	203.26	CP_2
8		0.85			203.345	
			0.19		204.005	Last point

Arithmetic check :

$$\Sigma \text{ B.S.} - \Sigma \text{ F.S.} = \text{Last R.L.} - \text{First R.L.}$$
$$6.59 - 2.585 = 204.005 - 200$$
$$4.005 = 4.005$$

3. Describe the temporary adjustment of dumpy level.

Ans. Refer Section 6.7.1.

4. What are different types of levelling ? Explain any one in brief. Calculate the floor to ceiling height of building if 4 m levelling staff is ketp in a such way that it's bottom is touching at ceiling and axial reading on dumpy level is 1.51 m and height of instrument is 1.6 m.

Ans. Floor to ceiling height = 1.6 + 1.51 = 3.11 m

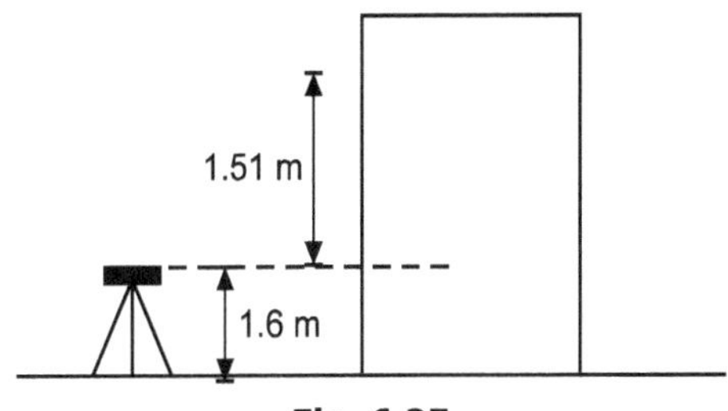

Fig. 6.25

5. Find the missing reading and apply the usual checks in reading taken in page of field book.

Station	Readings			Rise	Fall	Reduced level	Remarks
	B.S.	I.S.	F.S.				
A	3.500					x	B.M.
B		x		1.000		x	
C	x		2.700		x	100.00	C.P.
D		1.500			0.500	x	
E			0.400	x		x	

Ans.

Station	B.S.	I.S.	F.S.	Rise	Fall	R.L.s	Remark
A	3.5					99.2	B.M.
B		2.5		1.0		100.2	
C	1.0		2.7		0.2	100.00	
D		1.5			0.5	99.5	
E			0.40	1.1		100.6	

Remember : (1)   B.S./I.S. – I.S./F.S. = Rise if +ve

Fall if –ve

(2)   R.L. – Rise or + Fall = R.L. of preceding points.

R.L. + Rise or – Fall = R.L. of following points

6. What are the sources of errors in levelling ?

Ans. Refer Section 6.23.

7. Draw a neat sketch of dumpy level and name all the parts.

Ans. Refer Fig. 6.2.

Summer 2013

1. Define : (i) Level line, (ii) Horizontal line.

Ans. Refer Section 6.2 (2) and (4).

2. Differentitae between G.T.S. bench mark and permanent bench mark.

Ans. Refer Section 6.3 (1) and (2).

3. State the sources of errors in levelling.

Ans. Refer Section 6.23.

4. What precautions would you take while levelling with a dumpy level ?

Ans. Refer Section 6.18.1

5. Differentiate between height of instrument and rise and fall method of redution.

Ans. Refer Section 6.28.

6. Explain the procedure of profile levelling for construction of a road.

Ans. Refer Section 6.18.

7. Explain importance of change point and Bench mark in levelling.

Ans. Refer Section 6.3 and 6.15.3 (4).

8. State the fundamental axes of dumpy level. State relationship between the axes when dumpy level is in perfect adjustment.

Ans. Refer Section 6.3.

9. State advantages of auto level over dumpy level.

Ans. Refer Section 6.11.

University Question Papers
WINTER 2013

---

1. Attempt any Six of the following :   **(12 Marks)**

(i) State the principle of survey.

Ans. Refer section 1.5 on page 1.3.

(ii) Define ranging.

Ans. Refer section 2.3 on page 2.12.

(iii) State the principle of optical square.

Ans. Refer page 3.9.

(iv) Define long offset and short offset.

Ans. Refer page 3.6.

(v) State the principle of plane table survey.

Ans. Refer section 5.4 o page 5.4.

(vi) Define line of collimation.

Ans. Refer section 6.6.1 (ii) on page 6.6.

(vii) Enlist the component of prismatic compass.

Ans. Refer section 4.4 on page 4.3.

(viii) What is true meridian ?

Ans. Refer section 4.13 (i) on page 4.9.

(b) Attempt any Two of the following :   **(08 Marks)**

(i) What is perpendicular and oblique offset ?

Ans. Refer page 3.5.

(ii) Explain the method to overcome an obstacle in chaining, where vision and chaining both are obstructed.

Ans. Refer page 3.20.

(iii) Explain with neat sketch differential levelling.

Ans. Refer section 6.17.2 on page 6.22.

2. Attempt any Four of the following :   **(16 Marks)**

(a) What is plane and geodetic survey ?

Ans. Refer section 1.4 on page 1.2.

(b) Explain with neat sketch the procedure of indirect ranging.

Ans. Refer section 2.3.2 on page 2.15.

(c) State the procedure of setting offsets with optical square.

Ans. Refer page 3.11 (Use of optical square).

(d) Compare whole circle bearing and quadrantal bearing system.

Ans. Refer section 4.14 on page 4.10 and 4.11.

(e) Explain temporary adjustment of plane table.

Ans. Refer section 5.5 (i) and (ii) on page 5.4.

(P.1)

(f) State the fundamental lines of dumpy level and give their relationship.

Ans. Refer section 6.8 on page 6.8.

3. Attempt any Four of the following :   **(16 Marks)**

(a) Draw conventional symbol for :

 (i) Cutting

 (ii) Embankment

 (iii) Marshy land

 (iv) Forest.

Ans. Refer section 1.9 on page 1.8.

(b) Explain the procedure of chaining of sloping ground.

Ans. Refer page 2.18.

(c) Explain with neat sketch the construction of optical square.

Ans. Refer page 3.9.

(d) B and C are two points on the opposite banks of a river along a chain line ABC which crosses the river at right angles to the bank. From a point P which is 150 m from B along the bank, the bearing of C is 305° 30' and the bearing of A is 215° 30'. If the length AB is 200 m, find the width of river.

Ans. Refer Example 3.4 on page 3.22.

(e) Calculate back bearing for following bearings :

 (i) 135° 30'

 (ii) 230°

 (iii) S 40° 30' W

 (iv) N 50° W

Ans. (i) B.B. = 180 + 135° 30"

  (ii) B.B. = 230 – 180

  (iii) B.B. = N 40° 30'

  (iv) B.B. = S 50° E

(f) Convert following bearing from R.B. to W.C.B.

 (i) N 30° 30' E

 (ii) S 60° E

 (iii) S 70° 30' W

 (iv) N 65° W

Ans. (i) W.C.B. = 30° 30'

  (ii) W.C.B. = 180° – 60° = 120°

  (iii) W.C.B. = 180° + 70° 30' = 109° 30'

  (iv) W.C.B. = 360 – 65° = 295

4. Attempt any Four of the following :   **(16 Marks)**

(a) State the code of signals for ranging.

(b) A 30 m chain was tested before commencement of chaining work. Line PQ was chained by it and observed length of PQ was 1230 m. The chain was tested at the end of days work and was found to be 12 cm too short. Find the correct distance PQ.

Ans. Refer Example 2.2 on page 2.20.

(c) Plot the following cross staff survey of field and calculate its area in m^2 as shown in Fig. 1.

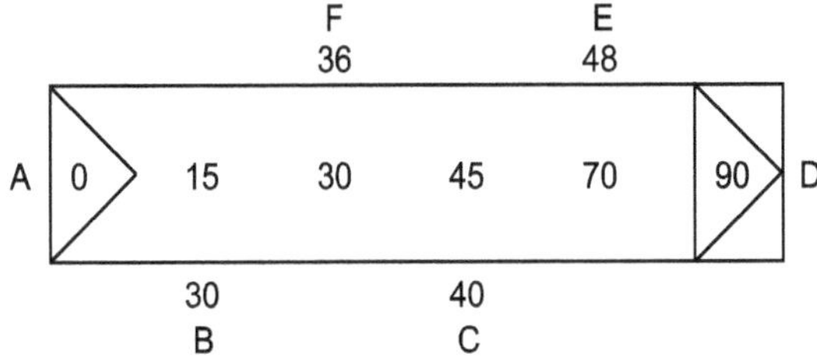

Fig. 1

Ans. Refer Same Example 3.8 on page 3.26

(d) What is temporary adjustment of prismatic compass ?

Ans. Refer section 4.7 on page 4.6.

(e) What is fore bearing and back bearing of line and give their relationship.

Ans. Refer section 4.16 on page 4.12.

(f) Given below are the bearings observed in a closed traverse. Determine which of the stations are affected by local attraction. State the values of corrected bearings.

Line	FB	BB
AB	124° 30'	304° 30'
BC	68° 15'	246° 00'
CD	310° 30'	135° 15'
DA	200° 15'	17° 45'

Ans. Refer Example 4.24 on page 4.43.

5. Attempt any Four of the following :   **(16 Marks)**

(a) Explain with neat sketch open and close traverse.

Ans. Refer page 4.22.

(b) State the different accessories with their use for plane table survey.

Ans. Refer section 5.3 on page 5.3.

(c) What is orientation of plane table ? Explain back sighting method of orientation of plane table survey.

Ans. Refer page 5.5

(d) Explain intersection method of plane table survey.

Ans. Refer section 5.6.2 on page 5.7.

(e) Define the following terms used in levelling :
  (i) Level surface.
  (ii) Datum line.
  (iii) Reduced level.
  (iv) Axis of telescope.

Ans. Refer section 6.2 on page 6.2.

(f) What it temporary adjustment of dumpy level ?

Ans. Refer section 6.7.1 on paeg 6.7.

6. Attempt any Two of the following :   (16 Marks)

(a) The following readings were taken with a level and 4 m staff. Draw up a level book page and calculate reduced levels by height of instrument method. 0.578, 0.933, 1.768, 2.450, 3.005, 0.567, 1.181, 1.888, 3.679, 0.612, 0.705 and 1.810. The instrument was shifted after 5th and 9th reading. The R.L. of first station is 58.250 m. Apply usual checks.

Ans. Refer Example 6.5 on page 6.39.

(b) What are the sources of errors in levelling ? What precautions should be taken to guard against it ?

(c) Below is the page of a level book in which some of the readings are missing and are marked as 'X'. Find the values of the missing readings. Calculate RL's of all points. Apply using checks.

Level page of the field book

Stn.	B.S.	I.S.	F.S.	Rise	Fall	R.L.	Remarks
A	X					275.000	B.M.
B	1.060		1.975		1.500	X	C.P.1
C		1.550			X	X	
D		X			X	272.440	
E	2.380		1.785	X		X	C.P.2
F	1.325		0.895	X		X	C.P.3
G			X	X		X	Last point

Ans. Refer Example 6.16 on page 6.52.

1. Attempt any Six of the following : (12 Marks)

(i) State the primary classification of survey.

Ans. Refer section 1.6 on page 1.5.

(ii) State different objectives of survey.

Ans. Refer section 1.3 on page 1.2.

(iii) Define ranging and list the instrument required for ranging.

Ans. Refer section 2.3 on page 2.12.

(iv) Write the bearing of line AB and line CD.

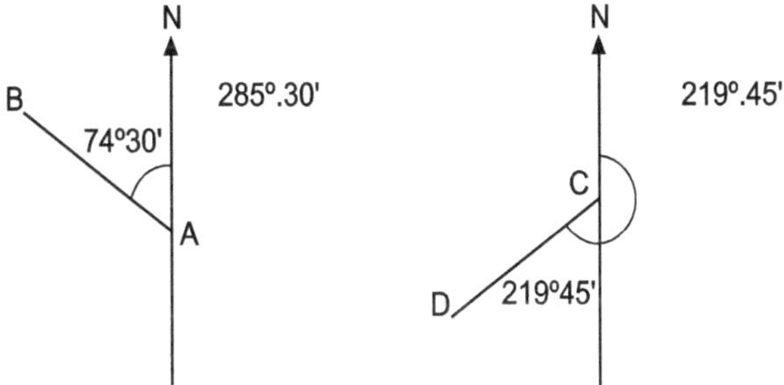

Fig. 1

Ans. (1) Bearing of line AB = 360° – 74° 30' = 285° 30'

(2) Bearing of line CD = 219° 45'

(v) Write any four personal errors in compass survey.

Ans. (1) Inaccurate levelling of the compass box.

(2) Inaccurate centering of the compass over the stations.

(3) Inaccurate bisection of the object.

(4) Taking wrong reading and recording wrongly.

(5) Reading the bearing in wrong direction.

(vi) List the accessories required for plane table survey.

Ans. Refer section 5.1 on page 5.3 and 5.4.

(vii) Define Datum line and Bench mark.

Ans. **Datum line :** "It can be defined as the line parallel to the mean spheriodal earth surface from which the vertical distances are measured".

Bench mark : "It can be defined as the point known elevation".

(viii) Describe in brief negative staff reading.

Ans. Refer section 6.2 (6) and 6.3 on page 6.3.

(b) Attempt any Two of the following : (08 Marks)

(i) Explain the principles of surveying.

Ans. Refer section 1.5 on page 1.5.

(ii) State the uses of survey.

Ans. Refer section 1.4 on page 1.4.

(iii) Explain linear measurement by pacing and by speedometer.

Ans. Linear measurement by pacing : This method is used only for knowing approximate distanced between the objects. In preliminary survey this method can be used for linear measurement. This method consists of counting the number of paces between the two points of a line. The length or the line can then be computed by knowing the average length of the pace. The length of the pace varies with individuals and also with the nature of the ground and the speed of pacing.

Linear measurement by speedometer : If the nature of the ground is the smooth than speedometer of an automobile can be used to measure the distance approximately. It works on the principals that the no of revolutions registered by the wheel and multiplied by the circumference of the wheel to get the distance.

2. Attempt any Four of the following : (16 Marks)

(a) Differentiate between Direct ranging and Indirect ranging.

Direct ranging	Indirect ranging
It is done when terminal stations are visible.	It is done when terminal stations are not indivisible.
It is suitable when the distance is less.	It is adopted when distance is more and if obstacle like hill is intervening between the stations.
Intermediate points are located on the survey line by line ranger.	Intermediate two points are located approximately in between terminal stations.
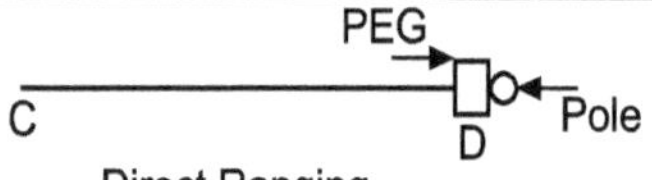 Direct Ranging **Fig. 2 (a)**	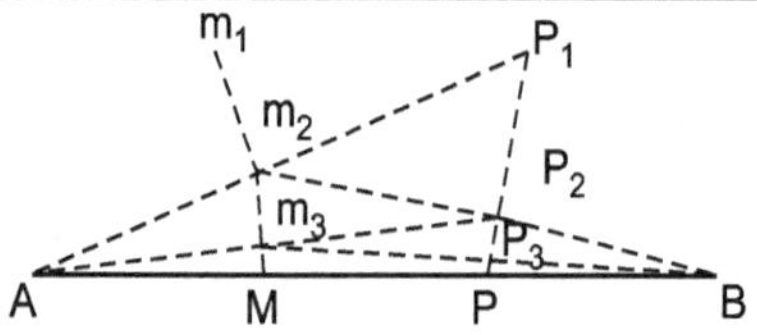 Indirect Ranging **Fig. 2 (b)**

(b) Explain the process of chaining on sloping ground by stepping method with neat sketch.

Ans. Refer section 2.5 on page 2.17 and 2.18.

(c)   A 30 m chain was found to be 5 cm too short after chaining 1200 m. It was found to be 10 cm too short after chaining 2100 m. If the chain was correct before commencement of the work find the true distance.

Ans. Part I : Chain was correct before commencement of work.

Length of chain L = 30 m, Error in chain 5 cm = 0.05 m too short.

Measured distanced D' = 1200 m

$$L' = \text{Incorrect length of chain} = 30.00 - \left(\frac{0.05 + 0.00}{2}\right) = 29.975 \text{ m}$$

$$D1 = (\text{True distance}) = \text{Correct distance} = \left(\frac{L_1}{L}\right)D = \left(\frac{29.975}{30.00}\right)1200 = 1199 \text{ m.}$$

Part II : Length of chain L : 30 m.

Measured distanced D' = (2100 – 1200) = 900

$$\text{Error in chain} = \left(\frac{0.05 + 0.10}{2}\right) = 0.075$$

$$L' = \text{Incorrect length of chain} = 30.00 - \left(\frac{0.05 + 0.10}{2}\right) = 29.925 \text{ m}$$

$$D2 = (\text{True distance}) = \text{Correct distance} = \left(\frac{L_1}{L}\right)D' = \left(\frac{29.925}{30.00}\right)900 = 897.75 \text{ m}$$

Total true distance = 1199.00 + 897.75 = **2096.75 m**

(d)   State the points to be considered while selecting survey stations.

Ans. Refer section 3.5 on page 3.3.

(e)   Draw the sketch of chain triangulation and label different lines.

Ans. Refer Fig. 3.2 on page 3.4.

(f)   Explain principle of optical square with neat sketch.

Ans. Refer page 3.9.

3.   Attempt any Four of the following :   (16 Marks)

(a)   Write the obstacles in chaining and explain how you overcome when building comes across the chain line.

Ans. Refer page 3.20.

(b)   Distinguish between true meridian and magnetic meridian and explain dip of needle.

Ans. Refer section 4.13 on page 4.9.

(c)   Why zero is marked at south end on a prismatic compass ?

Ans. Refer section 4.5 para 2.

(d)   Draw a labelled sketch of prismatic compass and give example of reading taken on prismatic compass.

Ans. Refer Fig. 4.1 (a) on page 4.3.

(e)   Define bearing of a line and convert following fore bearing into back bearing :

    (i)   127° 30'

    (ii)   S 38° 30' W

    (iii)   54° 45'

Ans.   (i)   BB 307° - 30'

    (ii)   N 38° - 30' E

    (iii)   234° - 45'

(f)   Define closing error and explain graphical method of adjusting closing error.

Ans. Refer section 4.31 on page 4.26.

4.   Attempt any Four of the following :   (16 Marks)

(a)   Calculate interior angles in a closed traverse PQRST by following observational bearings :

Line	FB
PQ	S 37° 30' E
QR	S 43° 15' W
RS	N 74° W
ST	N 11° E
TP	N 57° 45' E

Ans.

Line	Fore bearing (R.B.)	Fore bearing (W.C.B.)	Back bearing (W.C.B.)
PQ	S 37° 30' E	142° 30'	322° 30'
QR	S 43° 15' W	223° 15'	43° 15'
RS	N 74° 0' W	286° 00'	106° 00'
ST	N 11° 00' E	11° 00'	191° 00'
TP	N 57° 45' E	57° 45'	237° 45'

Calculations :

Induced angle = Fore bearing of next line – B.B. of previous line

= Difference (if less than 180° then = interior angle)

(if greater than 180° than = Exterior angle)

And interior angle = 360° – Exterior angle

Induced angle P = 237° 45' – 142° 30' = 95° 15'

Induced angle Q = 322° 30' – 223° 15' = 99° 15'

Induced angle R = (286° 00' – 43° 15') = 242° 45' > 180° (i.e. exterior angle)

Interior angle = (360° 00' – Exterior angle)

                = (360° 00' – 242° 45')

                = 117° 15'

Included angle S = 106° 00' – 11° 00' = 95° 00'

Included angle T = 191° 00' – 57° 45' = 133° 15'

Total (< P + < Q + < R + < S + < T) = 540° 00'

(b)   State different accessories of plane table survey and their use.

Ans. Refer section 5.1 on page 5.3 and 5.4.

(c)   Write any two advantages and disadvantages of plane table survey.

Ans. Refer section 5.13 on page 5.14.

(d)   Explain traversing method of plane table surveying.

Ans. Refer section 5.6.3 on page 5.8.

(e)   Explain with neat sketch method of orientation by back sighting of plane table survey.

Ans. Refer page 5.5.

(f)   Define line of collimation and axis of bubble tube.

Ans. Refer section 6.6.1 on page 6.6.

5. **Attempt any Four of the following :**   **(16)**

(a)   Describe the advantages of auto level.

Ans. Refer section 6.11 on page 6.12.

(b)   Explain with neat sketch reciprocal levelling.

Ans. Refer section 6.22 on page 6.26.

(c)   Distinguish between the following :

    (i)   Back sight and fore sight.

    (ii)   Simple levelling and differential levelling.

Ans. (i)   Back sight and Foresight :

Back sight	Fore sight
It is a staff reading taken on a point of known elevation i.e. B.M. or C.P.	It is a staff reading taken on a point whose elevation is to be determined. i.e. C.P.
It is the first riding taken after the level is set-up and levelled.	It is the last staff reading denoting the shifting of the instrument or closing of levelling work.

(ii) Simple levelling and differential levelling :

Simple levelling	Differential levelling
In this difference in elevation between two point is determined, when two points are visible, small distance apart, small difference in elevation between two points.	In this difference in elevation between two point is determined if the points are too far apart, elevation between two point is more or any obstacle in between them.

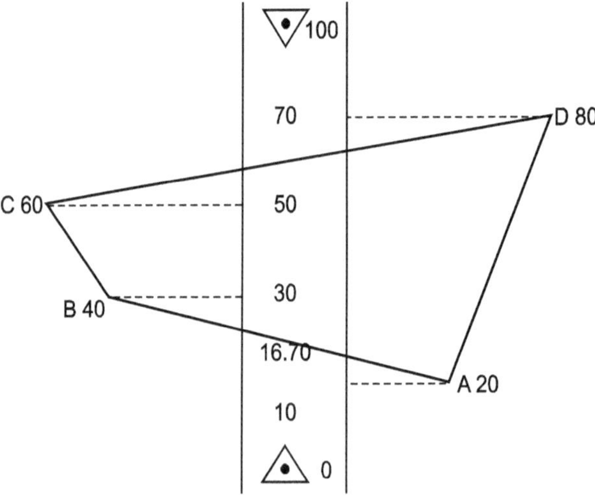

(d) Define fly levelling and explain the situations when fly levelling is required.

Ans. Refer section 6.16 on page 6.20.

(e) Enlist the sources of errors in levelling and explain any one source in detail.

Ans. Refer section 6.23 on page 6.27.

(f) Explain the precautionary measures in levelling.

Ans. Refer section 6.25.2 on page 6.29.

6. Attempt any Two of the following :   **(16 Marks)**

(a) (i) Find the area of the plot ABCD from the data collected in chain and cross-staff survey. (Refer Fig. 4).

Ans.

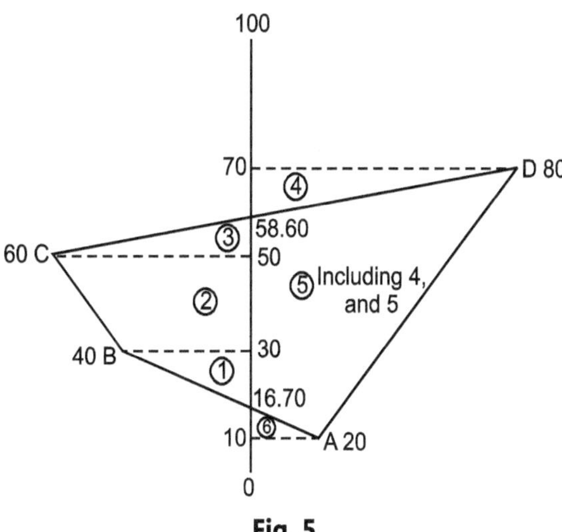

Fig. 5

| Fig. | Fig. | Chainage | | Base | Offset | | Mean | Area cm² | | Net |
No.		From	To		I	II	offset	+	−	Area (m²)
1.		16.70	30	13.30	0	40	20	266		
2.		30	50	20	40	60	50	1000		
3.		50	58.60	8.60	60	0	30	258		
4.		58.60	70	11.40	0	80	40		456	4001
5.		10	70	60	20	80	50	3000	67	
6.		10	610	6.70	20	0	10		67	
							Total	**4524**	**523**	

Area of the plot ABCD = 4001 m² (Note also consider area calculation of each figure separately).

(ii) Q and R are two points on the opposite banks of a river along a chain line PQR which crosses the river at right angles to the bank. From a point A which is 96.2 m from Q along the bank, the bearings of R is 305° 30' and the bearing of P is 215° 30'. If the length of PQ is 150 m. Find the width of river.

Ans. Using principle of similar triangle : $\dfrac{QA}{QR} = \dfrac{QP}{QA}$

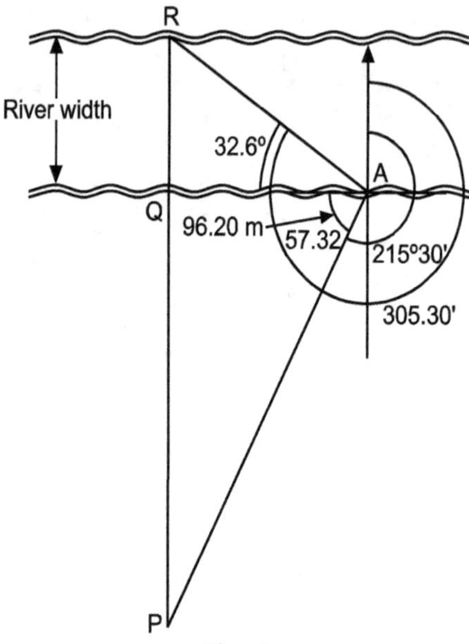

Fig. 6

$$\angle\,RAP = 305°\,30' - 215°\,30' = 90°$$

In right angle triangle RAP, $\triangle$ AQR and $\triangle$ PQA.

$$\frac{AQ}{QR} = \frac{PQ}{QA}$$

Given : PQ = 150.0 m,   AQ = 96.20 m

∴   QR = Width of river

∴ $\dfrac{96.20}{QR} = \dfrac{150.0}{96.20}$

∴   QR = 61.68 m **Ans.** Width or river.

OR In $\triangle$ QAP, $\angle$ A = $\tan^{-1}\left(\dfrac{150.00}{96.20}\right)$ = 57.32°

and In $\triangle$ QAR, $\angle$ A = 90° − 57.32 = 32.67°

∴   In $\triangle$ QAR, $\tan 32.67 = \dfrac{QR}{96.20}$

∴   QR = **61.96 m = Width of river**

(b) The following bearings were observed in running a closed traverse PQRST with prismatic compass.

Line	F.B.	B.B.
PQ	80° 10'	259° 0'
QR	120° 20'	301° 50'
RS	170° 50'	350° 50'
ST	230° 10'	49° 30'
TP	310° 20'	130° 15'

Calculate the included angle and find out corrected FB and BB with usual check.

Ans. Refer Example 4.26 on page 4.45.

(c) The following page of old level book having few staff reading missing find out the missing reading and rewrite the page. Apply usual checks.

Stn.	Staff Reading			H.I.	RL	Remark
	BS	IS	FS			
1	2.650			×	100.000	B.M.
2		×			98.910	
		3.830			98.820	
	4.640		×	×	98.380	CP1
		0.380			×	
	1.640		×	103.700	102.060	CP2
		2.840			100.860	
	×		3.480	104.900	100.220	CP3
			×		102.700	End Stn.

Ans. Refer Example 6.14.

Notes